Pacific Partnership: United States-Japan Trade

Prospects and Recommendations for the Seventies

The Japan Society is an association of Americans and Japanese actively engaged in bringing the peoples of their two nations closer together in understanding, appreciation and cooperation. Founded in 1907, it is a private, nonprofit, nonpolitical membership corporation organized under the laws of the State of New York, devoted to cultural, educational and public affairs, and to discussions, exchanges, and studies in areas of interest to both peoples. Its aim is to provide a medium through which each nation may learn from the experiences and accomplishments of the other. Japan House, the Society's new headquarters of contemporary Japanese design, located on Hammarskjold Plaza near the United Nations in New York City, was dedicated in September of 1971.

* * *

The Japan Society's Public Affairs Program, under which the materials for this publication were developed, aims to encourage informed public consideration of important issues involving Japan and the United States. This work is one in a series of Society publications in the public affairs area. As with all Society publications, this work represents solely the findings and views of the authors concerned, and should not be construed to reflect the views of the Japan Society, Inc., its Officers, Directors, Staff, or Members.

Pacific Partnership: United States- Japan Trade

**Prospects and Recommendations
for the Seventies**

Edited by
Jerome B. Cohen

Published for Japan Society, Inc.

Lexington Books
D.C. Heath and Company
Lexington, Massachusetts
Toronto   London

Published simultaneously in Canada.

Printed in the United States of America.

International Standard Book Number: 0-669-85316-X

Library of Congress Catalog Card Number: 72-10099

Contents

Acknowledgments

It seems not only appropriate but essential to express the very great appreciation of the "academic experts" and the "practical businessmen" to Mr. Rodney E. Armstrong, Executive Director of the Japan Society, and to Mr. F. Roy Lockheimer, Associate Executive Director of the Japan Society, for their most knowledgeable cooperation and tremendous and unswerving encouragement and support. They have both been exceedingly helpful and without their sustained effort this study would never have emerged. Our sincere thanks also to Mr. Philip van Slyck for serving as a most efficient and gracious rapporteur and to Ms. Teddy Oda for her most effective help with the manuscript and its organization.

Jerome B. Cohen
Chairman
Committee on Economic Policy
Studies

Introduction

Jerome B. Cohen

Bretton Woods, the Marshall Plan, GATT, OECD, IMF, IBRD, NATO, OEEC, aid to LDCs, Asian Development Bank, MFTA, the Kennedy Round, DAC, Group of Ten, SDRs—for a quarter of a century following World War II, under U.S. aegis, such ideas, institutions, and programs reshaped the free-world economy. An unprecedented effort by the United States, which emerged from the war as the world's then dominant economic power, to reconstruct and rebuild the international economic order, succeeded beyond expectation.

There were to be sure disappointments and delays and compromises, but, on the whole, the quarter century saw a vast expansion of world trade and production, a considerable improvement in the economic well-being of a considerable sector of the world's population, and the rehabilitation of shattered economies. The industrial world moved, in fits and starts, but rather steadily, toward a freer exchange of goods and services and relative monetary stability. Expanding output and expanding trade brought new levels of improvement and prosperity.

With an increasingly integrated world economy, barriers to the international movement of goods and money tended to diminish. Under the sponsorship of new multilateral and multinational institutions and programs, capital, management, and technology moved more steadily across national barriers. The massive economic transfusion, inaugurated and continued by the United States at a cost of over $150 billion in overseas aid, helped restore economic health and vigor to the European Community and to Japan and resulted in their emergence as major centers of economic strength. As this transfusion of energy and resources took hold and entrepreneurial confidence returned, these revitalized areas came to stand alongside the United States in economic magnitude. They came also to challenge the competitive position of the United States in world markets.

The burden of the quarter century of purposeful economic effort and ingenuity, while tremendously beneficial in world terms, was not without cost to the United States. The depletion of resources, economic and financial, higher taxes, fiscal deficits, inflation, the deep drain on gold reserves, the balance-of-payments hemorrhage of more than two decades duration, the enormous accumulation of some 50 billion U.S. dollars in foreign hands, the expensive financing of a world nuclear standoff, ultimately had its toll. When in 1971, the United States incurred its first annual trade deficit since the nineteenth century, $30 billion fled overseas, and the balance-of-payments deficit exceeded $22 billion, convertibility of the dollar had to be suspended and the Bretton Woods era appeared to be ending.

As Gabriel Hauge has so eloquently said:

The United States came to be regarded not only as the provider of last resort but, being so big and rich, as the absorber and adjuster of many problems of other nations as well. In the years after World War II, the U.S. was a towering economic giant among dwarfs. Now it is one among other giants and its role is changing.[1]

And, as Walter Wriston noted:

One of the reasons that world trade grew and prospered in the postwar era was the relative peace that the world enjoyed. In no small measure, this relative calm could be attributed to the fact that the United States paid the price to hold the nuclear shield, protecting both ourselves and our allies and preserving the uneasy balance of power. Over the years we have paid a disproportionate amount of the costs, which are now beginning to be shared more equitably. While we paid the check for the defense of the free world, on the commercial front the American dollar fueled the revival of Europe and Japan. In fact, the world learned to live off the U.S. balance-of-payments deficit and to enjoy it. The Japanese were able to permit the yen to become substantially undervalued relative to the dollar. Such undervaluation acted as a massive and continuing subsidy for its own exporting industries.[2]

The United States incurred balance-of-payments deficits in most of the postwar years. As long as those were of modest proportions, and the trade account was in surplus, they were no problem. As a matter of fact they contributed to international liquidity since the dollar had become the world's principal reserve currency. When the trade surplus narrowed and the payments deficit widened, a deluge of dollars inundated many trading countries. As long as foreigners were willing to absorb and hold dollars and not convert them into gold, the fixed exchange rate structure endured, though punctured from time to time by devaluations and revaluations.

In 1971, with the U.S. trade position impaired, with $45 billion surplus dollars in foreign hands and with the U.S. gold reserve down to some $10 billion, the fiction of the convertible dollar came to an end. The country most sensitive to the U.S. deficit and international financial conditions during the first half of 1971 was Germany. Faced with a particularly large inflow of dollars, substantial domestic inflation, and interest rates well above the Eurodollar and most European money market rates, the Bundesbank suspended its foreign exchange operations in the wake of a $1 billion inflow over May 3-4, and an additional $1 billion inflow in the first forty minutes of trading on the morning of May 5. Shortly after the German decision, speculative pressure shifted to other "strong" national currencies.

Confronted by an enormous deterioration in the U.S. external position and with a speculative flight from the dollar, President Nixon, on August 15, 1971 suspended convertibility of the dollar into gold. The president's program of August 15, 1971 imposed an additional temporary tax (surcharge) of 10 percent on goods imported into the United States. The apparent purpose of the surcharge was to set the stage for international negotiations to achieve a realignment of currencies and a better access to foreign markets for American producers.

An avalanche of dollars poured into Japan during 1971. Its official reserves rose from \$4.8 billion at the end of 1970 to \$5.9 billion in March of 1971, to \$7.8 billion in June, to \$13.4 billion in September, and to \$15.4 billion by the end of December 1971. The Japanese government initially tried to purchase all dollars offered at the ceiling rate, but in the face of a \$4 billion inflow in August, it was later forced to suspend the rate and limit intervention so as to permit about a 5 percent rise relative to the dollar in the subsequent month. Other administrative actions to limit the appreciation of the yen relative to the dollar were taken over the remainder of the year. Many of these exchange controls were relaxed in 1972 after the Smithsonian agreement of December 18, 1971.

A number of other countries also imposed restrictions on foreign exchange transactions but still permitted the value of their currencies to fluctuate relative to the dollar. By early December 1971, it was clear that a set of exchange rates between foreign currencies and dollars had emerged which was substantially different than at the beginning of the year. Many of these were formalized in the Smithsonian agreement of December 18, 1971 after the United States had announced its willingness to devalue the dollar by raising the dollar price of gold by 8.57 percent (from \$35 to \$38 an ounce) and to remove the import surcharge. Of all the currencies revalued, the Japanese yen appreciated the most by 16.88 percent. The Swiss franc was next, with an increase of 13.87 percent. The dollar-yen exchange rate went from 360 yen to the dollar to 308 yen to the dollar. In the Smithsonian agreement, countries decided to permit exchange-rate fluctuations within a 2.25 percent range on each side of the central value.

Thus in 1971, a quarter-of-a century dominance of the dollar came into question; the fixed exchange rate system faltered, underwent an operation, but reemerged. It was a particularly harrowing economic year for the United States. Its balance-of-payments deficit on an official settlements basis rose to an astonishing \$29.8 billion from a \$9.8 billion deficit in 1970 and a \$2.7 billion surplus in 1969.[a] The trade account, which is perhaps the most important

---

[a]On a net liquidity basis, the deficit was \$22 billion in 1971. The underlying assumption about the economic behavior of the *Net Liquidity Balance* is that all foreign holdings of U.S. dollar liabilities which mature in one year or less are potential claims on the U.S. gold stock and other reserve assets. As such, the net liquidity balance is measured by the actual change in the gold stock and other reserve assets, changes in U.S. liquid liabilities and liquid assets, and changes in certain nonliquid liabilities to all foreigners. The underlying economic rationale of the *Official Settlements Balance* is that only foreign official holdings of dollars represent a real claim on the gold stock and other U.S. reserve assets. Thus the *Official Settlements Balance* is equal to the *Net Liquidity Balance*, less foreign private holdings of U.S. liquid liabilities and liquid assets.

component of the current account, declined from a surplus of $6.8 billion in 1964 to a deficit of $2.9 billion in 1971. U.S. trade with Japan in 1971 was in deficit by $3.2 billion, thus exceeding in size the overall U.S. trade deficit, which meant that in its trade with the rest of the world, the U.S. had a small surplus.

The recent deterioration in the U.S. trade position has been attributed to a variety of factors. As higher prices and higher incomes spread, the domestic market became more attractive, both for domestic manufactures and for imports. Organization for export expansion was of relatively less interest than direct investment abroad with branch plants in leading overseas markets. U.S. exports became less competitive because productivity gains in manufacturing lagged behind those of other major trading countries in the later 1960s. This is clear from the fact that the rate of import growth and the rate of export growth were fairly close together prior to 1966, but from 1966 on, the rate of increase in imports became twice that of exports. The emergence of this disparity in rates of increase is traceable to changes in price-performance relationships between domestic and imported goods. Other countries were able to adjust exchange rates when necessary, but under the IMF system the United States did not have the same option to devalue when necessary. There had persisted a variety of restrictive practices limiting access to major trading markets, not only in the form of tariffs and quotas but also other discriminatory measures and administrative practices. Protectionist agricultural policies abroad blocked potential export growth in agricultural products, a sector where the United States enjoys a clear comparative advantage.[3]

While the U.S. trade and payments situation deteriorated, Japan's economic position improved substantially. For the past quarter of a century the Japanese have staged a unique, cooperative business-government effort to achieve rapid economic growth, expand output, and maximize foreign trade. How successful this endeavor was is now well recorded in the annals of economic history.[4] Japan has in recent years been the fastest growing of the world's industrialized countries. It has now become the third ranking economic power in terms of gross national product, after the United States and the USSR. The rate of growth tended to accelerate steadily during the past fifteen years. The GNP grew, in real terms, at an 8.9 percent per annum rate during the 1955-60 period, at a 10.0 percent per annum rate during 1960-65, and 12.2 percent per annum for 1965-70. Between 1950 and 1960 the Japanese economy grew (GNP at constant prices) at an average annual rate, in real terms, of 9.1 percent compared to 7.9 percent for West Germany, 3.2 percent for the United States, and 2.8 percent for Great Britain. For the 1960-1970 decade, the Japanese economy grew at an average annual rate, in real terms, of 11.3 percent compared to 4.7 percent for West Germany, 4.2 percent for the United States, and 2.7 percent for Great Britain.

Japan is now either first or second in world production of an ever expanding list of commercial and industrial products and has outdistanced many competitor nations. In 1960, for example, Japan produced 22 million tons of steel, West Germany 34 million, Great Britain 24 million. In 1970 Japan produced 93 million, an increase from 22 to 93 million; West German production rose from 34 million to 45 million; Great Britain's from 24 to 28 million tons. With respect to Japanese production of a relatively new product—automobiles—output rose from 165,000 cars in 1960 to 5.8 million in 1971 and exports jumped from 7,000 in 1960 to 1.7 million in 1971. For over a decade Japan has led the world in shipbuilding and exports thereof.

Japan's trade surplus has become the largest in the world. From a rough balance in the early sixties, the trade account moved to an annual surplus averaging $2 billion between 1965 and 1968. In 1969 the surplus rose to $3.7 billion, and in fiscal 1970 (April 1, 1970-March 31, 1971) it reached $4.5 billion, then jumped to $8.6 billion in fiscal 1971 (April 1, 1971-March 31, 1972). About half of the increase in Japan's trade surplus originated in its trade with the United States. Exports to the United States during fiscal 1971 were up some 25 percent, while imports from the United States actually declined by about 12 percent. As a result, Japan's bilateral trade surplus, on a payments basis, widened from about $1.6 billion to about $3.7 billion.

Up to 1964 Japan tended to have a deficit in its trade with the United States, and its payments position was at times precarious and restrictive. In more recent years, however, Japan has had the trade surplus, and its payments position has been strengthened steadily. When Japan had a trade deficit, its government pressed for an increase of U.S. imports of Japanese products. The U.S. position then was that Japan should aim at a multilateral rather than a bilateral balancing of its trade. Now that the position has been reversed, some voices in the United States are pressing for bilateral adjustment and the earlier stress on multilateralism appears to have receded. Protectionist sentiment, as epitomized by the Burke-Hartke bill, has tended to rise in the United States and U.S.-Japanese economic relations have in recent periods been strained.

This is unfortunate for a variety of reasons. For a quarter of a century the United States attempted to assist in Japan's economic resurgence. It sponsored Japan's reentry into world monetary and trade organizations, opened its vast domestic market relatively freely to Japanese goods and urged other major trading nations to do likewise. The United States became Japan's largest customer and for the United States, Japan is its second biggest trading partner, after Canada. In 1971 Japan became the world's first billion dollar market for U.S. agricultural output. The multilateral expansion of total world trade over recent decades has been of mutual benefit to the advanced economic countries and any serious disruption of the delicate fabric of world trade and payments would halt expansion and curtail economic growth over much of the world. There is thus a basic need and urgency for the European Community, Japan, and the United States to resolve economic differences and move ahead once again in the 1970s and 1980s for the economic and social benefit of the world population. Change is inevitable, hopefully conflict may not be.

Such, in brief, is the background and setting in which the directors of the Japan Society determined to establish a Committee on Economic Policy Studies aided by a Businessmen's Advisory Committee to explore U.S.-Japanese economic relationships and develop policy recommendations which would attempt to resolve difficulties and differences and suggest necessary accommodations. The society, a nonprofit, private organization, assembled a group of economic experts on Japan and commissioned a series of economic papers. For some years an informal Japan economics seminar has been operating on a private basis rotating once a month between Cambridge, New Haven, and New York. The Committee on Economic Policy Studies that the Japan Society assembled has drawn heavily on the personnel of that economics seminar. The Businessmen's Advisory Committee received the economic studies and together with the economists formulated the policy recommendations which are herein presented. Needless to say, the recommendations represented a consensus and not every member of both committees agreed with every recommendation. But the views expressed do clearly reflect the majority view.

Notes

1. "We Have Time to Take Time," Gabriel Hauge, Chairman of the Board, Manufacturers Hanover Trust Company, New York, May 15, 1972.

2. "The Global Attic," Walter R. Wriston, Chairman, First National City Corporation, New York, May 9, 1972.

3. See "U.S. Foreign Economic Policy and The Domestic Economy," A Statement by the Program Committee of the Committee for Economic Development, New York, July 1972. See also "U.S. Steel Industry is Dragging Its Feet: More Effort is Needed to Increase Exports," New York Times, Sunday, July 23, 1972.

4. See, for example, Chapter 3 "Japan: Problems of Change," in William Diebold, Jr., THE UNITED STATES AND THE INDUSTRIAL WORLD, published for the Council on Foreign Relations by Praeger Publishers, New York, 1972.

Pacific Partnership: United States–Japan Trade

Prospects and Recommendations for the Seventies

1 Japan's Economic Future: An Overview

Henry Rosovsky

During the late 1940s and early 1950s, before "futurology" had been elevated to its present status of a pseudoscience, most predictions concerning the economic future of Japan were pessimistic. Both Japanese and foreign observers tended to be obsessed by the defeat and destruction of World War II and even more by what seemed to be Japan's obvious disadvantages: a large population living in a destroyed country with sparse natural resources.[a] Today, the errors of twenty years ago may seem unimportant, but I believe that this is incorrect. The old forecasts were wrong because the great majority of analysts formed their picture of the future merely by extrapolating current trends. Therefore, they grossly underestimated the gains made possible by the rapid absorption of technological progress—these gains made Japan's resource endowment relatively insignificant and turned her large and educated labor force into a clear competitive advantage.

When one contemplates what is being said concerning Japan's economic future at present, it seems that we are in danger of once again falling into the

---

Parts of this essay were previously published in the author's "The Economic Position of Japan: Past, Present, and Future" in *United States International Economic Policy In An Interdependent World* (Washington, D.C.: U.S. Government Printing Office, 1971), vol. 2, pp. 111-128.

[a]A rather typical example is the University of Chicago's Round Table of the Air discussion on NBC, December 16, 1951. The following are excerpts from the printed version (no. 716).

Theodore W. Schultz: May I ask what do you see in prospect for the Japanese economy, taking both the short view, the next two or three years, and the next five or ten years? I judge that you see rather serious difficulties?

Norton Ginsburg: Yes, I think there will be very serious difficulties. The Japanese economy, insofar as it has been an export economy in the past, lies dependent, in large part, upon foreign markets and upon imported raw materials in large quantities. And the bulk of those markets and raw materials, with some exceptions, have been in the past in the Far East. . . . There are many complications, chiefly Japan's lack of basic raw materials. . . .

Earl Pritchard: I certainly agree with the general point which Ginsburg has expressed that Japan is going to have a very serious difficulty of making a go of it economically. She has the problem of finding markets, of getting raw materials. . . . Before the war she exported a lot to China. That is closed today; the Southeast Asian countries are not buying too much. Just where do you expect her to find a market?

For the record, it should be added that Professor Schultz took a much more optimistic and realistic view.

1

trap of seeing tomorrow exclusively in the framework of today.[b] Those who use the crystal ball most frequently appear to see the future with considerable clarity: the twenty-first century will be Japan's; by the year 2000 Japan will have the largest GNP in the world; even the United States will be surpassed in terms of industrial productivity and standard of living; etc.[1] All of this is possible, but the realization of these predictions depends on a few crucial assumptions. For the past twenty years the Japanese economy has been expanding at the unprecedented rate of slightly over 10 percent per year (in real terms). Most of the rest of the world has been growing much more slowly, on average at more or less one-half the Japanese pace. The gap between Japan and other advanced countries is still large—in 1970 GNP per capita was $1910 in Japan, $3020 in West Germany, and $4850 in the United States—and if she is to overtake the competition by A.D. 2000, two reasonable conditions must hold. First of all, Japan will have to continue running the race at more or less current speed. And secondly, the other runners must not significantly increase their speed.

Whether or not some advanced countries will be able to challenge Japan's rates of growth cannot be discussed here, although we fail to see how one can be very certain about such a matter in the long run. I do, however, wish to examine the first question: will the Japanese economy maintain present rates of growth in the future? The year 2000 is far away and as an economic historian I am naturally more comfortable in displaying the easier wisdom of hindsight. To make the question more tractable, let us first ask: is it likely that Japanese GNP will grow less rapidly—say, in the neighborhood of 6 ± 1 percent—towards the end of the 1970s?[c] And then, let us consider the year 2000 in a later section.

We will attempt to show that the possibility of a slowdown cannot be dismissed. For the past twenty years Japan has been a veritable businessman's paradise in which many factors worked towards maximizing the rate of growth of aggregate output. This situation may change during the decade of the 1970s, partly for reasons beyond Japan's internal control. Equally critical may be a conscious change of direction induced by a new set of national priorities. The highest possible rate of growth of GNP does not necessarily lead to optimal national satisfaction. Perhaps the Japanese, who have led the world in growth-manship, will also be first to redirect their energies towards socially more beneficial activities. None of these developments are certainties, but they deserve to be kept in mind when we contemplate—with fear or joy—the alleged dawning of the "Japanese Century."

---

[b]This had been the traditional predictive error concerning Japan. In the Meiji Era many foreign observers could not bring themselves to believe that modern economic growth was possible. They understood too well the difficulties of the 1870s and 1880s, they did not foresee that the economic and social regimen would undergo basic change in the 1890s and thereafter.
[c]If GNP continues to grow at present rates of over 10 percent per year, by 1980 Japan will reach a level of about $400 billion and a per capita output of about $3500—all in 1960 prices. U.S. GNP in 1980 is estimated at $1280 billion in 1958 prices.

Economic Growth, 1950-1970

Perhaps the best way to understand the implications of the future is to consider once again the reasons for Japan's spectacular economic performance from the middle 1950s to the present. Within this time span Japan not only developed much more rapidly than at any other time in her history, but she also did better than any other comparable economy. Why? No one "secret" exists, and the real factors are intertwined in necessarily complicated relationships. Nevertheless, the basic elements in Japan's so-called economic miracle can be identified.

Economists frequently use the concept of the aggregate production function which says that the growth rate of output is related to the growth rates of the conventional inputs: labor and capital. In specific cases, the relationship between inputs and output varies both in time and internationally. Two countries—or one country at different historical periods—may have identical rates of growth of inputs and very different rates of growth of aggregate output. This difference is usually called "the residual," and its existence has generally been ascribed to technological progress, to the possibilities of exploiting economies of scale, and to qualitative improvements in inputs. The point is that in postwar Japan—since the 1950s—the residual has been growing at an unprecedented rate; to put it in somewhat different words, the Japanese have succeeded in squeezing more output out of every unit of input than at any other time in their modern development. The rest of the world has not been able to match these results. Why? Surely a key element must be the massive inflow of foreign technology which in the eighteen years between 1950 and 1968 represented about 10,000 contracts and payments in excess of $1.4 billion. These inflows permitted the modernization of old and the creation of new industries under extremely favorable conditions. Foreign technology was, in almost all instances, superior to domestic types, and it was—until recently—cheap. Foreigners were content to sell know-how for reasonable royalties and license fees; this suited Japanese business and government, both of whom were anxious to keep foreign enterprise out of their home market. It was also cheap because the purchase and use of foreign processes finessed expensive and hazardous R and D efforts since the costs of pioneering were borne by others. Furthermore, Japanese enterprise raised the adaptation of foreign methods to a fine art through the development of what has been called "improvement engineering."[d]

The advantages inherent in acquiring advanced technology are not a Japanese monopoly, and one has to ask why they were so successful. In part, it can be argued that the opportunities were obvious and plentiful in a semideveloped

---

[d]This refers to systematic attempts at improving imported technology. It is largely an activity of "carefully taking apart and putting together a little better." I have been told by Japanese businessmen that they have frequently succeeded in running a foreign process at up to 130 percent of rated capacity, simply by making a set of minor—though carefully considered—improvements.

economy recently devastated by war and out of contact with more advanced countries for over ten years. But this was nearly equally true for most Western European economies.

A more distinctive Japanese feature is the level and growth of investment. In this area Japan has topped all competitors. During the 1950s and 1960s, fixed capital formation has averaged well over 30 percent of GNP, with most of this going into private productive investment embodying recent technological improvements. (Residential housing accounted for only a very small share of this total). Other countries produced far less impressive figures: for comparable periods, U.S. investment shares were 17 percent, in France they were 19 percent, and in West Germany 24 percent.

What made it possible for such a large share of GNP to be invested in an essentially free-market economy? One factor was the high return obtainable from private investment. Capital-output ratios, especially in those industries which imported technology, tended to decline leading to more output per unit of capital input. Giving the labor force more and better equipment also raised output per worker, but luckily for entrepreneurs this did not lead to a comparable rise in wages. During the fifties worker productivity rose more than wages; for most of the sixties productivity has kept pace with wage increases. In European countries as well as in the United States, wage increases outstripped worker productivity gains in this period.

The labor situation remained unusually favorable in Japan until the late 1960s. Real strikes—i.e., lengthy work stoppages—were almost unknown, and the national unions continued to dissipate their energies on problems of foreign policy. On the shop floor, where it counted, the employer dealt with docile and cooperative enterprise unions. Labor supply remained elastic due to the large reservoir of able, educated workers still available in agriculture and in assorted pockets of traditional underemployment. All this kept cost pressures under control while worker productivity continued to rise at about 9 percent per year in the aggregate—another record.

Undoubtedly, the government deserves considerable credit for Japan's high growth. It taxed moderately—19 percent of GNP, as opposed to 27 percent in the United States, and 35 percent in the United Kingdom—supported growth industries by controlling foreign exchange allocations and guiding the inflow of technology, and ultimately guaranteed the availability of industrial bank credit through the Bank of Japan. Business and government worked hand in hand towards the common objective of rapid economic growth—sometimes it was hard to know where one entity began and the other left off. Of course the fact that defense expenditures were less than 1 percent of GNP helped both government and business. It is, perhaps, worth recalling that Japanese defense was so inexpensive because of American guarantees.

The public also supported the all-out growth effort primarily by supplying the savings needed to finance the enormous investments. In the 1960s personal savings were about 20 percent of disposable income, as compared to 12 percent in West Germany and 7 percent in the United States. Why and how the Japanese manage to be so frugal is a frequently debated issue among social scientists. Some of the most crucial factors may be repeated here. The individual Japanese is largely responsible for his own welfare—clearly this is related to the low level of government expenditures—and he must provide for education, retirement, and "rainy day" emergencies. Welfare is private and not yet public and this heightens the incentive to save in order to make up for the inadequacies of Japan's social security system. It is also true that personal income has been rising rapidly during the past twenty years while consumption expenditures have risen—but only with a time lag of between one and two years. In other words, the Japanese have been rather conservative consumers, and the lag alone will assure a large and growing pool of savings. The reason for the lag—even its existence—may be puzzling in view of the manifest prosperity of the people. However, this prosperity has its misleading aspects. In the consumption of necessities and small consumer durables—food, clothing, radios, TV, refrigerators, etc.—the Japanese can compare themselves quite favorably with nearly all other countries. This is not so when it comes to housing or automobiles—only 7 percent of Japanese owned private cars in 1969, as opposed to 39 percent in the United States, and 18 percent in West Germany. These "big-ticket" items are difficult to acquire largely because consumer credit is still an underdeveloped commodity. When and if it does become available, the consumption lag may disappear.

Japan's postwar expansion has also been mightily supported by an expansion of exports running at about 15 percent per year, which is more than twice the rate of expansion of world trade. Again, we believe that the absorption of new technology is relevant in explaining this phenomenon. Foreign customers purchased a rising proportion of Japanese goods because these represented good buys in terms of price and quality. And indeed, while domestic consumer prices rose over 50 percent in the decade of the 1960s, export prices for many commodities declined and in the aggregate remained almost stable. The incongruity between domestic and export prices is complicated, but one reason undoubtedly is the fact that Japanese exports have increasingly concentrated on those commodities in which cost-reducing technological progress has made its largest contributions. In the last few years the most rapidly rising exports have been transportation equipment, machinery, and iron and steel. All of these industries have had especially rapidly declining capital-output ratios indicating the massive absorption of technical and organizational progress—in good measure of foreign origin. Obviously the government has also had a lot to do with building up these strong and increasingly competitive export industries through its explicit methods of preferential credit rationing, tax exemptions, extraordinary depreciation allowances, readier permission to import know-how and—at times—tight protection against foreign imports.

We should also keep in mind that the past twenty years created an especially congenial climate for trade expansion. Japan's largest customer, the United States, espoused free trade, and there was little difficulty in penetrating markets in South and Southeast Asia, and Latin America.

Finally, a word about the human element in Japan's recent success story. Thus far we have concentrated on relatively "pure" economic factors. Somehow account has to be taken of the tremendous burst of entrepreneurial energy in postwar Japan. The Japanese have a long history of entrepreneurial achievements; throughout this century they were strong, imaginative, and sometimes ruthless competitors. Still, as with so many other indicators, there is an extraordinary quality attached to the 1950s and 1960s—one need think only of the long list of triumphs in electronics, steel, shipbuilding, automobiles, and many other industries. Behind each one of these stand a group of innovating business leaders. Is there any reason for believing that recent years were—in some way—particularly hospitable to the flowering of entrepreneurial talent? This is the sort of problem which economists like to avoid and sociologists fail to study. I am convinced, however, that there was something special about the postwar era—and so are some very knowledgeable Japanese. World War II destroyed Japan's "proper order of things" and this may be the exceptional ingredient which favored entrepreneurship. One hundred years ago, the Meiji Restoration destroyed the Tokugawa system, and liberated the long pent-up energies of all classes. What happened after that is history: Japan became the only non-Western nation to achieve modern economic growth. With time, however, the new order developed rigidities especially from the point of view of new enterprise. New ventures and ideas came to be judged not only in terms of their intrinsic merit, but also in terms of who made the suggestion, what his connections were, where he had been to school, and so forth. These rigidities were wiped away when the World War II establishment was displaced. For a time, talent and ability counted more than age, university degrees from the right schools, and family or banking connections. A new and vital entrepreneurial class emerged, and it has served Japan brilliantly ever since.[e]

The 1970s

Next, we should consider the meaning of what took place during the last twenty years. What are its implications for the future—especially for this decade? Were these years a specific growth phase and the consequence of transitory economic opportunities, or do they represent a style of growth that will maintain itself for the next thirty years? There are two separate aspects to this problem. First, we have to speculate about the quality in the 1970s of those economic factors

---

[e]A leading Japanese businessman told me that the black market of the late 1940s provided a most useful lesson to the business community since it proved that people of ability could succeed regardless of connections or background.

which have been so vital in creating rapid growth in the past. Secondly, we have to speculate about the possibility of new factors affecting the direction of economic development in Japan. I will proceed in this order.

Let us begin with the inflow and absorption of foreign technology. There seems to be general agreement on the following points: that in the 1950s and 1960s Japan lagged behind the technological leaders (primarily the United States and to a lesser extent West Germany); that since the middle 1960s this technological gap has been rapidly growing smaller; that Japanese business is now making great efforts through increased R and D expenditures and similar devices to develop its own advanced technology. The facts have recently been thoroughly analyzed by James Abegglen.[2] He notes that since 1958 approximately 10 percent of total manufacturing in Japan was carried out using foreign technology. However, if only the modern sectors are considered, the dependency on foreign technology would rise 25 to 30 percent. Although the number of technical agreements has continued to increase all the time, "the proportion of agreements representing technology new to Japan and previously unlicensed is dropping steadily, from 70 percent in 1961 to only one third in 1966." This is one sign that the gap is closing, "both because Japan is achieving technical parity with the nations of the West and because of an increasing reluctance of Western business to make technology available on license."[3] As Abegglen points out, the private sector has responded to this pressure by a considerable research and development effort. In 1964 about 115,000 employees were classified as research workers—France and West Germany reported slightly over 30,000 each. Obviously these efforts have yielded some favorable results: "In 1960 Japan paid about $95 million for foreign technology, and received payments of only $2 million for sales of Japanese technology . . . in 1967 while Japan paid out about $239 million, receipts totalled about $26 million. . . ."[4]

It seems to me that the long-run implications of the present situation are frequently misunderstood. There are many reasons for believing that Japan will—in the coming decades—create numerous significant and profitable technological advances. No doubt Japan will also continue to avail herself of progress made elsewhere. There is, however, a fundamental difference between closing a gap (or eliminating a lag) and depending on the extension of a domestic or foreign technological frontier. In the former case one can—if other conditions are right—proceed at great speed. Gains can accrue in a relatively short time. In the latter case, one may face lengthy bottlenecks. The technological frontier is inevitably surrounded by uncertainties, hesitations, and false starts—soon an element of "cheapness" in Japanese development may disappear.

It would be fruitless to attempt to quantify the effect of Japan reaching technological parity sometime in the 1970s. On balance, however, it seems clear that reaching this point will make continued high-speed growth more difficult. Probably the rate of growth of residuals will decline, and it may not be possible for labor productivity to maintain a rate of expansion two or more times larger than that of competing countries. Of course, the residual can be said to contain technological *and organizational* progress, and reaching parity may have less impact on the latter item. But I remain skeptical. The recent waves of mergers and consolidations generally encouraged by the government may lead to a rise in efficiency. They may also bring about—once again—prewar style rigidities, together with all the adverse features that this implies.

Let us turn our attention now from technology and the productivity of capital, to labor, wages, and employment. Japan's current position has frequently been described as "second and twentieth": the second largest GNP in the capitalist world and number twenty from the top in income per capita. Low income per capita in the aggregate is a direct consequence of low productivity in certain backward sectors, primarily agriculture, forestry, and fisheries, service industries, and small and medium-sized enterprises. However, a growing body of evidence indicates that certain changes are now discernable within the long-established differential structure; these began in the first half of the 1960s.[f] A tendency towards both narrowed wage differentials and smaller labor supply elasticities have been widely noted. In 1967, for the first time since World War II, the ratio of labor demand to supply (active openings/active application job seekers) exceeded 1.00. (In 1959 the ratio was 0.44.) And the Japanese government estimates that from 1970 to 1980 the working age population will rise only by 1 percent per year. Since 1967 wage differentials have continued to narrow, though at a somewhat slower pace.

Productivity differentials, however, present a very different picture: the gap between advanced and backward sectors is still there, and it is still widening. This sharp contrast in wage and productivity gaps is a new phenomenon of the late 1960s, and its consequences must be taken into account in evaluating Japan's economic future. Two problems, in particular, require attention: wage-income-price relations, and patterns of labor shift.

The wage-income-price relations of Japan, up to the present, differ fundamentally from those of other advanced countries. In Western Europe and the United States, cost-push or inflationary wage increases have generally been recognized as one of the primary causes of rising prices. This has not been true in Japan, where the causes of inflation are structural. In the past—until the early 1960s—the differential structure meant that low productivity sectors also paid low wages, and the prices of their goods and services remained relatively low—though as a trend they were slowly rising. Now the situation has changed. Labor shortages are reducing wage differentials, without affecting productivity levels. Given the persistent strong demand for the output of the more backward sectors—they supply much of the food and many other daily needs—their prices have been

---

[f]The differential structure refers to a historical trend, in evidence since World War I, in which wages and productivity levels have been rising more rapidly in the modern (advanced) sectors than in the traditional (backward) sectors. The resulting "gap" which grew larger between World War I and the early 1960s—is called the differential structure.

rising. This is the mechanism of Japan's inflation in the 1960s and today: it is a new version of the differential structure.

The performance of Japanese prices clearly illustrates what has been happening. During the 1960s, these relative movements were observable: rising retail prices vs. stable wholesale prices;[g] rising consumer goods prices vs. stable investment goods prices; and rising domestic vs. stable export prices. All these contrasts reveal the key role of backward sectors in raising the price level as against the stabilizing influence of modern industry.[h]

The transfer of workers from less to more productive occupations has, as yet, been unaffected by the new differential structure. Higher wages are required to get the needed numbers, but the ever rising productivity attainable in modern industry has kept demand strong. Net outflows continue unabated, despite rising prices, wages, and incomes in agriculture and other traditional sectors.

So much for the current situation. What of the future? This is the crucial question. No easy answer is possible, but one can say what appears to be a distinct possibility. On the one hand, modern industry will continue to require a large number of workers. On the other hand, labor supply will be less plentiful and pressure for rising wages emanating in backward sectors should be powerful. If this is combined with more limited technological opportunities in the coming decade, the appearance of cost-push sometime during the 1970s is not only conceivable—rather it is highly likely.

The reaction of organized labor to this possible situation should also be considered. Until now the Japanese worker has done well. His real wages have increased despite inflation, and individually and collectively he has had a somewhat superficial sweetheart relation with his bosses—at the plant level. Yet one may have doubts about the future. Management has shown little resistance to sizeable wage increases largely because these were more than matched by gains in productivity. But will management not be tempted to resist if it becomes more difficult to raise productivity levels? If this happens, if prices continue to go up, if labor shortages still exist, we can safely assume more severe

[g]A division into wholesale prices originating in modern and traditional sectors would show divergent movements: stability and sometimes decline in the former and increases in the latter. In the aggregate, however, traditional wholesale prices are not very significant, since the important service sector does not enter into consideration.

[h]For a few years before 1970, some increases occurred in wholesale prices, and it was widely believed that signs of cost-push were appearing in modern sectors. But this turned out to be a premature conclusion. When the government adopted a tight money policy to curb an excessive rate of growth, wholesale prices stabilized. We may, therefore, conclude that the pressure came from the demand side.

Some might also argue that recently labor costs in relation to productivity or that labor's relative share have started to increase in modern industry, and this is offered as an explanation of the recent inflation. As a long-term trend labor costs per unit of capital have certainly been increasing. But to link this observation with rising prices is too simple. One has, at the same time, to consider output per unit of capital, and this gives no support to cost-push up to the present.

and open worker-management conflict in the 1970s. When will the Japanese economy experience a wave of Western-style strikes, defined as rather lengthy work stoppages against individual enterprises in order to achieve a set of economic demands? Many of the largest employers are peculiarly vulnerable to this tactic: they export a relatively large share of output and interruptions of shipments would lose foreign clients; they are heavily indebted to banks and therefore carry unusually heavy overhead burdens. Perhaps the Japanese labor unions will adopt these tactics in the 1970s. It could lead to some interesting changes.

Foreign trade is another area in which changes cannot be excluded, although these are always difficult to predict. The current boom which began in 1965 has relied far more on the contribution of exports than previous postwar booms.[i] Also, as a trend, Japan's share in world trade has more than doubled between 1955 and 1970, and plans for the future remain very ambitious. The Japan Economic Research Center estimates a 10 percent share of world exports by 1975, with an 18 percent share of the U.S. market and 35 percent of the Asian market.[5]

But targets for 1975 are too close at hand. My query is: Can this great expansion continue beyond the 1970s? Let us briefly dwell on some of the "straws in the wind" floating about. Japan's export capability depends not only on her prices but also on world prices. Should cost-push develop in the 1970s, it stands to reason that export prices will not escape this pressure, and no one can argue that this is a competitive advantage in world markets.

This is all the more dangerous because a rise in protectionist sentiment is in evidence in many parts of the world. Talk of Japanese dumping is more frequent, and various industries are seeking relief from foreign competition. If the United States adopts quotas, tariffs, and other restrictions, this will undoubtedly hurt Japan's trade account. In Asia also there is a rising nervousness about Japanese economic and political intentions usually expressed as a fear of "domination." Perhaps the Japanese will reach 18 percent of the American and 35 percent of the Asian market, but it is also likely that the attempt will generate strong resistance.[j]

I have tried to suggest that some of the very favorable factors in Japanese growth may be transitory. At least some of the possible changes are beyond simple policy control; they can perhaps be called part of the economic

---

[i]For 1965-69 exports contributed nearly 12 percent to total increases in Gross National Expenditure. During the preceding Iwato Boom (1958-61), the comparable contribution stood at 7 percent.

[j]In this discussion no attempt has been made to assess the impact of rising military expenditures, because I do not believe that Japan will—in the next ten years—engage in large-scale rearmament. I could easily be wrong, but everyone will agree on the following: (a) the low level of military expenditures up to the present has been a distinct advantage in maintaining rapid growth; (b) large-scale rearmament would contribute very little towards future economic development.

maturation process. Now I would like briefly to consider the likelihood and consequences of new socioeconomic priorities.

A recent article in the influential *Japan Economic Journal* said:

The Japanese economy has passed the time when it should be satisfied only with the expansion of gross national product. It, instead, has entered the state in which it should pay closer attention to the level and distribution of stocks.

Environmental improvement based on social investments is the principal theme in this stage.[6]

By now this has become a familiar refrain, and anyone concerned with Japan will be familiar with criticisms of "growth at any cost," *kogai* (public nuisances), and assorted horror stories concerning pollution. No longer can these topics be called a partisan matter. Both the ruling Liberal Democratic Party and the opposition parties agree that the "agonies of a growing economy" must—some-how—be rectified. The question is: are we confronting merely another fad of Western origin or do they mean it?

Given twenty years of great prosperity, the Japanese have—according to their own sources—accumulated an impressive list of agonies. The best known of these is the lag in social overhead capital. Despite a growth rate of government investment, measured against per capita national income, that exceeds those of more advanced nations, Japan continues to fall behind her needs. Measured in terms of number of rooms per person, diffusion of water supply and sewage, ratio of paved roads, or area of city parks, Japan lags sadly behind countries with which she likes to compare herself. (Medical facilities are the only exception.) The ratio of social capital stock to national income fell steeply from the early 1950s until the early 1960s, and since then it has not risen significantly. The ratio of living-related social capital stock—houses, environmental sanitation, health and welfare, education—which the government would like to see at 0.5-0.6 actually stood at about 0.35 in the late 1960s.[k]

---

[k]It may be helpful to provide some international perspective at this point. Taking Britain, France, and West Germany as 100, the Japanese situation in the middle of the 1960s was as follows:

Per capita annual consumption of vegetables	121.6
Per capita annual consumption of meat, eggs, and fish	46.7
Per capita daily intake of calories	77.3
Number of rooms per household member	68.4
Ratio of diffusion of sewerage	73.1
Ratio of population using public water supply	21.9
Extension of paved roads per motor car	20.4
Ratio of paved roads	13.4
Number of teachers per 1,000 elementary school pupils	107.9
Ratio of diffusion of electric washing machines	153.2
Ratio of diffusion of television sets	166.7
Per capita annual consumption of textiles	94.8

Economic Survey of Japan, 1967-68, p. 142.

Many reasons can explain the present impasse. Funds are always a problem especially when taxes are low. Public investments have been more affected than the private sector by price increases due to their larger labor content. A great inflation in land prices has been another stumbling block. However, the fundamental reasons lie elsewhere. As first priority the government consistently maintained a policy of maximizing the rate of growth of aggregate output; other needs remained in a subordinate position. This implied encouraging private capital formation, a balanced budget, and a chronic shortage of resources available for the enlargement of social consumption.

Modern economic growth has also led to an ever more unpleasant and dangerous set of public hazards or nuisances. To understand the problem, one only needs to know that Japan has the largest per area gross national product in the world. More economic activity takes place in less space than in any other country, and the consequences in terms of noise, water and air pollution are not hard to imagine.[1]

Japan also suffers from a deficiency in social security. The percentage ratio of social security payments to national income was 6.2 in 1966, and it has hardly risen since then. Comparative ratios were 7.6 percent in the United States, 13.8 percent in Great Britain, 19.9 percent in West Germany, 19.2 percent in France, and 15.0 percent in Italy.[m] Japanese (and United States) levels are inadequate, and are made more so by the rapid change in the age structure of the population. A declining birth rate and lengthened life expectancy have raised the proportion of people sixty-five or over from 5.3 percent in 1955 to a projected 9.9 percent in 1985. Family units consisting only of old people are on the rise, and they can rely less and less on traditional practices—support from children, family work, and so forth—to provide a comfortable old age. This may well be one of the saddest consequences of modern economic growth in Japan. Not long ago one could still see happy old people living in extended families, an especially impressive phenomenon for Americans who are unfortunately used to a different situation. In this respect—unless great care is exercised—Japan may soon reach U.S. levels.

The agonies and benefits of growth are related to different aspects of the economy. Benefits are closely correlated with the level of income per capita: other things being equal, the richest countries have the highest standards of living. Agonies or adverse side-effects also bear some relation to the level of income. However, they are equally closely tied to the rate of income growth, the progress of technology, and to a variety of noneconomic factors, such as geography. I have not made a systematic comparison of Japan with the rest of the industrialized world. Nevertheless, it seems to me that Japanese-style growth

[1]Air pollution problems are aggravated by Japan's almost exclusive reliance on high sulphur content Middle Eastern oil.

[m]More recent comparative statistics are not available to me, but there is no reason to believe that either absolute or relative expenditures have significantly changed during the last six years.

has produced a lengthy and worrisome set of adverse side-effects at comparatively low levels of income per capita. Partly this can be ascribed to the speed of economic development: no doubt the lag in social overhead capital was in some measure due to the steep rise in demand for these services. Partly it is a consequence of resources and physical configuration: air and water pollution are more severe because of population concentration and enforced reliance on certain types of fuel. When Western Europe and the United States were at Japanese levels of income, one heard rather little concerning these unpleasant side-effects. Another historical era was involved, society was organized along different lines, and current social priorities were as yet insignificant. All of this is true. It is also true that the problems were less severe in the United States or Europe at these lower levels: in the United States the vastness of our country allowed more leeway, and in Europe both the slower pace of growth and an earlier start permitted some problems to be postponed. Whatever the reasons, we come back to the same conclusion: Japan faces the so-called agonies of growth at lower levels of income per capita than her predecessors in the development race—and postponement of solutions may be neither possible nor desirable.

Japanese planners are well aware of the trade-off issues posed by these problems. Most of them stem from a peculiar political situation. A higher ratio of public investments, badly needed at this time, has in the past been vigorously and successfully resisted by a powerful private sector. Given the fact that sources for financing capital formation are limited, intensified social investments compete with business expansion plans, and leading enterprisers have used their considerable influence within the government to minimize the impact of desirable social policies on their affairs. Thus far, obvious steps like increased interest rates or higher corporate taxation have been successfully avoided despite much lip service by business and government leaders in favor of improving the quality of life. Since the 1950s, Japan has not only been a businessman's economic paradise—it has been an economic *and* political paradise: therein lies the problem. But, we should also remember that the Japanese are good at institution building, and what is needed now is some national machinery that could reach a new consensus concerning overall investment allocations. Presumably the voices of all citizens—labor, capital, farmers, small business, and so forth—would be heard.

There are, of course, difficult political problems associated with the trade-off between public and private expenditures. Shifting resources from private to public capital formation may lower the output effect of these expenditures because the capital-output ratio is generally higher for social overhead investments.

Undoubtedly these trade-offs have been stated in naive form. An improvement of the social overhead capital stock should raise the efficiency of private investment. Other types of social expenditures may favorably affect labor force quality. Offsetting possibilities, however, are not likely to change the net trade-offs: the choice of the future lies either in curbing private investment or private consumption. It is this latter alternative that is especially difficult to imagine as Japanese policy, for it would entail asking the population to make consumption sacrifices while their income per capita was still low. This is just the time when desires for more and better consumption are great—and they are growing greater. Japan is on the threshhold of becoming a mass consumption society, not a time when any politician—in or out of office—will advocate a large dose of austerity on behalf of the public good.

A Longer Perspective

In the preceding section, I spent some time on Japan's economic future in the 1970s. What about the longer-run destiny of Japan? This is, at the moment, a rather popular and timely question, and I would like now to speculate about the coming twenty or thirty years. No formal forecast or quantitative projections will be attempted. Instead, I intend simply to pursue some of the future implications stemming from the analysis of the past. In this type of exercise, unknown factors are numerous, and history may be a poor guide to the hereafter. Nevertheless, the temptation to conjecture is irresistable, and there is probably no sounder method than to consider how the "normal" historical path might change. In doing so, external factors beyond Japan's control have to be largely excluded; there exists no systematic way of discussing them, although I will come back to this matter later.

Towards the end of the 1970s, for reasons already described, I have predicted a slowdown in the rate of growth of Japan's national product. To pursue this prediction beyond the 1970s, it is most practical to concentrate on the demand and supply for labor. For this particular market, the future can be predicted with a fair degree of certainty; it is, after all, widely accepted that sometime soon labor will take the place of capital as a limiting or scarce factor.

By the end of this decade, it is likely that Japan's rate of growth of aggregate output will have fallen from its postwar rate of 10 percent to somewhere in the neighborhood of 6.5 percent—this was the previous conclusion. Let us now assume, just for discussion's sake, that this rate represents a new long-term average for the next twenty years. Then, the following other average annual rates of growth are implied:

	Projections, 1970-90	Actual, 1955-68
(1) Manufacturing output:	10.5 %	11.4 %
(2) Agriculture output:	2.0 to 2.5 %	2.8 %
(3) Labor demand in manufacturing:	3.6 %	4.1 %
(4) Labor productivity in manufacturing:	6.9 %	16.0 %

(5) Labor force in agriculture:	-3.0 to -3.5%	-3.0%
(6) Labor productivity in agriculture:	5.0 to 6.0%	5.3%
(7) Total labor force:	0.7 to 1.0%[n]	1.6%

Just a few additional comments concerning these figures. With these assumptions, labor productivity in manufacturing continues to expand more rapidly than in agriculture: the productivity gap is still being widened. Since the total labor force can only expand slowly due to demographic reasons, the high labor requirements of manufacturing can be met only by a continuing reallocation of workers from agriculture to industry.[o] And this is a crucial matter because I believe that the possibilities of substituting capital for labor are technologically limited, although to some degree it will be accomplished so as to combat the trend of rising wages.

If this simple growth path continues until (say) 1990, a picture of the Japanese economy emerges at that time:

1. The proportion of the labor force in manufacturing will be 43 percent if the total labor force rises at 1 percent per year, or 48 percent if the total increases at 0.7 percent per year.
2. Agriculture will contain 8.0 to 9.5 percent of the employed population.
3. The differential of average labor productivity between agriculture and manufacturing will be much larger than it is today. Compared to 1970, the relative position of agriculture will fall either 22 percent if the sectoral productivity growth rates differ by 1 percent, or 48 percent if the sectoral difference is 2 percent.

From the present until 1990, therefore, if these assumptions are at all nearly correct, the differential structure will still be a feature of the Japanese economy despite the maintenance of a high net outflow of workers from the backward sectors. Of course, between 1970 and 1990 the weight and significance of those in lower productivity sectors will have declined very much.

This is one way of looking at the future, and one certainly should not take these numbers too seriously. It may be interesting, however, briefly to pursue some of the inferences suggested by the numerical example.

---

[n]These projections are based on a variety of regressions fully discussed in a forthcoming book jointly authored by Professor Kazushi Ohkawa and myself, and entitled *Trend Acceleration: Japanese Economic Growth in the Twentieth Century*. For example, between the growth rate of aggregate demand (G_v) and manufacturing output (Gy_m) the following long-run relation (1908-64) exists:

$$Gy_m = \frac{1.55}{(0.885)} + \frac{1.366\, G_v}{(0.138)} \quad (\bar{R}^{-2} = 0.707).$$

[o]Of course, labor can also be shifted out of lower productivity service occupations into manufacturing. It is also possible to transfer workers from small-scale to larger-scale enterprises. For simplicity's sake these possibilities are not considered, although they would contribute towards a somewhat more favorable labor supply position.

With the perspective of history, we can say that in the nineteenth century Japan experienced initial modern economic growth, and that the period 1900 to 1965 represented a much bigger step which I would label "the leap toward a semideveloped state." These were the years of the great private investment spurts and trend acceleration (in the sense that the rate of growth of aggregate output climbed to ever higher levels). For reasons already indicated, I believe this phase to have ended at about the present time. Both the easy availability of technology and labor are less certain assets from now on. National priorities may also be redirected. For these reasons, I am inclined to call Japan's next long phase of growth "the movement from semidevelopment to economic maturity."

This is likely to be quite a different process. *Economic maturity* is a difficult term to define, but as used here, it has a narrow meaning. Let us call it that state in which the incentives of sectoral labor force reallocation have become minimal—in the extreme case impossible. In proceeding from initial growth to semidevelopment, opportunities for labor reallocation increased: that is one way of looking at the creation of the differential structure. In moving towards maturity, we can expect that, at some point, these opportunities will diminish.

When will this situation be attained in Japan and what will be its consequences? A rough indication of "when" is the proportion of the agricultural labor force, and according to the numerical example, in 1990 it will be about 9 percent. This is in excess of current proportions in the United States and the United Kingdom, but for Japan a level slightly below 10 percent may well be a point beyond which labor force shift incentives are minimal. Land resources are unusually poor, and a combination of farm and nonfarm employment is commonplace. We may reasonably assume that when the agricultural labor force declines to about 10 percent, some kind of intersectoral equilibrium will exist in terms of income per head.[P]

No one can name the year when Japan will reach this equilibrium. Perhaps in 1990; perhaps earlier or later. It all depends on the long-run rate of growth, and to make a firmer prediction is hazardous. More to the point are the implications of attaining this position—no matter when. From 1900 to the present I spoke of "trend acceleration," and perhaps we can characterize the future as *trend deceleration*. Towards the end of the century the labor bottleneck should loom large, and if the possibilities of substitution are indeed limited, a trend of slower growth is most likely. The previous assumption of 6.5 percent national product growth from now to 1990 was stated as constant average. In reality a decline from, let us say, 8 to 4 percent during this interval is even more likely.

These prognostications can in no way be considered pessimistic. Compared to other advanced countries, Japan's growth will still be rapid during the coming fifteen or twenty years; only the gap may become somewhat smaller. Rapid growth will continue because labor reallocation has a long way to go, and

---

[P]At that point there is no reason whatever for assuming that per capita product in Japan will be the same as that of the United States.

income levels will continue to rise creating opportunities for further domestic technological growth combined with continued improvement engineering. In a word, Japan is still a quarter of a century away from facing the difficulties of mature development. To project beyond that stage is quite impossible.

A Japanese economy growing at 6.5 percent per year presents considerable problems for the world, and possible international repurcussions must be considered in any estimate of the future. Japan's sustained rapid growth will almost certainly continue to be led by manufacturing. As a result, the growth of exports will have to be large and above the growth of world trade. Whether or not the rest of the world can or desires to swallow the flood of Japanese manufactures has to be a matter of grave concern. The Japanese may face repeated pressure for upward yen revaluation, and/or a rise of protectionism. To some extent they can attempt to alleviate the situation by larger capital exports, but this raises the spectre of Japanese economic domination and has explosive political consequences especially in Asia. One should not be surprised if, in the coming decade, Japan assumes a most unaccustomed role as champion of free trade, while other advanced countries turn more to defensive tariffs, quotas, and other restraints. Any or all of these eventualities could seriously undermine the projected rates of growth.

On the import side, Japan faces equally serious international repercussions. Import substitution has nearly reached its limit, and now this large and rapidly growing economy displays an ever more voracious appetite for the world's raw materials, of which Japan possesses almost none. It is true that Japan is anxious to exchange her excellent manufactures for the raw materials of less developed countries, and that her large purchases are beneficial to many nations. But few countries see their future as raw material exporters, and Japan's enormous needs now—and more enormous needs in the future—create economic and political apprehensions in diverse parts of the globe. Japan has to face the very real possibility that the world may be unwilling to supply, under any reasonable conditions, the raw materials necessary to sustain for twenty-five years a growth rate of 6.5 percent. A growth rate of 10 percent, as at present, is almost surely out of the question with this constraint. Even a lower level will demand a kind of economic statesmanship—for example, repeated upward revaluations—that the Japanese have only rarely displayed in the past.

In discussing Japan's future, my frank purpose has been to act as devil's advocate. This necessarily entails a certain amount of "viewing with alarm" and some will no doubt consider the conclusions excessively pessimistic. Still, I firmly believe that the two major themes which have been stressed are correct: (1) that there are certain factors inherent in a higher level of economic maturity which will make it increasingly more difficult to maintain a real annual growth rate of 10 percent, and (2) that a government financed improvement in the quality of life will have the same result. There is no cause for pessimism in these conclusions. If the rate of growth is reduced for the right reasons, Japan may not surpass the West in aggregate income by the year 2000. It may, however, surpass it in aggregate happiness, and this might yet be the real meaning of "Japanese Century" when it arrives.

Will it actually happen? My intuition tells me that it will. For a number of reasons I think that the Japanese have a better chance of achieving an intelligent and rational industrial order than many other democratic countries. The level of consensus in the society is still impressive, central government is strong, and the nation has frequently demonstrated a social capability to make basic changes. As Americans, we should hope for and welcome these eventualities since they will bring about a more stable Japan, capable of more intelligent leadership in Asia.

Notes for Chapter 1

1. For example, see Herman Kahn, THE EMERGING JAPANESE SUPER-STATE: CHALLENGE AND RESPONSE (New York: Prentice-Hall, 1970).

2. See James Abegglen (ed.), BUSINESS STRATEGIES FOR JAPAN (Tokyo: Sophia University, 1970), ch. 7.

3. Ibid., p. 117. Of course, overall parity is still a good distance away. At this time, technological renovation is moving from production and processing sectors to packing, marketing, and leisure industries. Technical advances are also moving from large to small-scale establishments. See ECONOMIC SURVEY OF JAPAN (1968-69), p. 110.

4. Ibid., p. 131.

5. See Saburo Okita, ESSAYS IN JAPAN AND ASIA (Tokyo: The Japan Economic Research Center, 1970), p. 19.

6. "China Trade Causing Headache," THE JAPAN ECONOMIC JOURNAL, May 19, 1970.

2

The Competitive Impact of Japanese Growth

James C. Abegglen and William V. Rapp

Close and cooperative relations between Japan and the United States are essential to maintaining a secure position for Japan and the West in today's world. On this relationship depends the security of the North Pacific and the feasibility of a viable order in the 1970s in Southeast Asia. Fast becoming an economic superpower, Japan is a large market for U.S. goods, and has been a dependable ally in maintaining order both in the world monetary system and in security arrangements.

Over the past two decades, while Japan moved from the status of a client to that of an associate of the United States, the relationship remained close and cooperative despite the inevitable strains associated with this change. This was true despite the fact that the two countries have little in common. Neither history, religion, culture, language nor race provide a basis for an identity of interests. Economic interests and their associate, military interests, have provided the real basis for cooperative efforts between the two countries.

Yet present relations are in a state of considerable tension. This is especially hazardous since these tensions are building with respect to trade—precisely the area in which common interest is most widespread and most likely to continue. For example, the inability to find even a basis for real negotiations over the textile issue, much less agreement, was a clear signal that relations are in serious trouble.

The crux of the issue has been, of course, Japan's increasing competitiveness in world markets, particularly in manufactured goods. Japan has broadened the spectrum of its penetration of the U.S. market from textiles and toys to steel, consumer electronics, and autos. In addition, it has replaced the United States as the main supplier of heavy equipment to such countries as Taiwan, Korea, and the Philippines. From the U.S. viewpoint, this situation has been further exacerbated by a shift of Japan's trade balance with the United States from deficit to growing surplus.

The major realignment of the yen-dollar parity in December is another sign of this changing economic relationship. However it is viewed most appropriately as a sign of Japan's increasing international competitiveness, as evidence of Japan's successful industrial policy, and as an indication of other countries' competitive failures. The purpose of this paper is to explore the underlying dynamics of Japan's success and the probability of its continuation.

19

The Problem

Since World War II, Japan has increased its share of world exports and almost totally in manufactured goods. Though this largely reflects a recovery of its prewar position, there is no abatement in its recent export growth rate. During the last decade, this has been two and one-half times the United States (17.2 percent versus 7.7 percent), and the United States has been steadily losing world export market share. This was almost inevitable given the economic anomalies of the early postwar period. In recent years, however, U.S. export growth has continued below world averages, especially in manufactured goods.

The net result of this process has been an increase in Japan's competitive export position vis-à-vis the United States in share of world exports from one-twentieth of U.S. exports in 1948 to not quite half in 1970. Further, Japan's exports are almost all manufactured goods (1970: 93 percent), whereas the U.S. exports large quantities of raw materials and agricultural commodities (1970: 32 percent). Therefore, in the world export market for manufactured goods, where the two countries really compete, the U.S. is less than twice as large and is losing ground fast (7.0 percent growth versus 17.8 percent). Most world trade is manufactured goods and, as their share is increasing, the Japanese are gaining world market share relative to the U.S. in the fastest growing portion of world exports.

This situation, as will be analyzed below, accelerates the improvement in their competitive cost position and a continuation of this trend will ultimately give Japan a larger share than the U.S. of world manufactured exports. For instance, by 1975 Japan's GNP may well be close to $500 billion in current prices. If exports continue to be about 10 percent of GNP, the total value of exports will be $50 billion compared with $20 billion in 1970. Most will be manufactured goods.

Concomitant with these world market developments Japan has increased her share of total U.S. imports from 7.8 percent in 1960 to 14.7 percent in 1970 and of U.S. manufactured imports from 16.8 percent in 1960 to 21.6 percent in 1970. As significant as these developments are, however, they do not completely reveal Japan's current dominance of U.S. imports of particular products such as textiles, steel, and consumer electronics that compete directly with U.S. producers of these items.

A typical assessment of Japan's ability to compete effectively in world markets, particularly the U.S. market, focuses on Japan's lower wage rates, special export incentives together with controls on imports, and "dumping" practices. Paradoxically, Japan's competitiveness has increased as wage differentials with respect to the United States and Europe have narrowed sharply and as she has dismantled her incentives and protectionism. In addition, Japanese companies have been profitable both domestically and overseas, an unlikely result of sustained "dumping."

Regarding the wage rate issue, during the 1920s Japanese wage rates and per capita GNP were about one-tenth U.S. levels, but Japan's only significant export to the U.S. was raw silk, accounting for perhaps 80 percent of Japanese exports to the United States. At present, Japanese labor rates are at West European levels, about one-third comparable U.S. rates, and several economists are predicting wages and per capita GNP at or above U.S. levels by the 1980s. However, the diversity, technological sophistication, and effectiveness of Japanese competition have increased as wages have increased and will continue to do so.

The question of trade policy, of protectionism versus free trade, is a changing one. Japan, like the United States in its earlier turn, pursued a vigorously protectionist policy as its industries were developing. Rather clearly the century of experience with a precarious payments balance resulted in a considerable awareness of the desirability of exporting as much as possible and importing as little as possible. And there is little question that this attitude persisted both in government and business longer than was warranted or economically desirable.

For its part, most of the American business community has for many years prided itself on being dedicated to a free trade policy and has felt that under reasonably free competitive rules, the United States is likely to outcompete other countries in any market. Just as the Japanese were slow to recognize the desirability of shifting away from protectionism, so the Americans have been slow to appreciate the reality of a U.S. shift toward protectionism.

According to the U.S. Department of State,[1] over the past decade from 1963 to late 1971, Japan moved from an extremely high level of quantitative import restrictions (132) to a rather low level (50, soon to be 40). The United States on the other hand went from the very low level of seven in 1963 to 67 in late 1971 not including the most recent textile quotas. Japan then has been moving with extraordinary speed given the obvious domestic problems in doing so to dismantle her protectionism while U.S. policy is moving about as rapidly toward protectionism. (The failure of many Americans to recognize these facts does not assist the dialogue between the two countries.)

The important fact about trade policy is not that one or the other nation is protectionist; the two nations appear now to be about equally "free-trading," although the trend lines are diverging. The important fact is that Japan, with a coherent and economically rational industrial policy, is protecting her high technology, high growth sectors while the protectionism of the United States is directed to the low growth, low technology sectors. It is evident, and will be further demonstrated below, that these respective positions tend to accelerate Japan's growth and hence her international competitiveness while depressing U.S. growth and competitive capability.

It is apparent that Japan is committed to a course aimed at eliminating all export incentives and opening most major industries to competition from imports and foreign investment. By the mid-1970s, Japan could well be the least protectionist country in the world and the most competitive. Excessive attention to issues like wage rates, trade policy or pricing methods only masks the underlying dynamics, with grave consequences of misperception for Western industries and governments. For this reason, it is imperative to clarify the cost effectiveness of Japan's rapid growth and the interaction of this growth with Japanese pricing behavior. The dynamics of Japanese competition are not being phased out; they will continue.

Cost Effectiveness of High Growth

A critical aspect of Japan's competitive development has been its industry's demonstrated ability rapidly to lower a product's costs and price. In product after product, Japanese firms have begun as high cost producers internationally but in a few years have become very competitive. We shall illustrate this shortly for television, and it will be demonstrated again later for steel and automobiles. Traditional product cycle analysis explains this as a result of market growth and changing factor supply availabilities. Yet, this explanation has a ring of historical inevitability, and on further examination is analytically inadequate. A firm's ability to lower a product's cost and price in fact depends on the volume it produces.

The Boston Consulting Group and other researchers have demonstrated for a variety of products in many industries that total cost per unit in *constant* dollars (or yen) will decline by a characteristic amount (usually 20-30 percent) each time accumulated production experience (total amount ever produced) doubles.[2] This statistical phenomenon is reflected in prices for entire industries as well as in unit costs for individual firms. It is observed in many countries, including the United States, Europe, and Japan and is an accepted part of cost projection formulations in the aircraft and semiconductor industries.[a] Because the concept relates the *rate* of cost decline with the *rate* of accumulation, a company's cost-experience relationship is plotted on log-log paper and is usually a straight line (Figures 2-1 and 2-2).

The cost-experience effect is temporally more noticeable in new products than in older, mature products. New products have a small experience base and a high demand growth. These products' accumulated production can double rapidly, and costs will fall accordingly. In mature industries, the effects of inflation will obscure the decline in real dollar (yen) cost. To obtain an accurate picture, one must factor out inflation.

The distorting effect of inflation is eliminated by deflating the current dollar

---

[a]Cost data are not always available, but one can derive curves from price data on the assumptions that prices follow costs over time and that market shares change slowly. Price curves are displayed in this paper and later for steel and autos. Cost is total cost to the end user, including direct overhead and marketing.

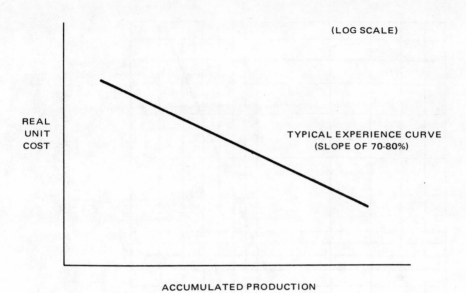

Figure 2-1. Schematic Cost-Experience Curve.

(yen) unit costs by the GNP deflator. Given a product's historical experience curve, one can predict future real costs at various levels of accumulated experience. To estimate actual future dollar (yen) cost, though, one must reinflate by multiplying the constant dollar (yen) cost projections by the expected rate of inflation.

Given this relationship between cost and volume, an individual firm's cost position within an industry depends on its growth relative to the entire industry, that is, on its market share. Conversely, an industry's ability to lower prices for a given amount of production depends on the market shares of the individual producers, that is, on the industry's concentration. (With greater concentration, industry experience is spread among fewer producers.)

The implication of the cost-experience effect for Japanese competition is that growth directly determines the Japanese firm's ability to accumulate experience and lower costs. And market share determines its ability to lower costs relative to competitors both domestic and foreign. The successful Japanese firm is the one who captures a dominant share of the world demand represented by Japanese market growth and subsequently export demand. This is evident from the direct relationship between Japanese firms' profitability and production share (see Table 2-1).

If a Japanese firm accumulates experience at 30 percent per year, it will double experience in less than three years and will lower *real* costs 20 to 30

24

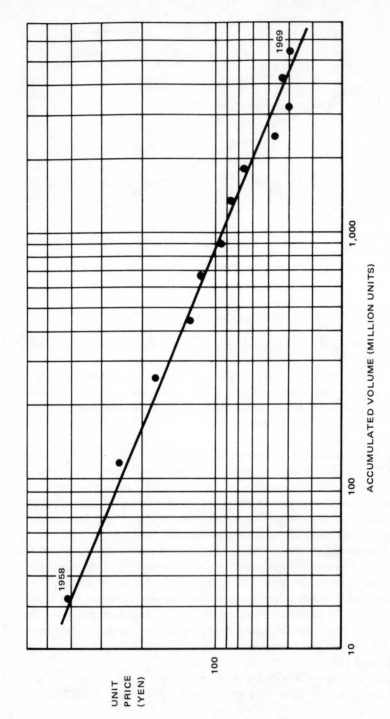

Figure 2-2. Price-Experience Curves (Japanese Transistor Prices vs. Accumulated Production: 1958-69). Data Source: MITI.

Table 2-1
Profitability and Market Share

	Profit after Taxes	Share
Tires		
Bridgestone	5.4	50%
Yokohama	1.4	24
Toyo Rubber	1.5	11
Synthetic Textile Fibers		
Toray	6.1	35
Teijin	4.0	25
Unitika	3.2	12
Bearings		
Koyo Seiko	4.7	32
Nippon Seiko	5.2	26
Toyo Bearing	4.5	31
Home Appliances		
Matsushita	11.0	23
Sanyo	7.5	14
General	4.5	2

Source: The *President Directory*, 1972, and the Boston Consulting Group, K.K.

percent. If inflation is 5 percent per year, its current costs will decline anywhere from 5 to 15 percent over the three-year period. If industry demand is growing at 15 percent, and the industry's accumulation rate has approached industry demand growth, the firm is capturing more than its share of incremental industry experience.[b] It is gaining market share relative to competitors and is improving cost position.

At a fixed exchange rate, the Japanese firm also lowers current dollar costs. If a mature U.S. market is growing at 5 percent with the same 5 percent inflation rate as Japan, the Japanese firm is rapidly gaining absolute cost advantage relative to U.S. producers (assuming relatively stable U.S. market shares). As most Japanese production has served, however, to satisfy domestic demand for products produced elsewhere first, frequently the United States, U.S. companies have begun or gone through the product's development and growth phase. They

---

[b]If industry growth is *go*, and the growth in accumulated experience at time *t* is *gn(t)*,

$$\frac{1}{\overline{Z}(1+go)t} + go = gn(t),$$

Thus the accumulation rate substantially exceeds the market growth rate in the early production stages but approaches it as the market matures.

have substantial cost-experience advantage relative to Japanese firms. Initial Japanese production has depended therefore on transportation cost differentials, Japanese government protection (tariffs, quotas, and subsidies), and/or no foreign marketing effort. Once beginning production, though, the firm's ability to become competitive has been a function of its initial real production costs, the slope of the experience curve, Japan's inflation rate, Japan's exchange rate, and the firm's accumulation rate.

Conversely, U.S. manufacturers' ability to maintain price competitiveness and dominance in products they have introduced would depend on an appropriate combination of the following:

- lower real start-up and initial production costs in the United States than Japan,
- steeper experience curve slope,
- lower inflation rate
- continuous devaluation
- faster accumulation rate.

In reality, few of these conditions can be met. The United States tends to have higher initial production and development costs than Japan. The cost of transferring a given technology decreases over time, and thus Japan need not accumulate equivalent-experience to become competitive. Secondly, actual comparisons by the Boston Consulting Group have yet to show any appreciable slope differentials between the United States and Japan for the same product. Real price reductions for a doubling of experience are similar. This indicates that technological factors and industrial organization at a given stage of development are analogous for the same product, and cost-experience curves for successful United States and Japanese firms producing a product are roughly equivalent.

Inflation and exchange rates are primarily macroeconomic variables over which firms have little control. Nevertheless, U.S. inflation rates approaching Japanese levels since 1967 have heavily affected U.S. competitiveness. Until that time, the 3 percent inflation differential between the United States and Japan offset the real cost reduction effect of Japan's higher manufacturing growth rate. The current revaluation compensates for the absence of this inflation differential during the last 4 to 5 years.

However, U.S. firms do have some control over Japanese firms' ability to capture world market share and accumulate experience even if they have not done so in many products. United States firms have lower current costs when Japan begins production, comparing each industry's starting point, even if not lower real costs. There is thus a calculable accumulation rate over some time period that Japanese firms require to become cost competitive. United States producers can remain dominant if Japanese firms fail to grow at this rate. During Japan's initial production stage, the United States can rarely accumulate experience as rapidly as Japan. The United States is the initial producer and has a larger accumulated production base, consequently taking longer to double experience. As Japan's smaller market saturates and its experience base gets larger, though, further doublings and cost reductions become more difficult for Japanese producers too. United States firms' must use their initial cost advantage, therefore, to participate in the Japanese market and/or shut off export development. They can deny Japanese manufacturers the growth necessary for fully competitive cost reduction, but the time horizon is limited.

Product Cycles and Economic Development

Product and industry life cycles are a recognized and logical economic phenomenon. We see currently and historically that the scientific and material resources needed for the invention and commercialization of any new product are concentrated in a few advanced countries (frequently the United States). A wide range of innovations are stimulated by the conditions of domestic demand and supply these countries enjoy:

- high wage rates promote labor-saving innovations;
- high personal incomes stimulate demand for new products;
- large military and space programs support technical innovations which may ultimately have consumer applications;
- the availability of large amounts of capital and skilled labor permit development to occur.

These demand-and-supply conditions do not occur in the LDCs until their income levels rise; therefore, they lag behind the advanced countries in the development of a particular product. They generally attain the required levels of demand and begin to make these products at the same time that demand is slowing down in the advanced countries. This process results in intra- and interindustry shifts within a country, and from country to country. Industrial emphasis moves continually from products less technically sophisticated and capital-intensive toward those requiring more capital, more skill, and more technological inputs. This historical evolution is apparent for Japan.

That is, after being introduced in the United States, new products and processes diffuse abroad, first to advanced countries like Japan that have the technical capabilities and resources needed to identify and imitate the technology. The less developed countries adopt the innovations more slowly depending on the upward shift in their demand and supply structures.

This process is well documented for many Japanese industries and products. Consider the cotton textile industry: U.S. and European dominance gave way first to Japanese competition, and later to competitors from Hong Kong, Korea, and Taiwan. Today the cycle is entering a new phase, with India and Pakistan developing their cotton textile industries. Wool and synthetics follow a similar evolutionary path.

These product or industry life cycles are continually evolving for all industries in each economy, new industries emerging all the time. In each country one finds a constantly changing spectrum of industries in various stages of development (initial development, growth, maturation, decline, export and import).

Because this is an ongoing process, it is unreasonable to expect a particular country to dominate production of any product forever. The reasons for this are apparent from comparative experience development. That the Japanese understand this process better than the U.S. is indicated by their willingness to phase out and rationalize declining industries, such as cotton textiles or sewing machines, in favor of newer high-growth products. It is these high-growth industries the Japanese have protected and are continuing to protect by controlling imports and foreign investment. Japan consciously pursues a policy of shifting its economic and industrial emphasis from low-growth, less sophisticated products toward high-growth, more sophisticated products—a very rational policy that has contributed substantially to Japan's postwar success. On the other hand, U.S. policy in direct contrast to Japan's, protects slow-growth, declining industries, leaving high-growth industries on their own. This is self-defeating in terms of resource allocation, growth, and meeting Japanese competition.

The Relationship between Experience and Product Cycles

A typical life-cycle pattern vis-à-vis Japan has run as follows:

In the early years of production U.S. demand, production, and experience have grown rapidly. Increases in productivity and relative price declines have been large. As domestic demand leveled off, increases in growth rates and productivity decreased so price declines slowed both relatively and absolutely. During this second phase, an industry shakeout usually occurred as one or two firms gained dominance and market shares stabilized.

Subsequently U.S. firms' international competitive strategy has been inadequate. United States firms have generally failed to capture increased world demand emerging abroad (because of international trade barriers and/or strategic errors). They have lost world market share to Japanese competitors who have begun production and have dropped costs rapidly. Since their initial real production costs have been lower than they were in the United States (the United States even facilitating this process by licensing and patent agreements), they did not have to repeat U.S. production experience to become competitive.

Japan's actual initial costs have been higher though than current U.S. costs. Some protection or lack of competition was thus required to get started. But the very rapid expansion of demand and production lowered costs quickly and established competitive equality in a few years.

Given a similar demand growth in both countries, the ability to sustain high growth (therefore a high accumulation rate) is a function of capital availability to expand capacity, which is a function of retained earnings, debt usage, and tax rates. A corporation's ability to increase its domestic and international market share thus depends on its financial policies and its financial environment. More specifically, a larger use of debt by Japanese companies facilitates higher growth rates and lower margins for the same return on equity than U.S. financial practices. Combined with a higher breakeven due to fixed labor costs and high fixed capital charges, this policy tends to stimulate penetration pricing and continuous operation at full capacity. The section on Japan's approach to pricing which follows will discuss more completely the Japanese practice of dropping prices as costs decline.

To catch up, Japan has accumulated experience faster than the current U.S. rate. Reduction in relative costs has proceeded particularly fast during Japan's initial production phase because the accumulation rate is higher at this stage of product development. In addition, during this initial production period, Japan has enjoyed greater growth in demand than the United States, the U.S. market usually being mature. Still, it has only been after this initial period of rapid cost reduction that Japan has become competitive enough to export.

The successful Japanese follower has generally increased his export market share first in less developed countries, where there is no domestic competition, where demand is growing, and where the United States has no innate advantage. These exports have served multiple competitive functions. They impaired the ability of U.S. firms to grow and to lower costs relative to Japan. They also enhanced Japan's ability to grow and lower costs. Competitively, there was a double effect. This was very important if the Japanese domestic market was relatively small and quickly saturated, or if costs had to be lowered further to stimulate additional domestic demand. Finally, these exports developed Japan's overseas marketing experience.

All these developments were critical if Japan was to gain enough strength to penetrate the U.S. market. This task was difficult because U.S. market demand was growing slowly, in-place capacity was difficult to dislodge, and domestic competition existed. However, quotas and high tariffs were seldom applied until after significant import market penetration, when the U.S. industry was in trouble.

Japan has often benefited from other economic conditions present in the United States as well. The United States has higher wage rates than Japan. As growth slowed, productivity increased slowly and higher wages were not offset as in earlier stages of product development. As the U.S. domestic market matured, the manufacturer has also frequently decided to forego continued growth (requiring investment and aggressive pricing) and has attempted, instead, to earn a return on past investment by maintaining a constant real price level.

Moreover, he has often felt that the foreign market's size and the foreign competitors, particularly Japanese, were not large enough to justify fighting Japanese protective policies, (though this thinking may be changing). Yet as the U.S. market matured it became increasingly price sensitive and vulnerable to low-priced imports.

Therefore, despite the difficulties encountered, Japanese firms penetrated the U.S. market and local producers declined in their own market, feeling even more the competitive pressures resulting from a smaller market share and a deteriorating cost position. Thus, in spite of U.S. protectionist policies, competitive forces have constantly pushed U.S. industry toward the development of newer and more sophisticated products, initiating the process once again.

The repetition of this competitive evolution with respect to Japan by the LDCs would only seem limited by product obsolescence, by the minimum internationally competitive plant size, and by follower's ability to capture world demand growth represented by its domestic demand. This appears to be happening in textiles and other simple manufactures. It has been made possible by the protective policies of local governments, by changes in U.S., European and Japanese financial strategies, and by the domestically restricted market perception of U.S. and European companies. Inflation and yen appreciation have also obviously contributed, decreasing the competitive advantage of mature Japanese business, for example (apparel and handicrafts). Exports of these products from the LDCs are increasing, both to Japan and third country markets.

Japanese firms compensate for these developments, however, by investing in these industries offshore and by playing the follower in new products at home. They are thus upgrading their employment structure and are participating in growth areas domestically and overseas. They make use of economic forces; they do not try to oppose them.

Their alternative strategy indicates the sensitive points within product cycle evolution for each country and firm: initial foreign production, initial foreign export development, and initial domestic market penetration. At these times, key variables such as margins can be effectively influenced by external pressures. The ability to apply or resist such pressure is related to:

— a firm's investment strategies (foreign and domestic);
— its marketing strategies (including exports);
— its pricing strategies (domestic and foreign); and
— its financial strategies

within the context of a country's current position in the product cycle and likely position five or ten years hence.

Policy Implications

The above analysis has immediate and profound implications for U.S. policy vis-à-vis Japan. Until now, Japan has quite rationally protected her growth industries from foreign (U.S.) exports that would keep her industry from developing, and from foreign (U.S.) investment that would merely serve the Japanese domestic market and would not develop into a major export industry. Japan has been able to adhere to this policy in part because the United States, in its trade negotiations, has been preoccupied with protecting its declining industries (for example, shoes and textiles) rather than its established or growth industries. U.S. antitrust policies—which have prevented various industries from combining into more competitive units better able to accumulate experience— have only exacerbated the unfavorable situation.

The Japanese have also demonstrated a better understanding of the economic forces determining their competitive development. This is apparent in many policy statements by Japanese business and government officials. The United States, on the other hand, has failed to respond with any integrated trade strategy or basic understanding of the competitive process. It has instead continued to react to *ad hoc* political pressures, pressures naturally favoring declining industries rather than growth industries, where we tend to be over-confident.

Furthermore, Japanese financial strategies, incorporating high debt and high breakeven characteristics, have helped create a finely tuned growth system—a system which, given the same initial costs as in the United States, normally sets lower prices and ultimately achieves lower costs and still lower prices. This is particularly true in export markets where trading companies offer a more efficient distribution system than the one existing in Japan itself. Given this competitive challenge, the United States can only respond effectively by thinking its way through some necessary changes in its present business practices and government economic policies.

More specifically, the United States has tended to give away experience by investing overseas rather than exporting. This is a second-best solution to the problem of access to foreign markets from the point of view of U.S. costs and contribution to GNP. In some cases, overseas investment is the only way to gain or maintain access to foreign markets, but in general U.S. firms simply prefer to invest overseas rather than export. This is probably a logical preference; its large volume of exports notwithstanding, the United States is not really structured for export. The U.S. export distribution system is fragmented and expensive, and there have been legal restrictions on the integration of functions which might otherwise have reduced costs. United States antitrust laws deter cooperation by U.S. firms in export marketing and in the creation of joint or cooperative trading companies that could spread export marketing costs over several products. For example, what would the U.S. government do if Ford and GM cooperated to defeat Toyota competitively overseas? Some relief from antitrust is required if the United States is to meet Japanese competition, competition that concentrates experience and invests overseas only in raw materials or declining industries.

United States antitrust policies also erode the experience base for export and accelerate the decline of maturing industries by preventing concentration of experience in one or two producers. The U.S. government currently thinks of competition only in domestic terms; it needs to extend its view to worldwide competition. Such a change in viewpoint would lead to more efficient U.S. production units, a more competitive position; and lower consumer prices. It would coincide with our traditional free trade posture as well since heavy protection would not be required even for traditional industries.

Such a change in outlook implies a reversal of U.S. policy—from protecting declining industries to protecting those industries whose growth rate is faster than that of the GNP or industry as a whole. The United States needs to be more conscious of the benefits derived from the huge U.S. market, from U.S. R&D capability, and from high growth. The U.S. market is twice the size of Japan's and will remain so, even if per capita purchasing power becomes the same. This means that the U.S. experience base and its potential cost advantage will always be larger than Japan's if equivalent industry concentration exists in the two countries. By protecting this base, the United States should be able to remain competitive if it exports and invests effectively, capturing world market growth.

Conversely, Japan must have access to the huge U.S. market if she is to maintain cost advantage and continue to grow once her own market is saturated. Her alternative overseas markets are limited, at least in the near future. These markets are growing fast but they cannot quantitatively provide what is required to add to Japan's increasingly larger experience base at a rate that will lower costs significantly. However, effective penetration of the U.S. market, the largest and most developed in the world, can provide such additions. Although Japan is gaining a greater position in Western Europe; although Southeast Asia will remain important for initial export development; and although some specialization agreement with China may be worked out, the United States will remain Japan's major foreign market for the foreseeable future.

One must conclude therefore that a rational U.S. trade posture would be to require Japan to pay for access to certain U.S. markets with access to certain Japanese markets (e.g., the U.S. auto market in exchange for the Japanese computer market). Since Japan's ability to develop an industry depends on protection and her ability to sustain cost advantage depends on access to overseas markets, particularly the U.S. market, this policy would naturally force a decision as to who would specialize in which products. The United States must stop Japan's progress in industries in which she still has a cost advantage;

protection is of little use in a declining or slow-growth industry. Also, in areas in which the United States is following Japan (e.g., video cassettes or four-channel stereo) it can use protection of high-growth industries to even greater advantage than Japan as the size of the U.S. market permits faster and greater accumulation of experience.

Japanese Pricing: "Dumping" or Sound Strategy?

The cost consequences of Japan's rapid growth have been discussed in terms of the whole economy or of industry and product groupings. Turning now to the firm, one can ask how these cost effects translate into pricing behavior. Why are Japanese firms often seen as pricing in "unfair," "irrational," "uneconomic" ways? Japanese companies are commonly accused of "dumping" into world markets. Yet it is clear that if Japanese companies were persistently dumping, they could hardly exist for long periods, much less finance very rapid and continued growth. Is there then a basis for analyzing Japanese pricing behavior which, taken with the effects of rapid growth, demonstrates a real competitive advantage? We believe there is.

The Price Implications of Corporate Debt

To understand Japanese pricing behavior, one must first note an aspect of Japanese corporate practice strikingly different from the West. As Figure 2-3 suggests, Japanese companies characteristically depend very heavily on debt for corporate financing. The typical level of debt financing is so high as to suggest to Western businessmen that the average Japanese firm is virtually bankrupt. For the typical Japanese firm, less than 20 percent of total capital is owned (equity and retained earnings) with more than 80 percent composed of short- and long-term borrowings and the financing of trade receivables. United States companies characteristically source most of their capital from equity and retained earnings; debt comprises a third or less.

The effects on pricing behavior of this difference in financial practice are startling (Table 2-2). Assume two competitors, a U.S. company and a Japanese company; assume their costs are roughly equal, but the Japanese company follows Japanese financial practices, and the American company uses somewhat more debt than customary in the United States. If both provide their shareholders an equal return (10 percent on equity) and grow on a sustained basis at 10 percent annually, the margin of the Japanese company will be roughly half the U.S. company's. Therefore, given equal costs, the Japanese company can service its debt, pay an equal return to shareholders, and maintain a growth rate equal to that of the U.S. company but at a far lower price level.

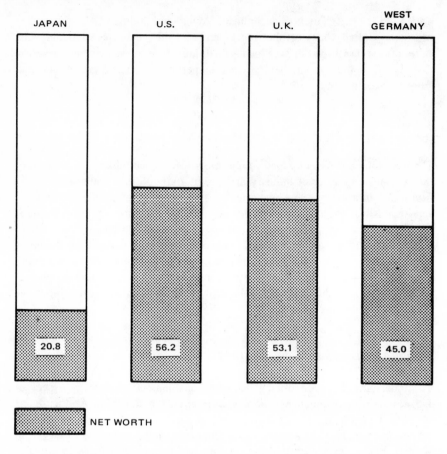

Figure 2-3. Capital Structure: 1968. Source: Bank of Japan.

While Table 2-2 is a generalized example, companies in the two economies display the effects of these differing financial approaches. The Bank of Japan reported 1968 results for major companies in both countries. Japanese companies were far less profitable in terms of after-tax return on sales (2.6 percent compared to 5.1 percent) but provided a higher return to shareholders (13.7 percent compared to 11.8 percent).

The generous use of debt by Japanese firms in effect uncouples their growth rate from their profitability as long as they can cover their debt service and dividend payout. This practice permits the continued financing of rapid growth even though sales are made at significantly lower margins.

But if the high use of debt confers a substantial competitive advantage, why

Table 2-2
Margins Required to Grow at 10%

	Japan	U.S.
Assets	100	100
Debt	80	40
Equity	20	60
Sales	100	100
Profit		
Before interest and tax	14.4	27.2
Interest	6.4	3.2
Profit before tax	8.0	24.0
Profit after tax	4.0	12.0
Dividend	2.0	6.0
Return on equity	10.0	10.0
Reinvestment of earnings	2.0	6.0
Additional debt	8.0	4.0
Growth Rate	10%	10%

do U.S. companies not follow a similar strategy? A full answer is both complex and outside this discussion. Briefly, however, Japan's business environment reduces the risk and makes tolerable for large Japanese companies a debt level unattainable and intolerably risky in the U.S. environment. The financial risks associated with high debt levels are reduced in Japan as the central bank stands implicit guarantor of major Japanese companies' debt position. No American company can assume similar support from the Federal Reserve. Further, an American company is vulnerable to the threat of prolonged strikes which make enormous demands on liquidity. The thin cash position of Japanese companies would make such strikes devastating, but Japanese labor relations and personnel practices make these labor conflicts unlikely.

In looking at Japanese price behavior, then, one must first appreciate that the Japanese business system permits an extraordinary level of debt financing for corporate growth, and that this in turn makes possible operation at significantly lower margins than in the United States.

The Full Capacity Policy

One consequence of this financial policy is the pressure on the Japanese company which results from its large debt service. Sizeable interest charges contribute to a high level of fixed costs for a Japanese company compared to a U.S. company. This too has direct implications for Japanese pricing behavior.

To take a specific product, Table 2-3 compares costs for Japan and the United States in nylon production. The Japanese advantage in labor costs is somewhat offset by higher overhead costs and by interest charges. Total costs are similar. However, given personnel relations in the large Japanese company, with employees hired for their entire careers, all labor costs as well as sales, overhead, and interest costs, are in fact fixed. For the American firm, labor is partially a variable cost (this analysis assumes about one-third U.S. labor costs are fixed). Taken with lower overhead and little debt service, a much smaller proportion of the U.S. firm's total costs are fixed.

These high fixed costs typical of a Japanese company result in what might be called a "full-capacity policy." Since most costs are fixed, there is considerable incentive to operate at full capacity so long as the product is sold at prices somewhat above variable costs—in fact, somewhat above raw material costs. Since the breakeven point is high and cannot be significantly reduced in the short run, management is constantly pressed to lower prices as necessary to ensure full operations as long as these prices do not drop below variable costs. In the United States this price point is reached much sooner than in Japan, since a substantially larger share of U.S. costs are variable and can be reduced.

Taken together with Japanese financial practices, this "full-capacity policy" means that the Japanese firm can price lower while maintaining required levels of return and a high growth rate, and has a powerful incentive to price lower to maintain full capacity.

Pricing Implications of Rapid Growth

These facts must also be seen in the context of rapid economic growth. The implications of Japan's high growth rates have been analyzed in the national context, but rapid growth impacts on individual firms' pricing behavior as well. The experience of the current generation of Japanese businessmen is unique. They have known twenty years of uninterrupted growth, and for most of this time, growth at rates virtually unprecedented in history. Further, they have a government committed to continued rapid growth, and the credibility of that commitment is strongly reinforced by success. Indeed, their government's generous growth estimates have nearly always fallen short of actual economic expansion.

The confidence that demand will increase rapidly, and long experience with rapidly expanding markets, has in turn confirmed the necessity to invest in anticipation of demand. In national terms, this makes for a self-fulfilling prophecy—investment in anticipation of demand creates the economic conditions that bring about increased demand. For the individual company, it means that since capacity does not increase smoothly but rather expands in large increments, there will be periods of temporary excess capacity. And Japanese

Table 2-3
Cost Comparison: U.S. and Japan Nylon Production

	Japanese Company	U.S. Competitor
Materials	20	22
Labor	10	15
Sales and administration	20	20
Overhead	15	13
Debt Service	2	0
Total Cost	67	70
Fixed Cost to Total Cost[a]	70%	54%

[a]Assuming all Japanese labor cost fixed and one-third U.S. labor cost fixed,

$$\text{Japan} = \left(\frac{10 + 20 + 15 + 2}{67}\right); \text{U.S.} = \left(\frac{5 + 20 + 13}{70}\right)$$

management is likely to clear that capacity at temporarily lowered prices and into world markets. This fact, in conjunction with the typical approach to export marketing discussed below, helps explain the part of Japanese pricing behavior that Japan's competitors object to and often find inexplicable.

But from the Japanese point of view, their preoccupation with investment and market share in the domestic market is entirely reasonable. At Japanese growth rates, failure to maintain market share can very quickly lead to a disastrous competitive position. Japanese industrial output has been growing in real terms at some 13 to 14 percent per year. The modern sector of most industries is thus doubling in size every five years or less. Put another way, if a competitor enters a market with zero share and simply takes the market growth without reducing the sales volume of other companies, he will hold half the market in only five years. Given the cost-experience effect, the competitive implications of this kind of market share loss are clear. The same phenomenon would occur in the United States, but since U.S. growth rates are generally much lower, management's appreciation of the effects of market share loss is less. In the Japanese context, however, it is appropriate that management accept market share as a primary objective even at the expense of short-term profitability.

Some additional special characteristics of the Japanese business environment reinforce this attention to market share. As Japanese industry swings away from labor-intensive toward capital-intensive industries, the effects of scale on cost are increasingly clear. Further, growth and market share have a direct effect on labor costs. Employees are hired directly from school for their career. Since their pay is essentially a function of their age, the average labor cost for a Japanese company is directly related to the average age of the work force. A rapidly growing company is hiring large numbers of young people; as the average age of the work force drops, labor costs also drop. Conversely, a slow-growing Japanese company has a work force aging steadily, and its labor costs are rising. The payoff for growth is immediate and clear.

Japanese Pricing and the Experience Curve Effect

All these factors come together to create a business system in which rapid growth in demand stimulates rapid investment; rapid investment and maintained or increased market share translates directly into visible cost advantage; high fixed costs ensure the additional capacity will be fully utilized; and financial and competitive practices are such that margins in excess of the financial requirements for growth penalize firms in high-growth business. Under these conditions, it is hardly surprising that price becomes the primary competitive weapon. U.S. firms characteristically prefer to compete through increased services, additional merchandising or product differentiation, and use price competition as a last resort. U.S. laws, notably the Robinson-Patman Act and ultimately the antitrust laws, reinforce this tendency and place sharp limits on the use of price as a competitive weapon. The results for international competition are unfortunate.

It is evident from this discussion that the Japanese firm is under considerable pressure to translate into immediate price reduction cost improvements resulting from rapid growth. The situation found in the United States of a "price umbrella" held over the market by the leading producer for an extended period is not commonplace in Japan. The risk of market share loss is too evident and urgent. Japanese prices thus tend to follow costs directly down the experience curve. This phenomenon, together with rapid growth, makes Japanese goods increasingly price competitive in world markets quite apart from other aspects of Japanese price behavior already noted.

What Are Real Prices?

This discussion has so far dealt only with the individual producer, and with some of the factors that make for differences in pricing practices between manufacturers in Japan and the United States. The issue is made more complex, however, by differences in distribution methods and their effect on pricing behavior.

In Japan the traditional, and still general, approach to distribution both domestically and for export has been the trading company, rather than direct management of sales activities by the manufacturer. The Japanese trading company is unique to Japan. The large ones are very large indeed, with sales over $10 billion annually and worldwide office networks, dealing in virtually all kinds of goods. But the trading company is basically interested in rapid turnover, and in handling large volumes at low margins. In contrast to a manufacturer selling for his own account, the trading company has less interest in market stability and permanence. The pricing effects in world markets are obvious.

At the same time, the trading company is a highly efficient export distributor. Especially for producers whose export sales are below the threshold volume making an export effort economic, the trading company offers an efficient and inexpensive way of arranging transport, establishing inventory and reaching customers. The result is worldwide export market access for relatively small Japanese companies, for products with limited export potential, and to countries with small markets. The lack of a comparable U.S. business institution hampers U.S. export efforts by many companies that cannot economically justify entry to export markets, much less to markets of limited size.

The efficiency of the trading company as an export distribution mechanism raises a difficult question, however, regarding the issue of "double pricing." It is commonly argued that Japanese companies "double price," with a higher price for their domestic market than for export markets. The real possibility of this kind of pricing has been indicated above with respect to the full capacity policy. It must be noted however that distribution costs in Japan are high: distribution channels are multilayered with compounding margins; customers are numerous, small, and expensive to reach; and payment terms are extended and difficult to enforce. Under these different conditions of domestic versus export sales, it is clear that caution must be exercised before charging "double pricing" against Japanese manufacturers.

Some Implications for Policy

It is not easy to discuss pricing behavior without seeming to justify the Japanese approach. U.S. producers are at an inherent competitive disadvantage. Japanese companies with costs similar to Western producers can price lower while being as profitable to shareholders and financing faster growth—which in turn leads to lower costs, and under Japanese conditions this is promptly translated into still lower prices. This advantage, unless compensated for by a higher Japanese inflation rate, must soon be balanced by exchange rate adjustment. The alternative—that U.S. companies might adopt Japanese financial practices—is not available given U.S. government-business relations.

This does not rule out however a critical review by U.S. firms of their own export pricing policies. It seems appropriate that roughly as many "dumping" charges should be brought against U.S. firms as are registered by U.S. firms against foreign competition. The current disproportion suggests U.S. companies are not pricing as aggressively in international markets.

The "dumping" issue also suggests a new U.S. response might be useful. By definition, dumping means Japanese domestic prices are high and a price umbrella is being held over the domestic Japanese market, providing the cash flow to finance expansion. At present, the U.S. response to this is to close or limit access to the U.S. market. Strategically, an interesting alternative would be to trade off closure of the U.S. market against wide-open access to the Japanese market. If Japanese prices are disproportionately high, U.S. producers should be able to penetrate the market and shut off the cash source financing further Japanese growth.

It also seems useful for the United States to examine the trading company. It is clear that most large American companies are prepared to handle their own export sales (although even these might find a joint export effort to smaller overseas markets economic). But many smaller, specialized producers that only the huge U.S. economy makes possible have export markets that their scale and experience prevents them from penetrating. Are there perhaps, in the trading company, some of the elements that might be used to expand U.S. exports and make U.S. producers better able to compete with the Japanese even outside the United States?

A Case History—Monochrome Television

Japanese television producers offer a poignant and pointed illustration of Japanese competitive development along the lines described above. It is a pattern systematically repeated throughout Japan's industrialization. Television is especially interesting, however, because U.S. strategic errors were illustrated not once but twice.[c] In addition, the rapidly growing Japanese market was unprotected compared to textiles, steel, or autos. The government never considered consumer electronics strategic or an important industry. Its development has not depended on special quotas, marketing restrictions, high tariff barriers, or other protections. There was little to prevent U.S. exports and market penetration when the United States was the world's low-cost producer. But no real effort was made. The eventual size and competitiveness of Japanese producers testifies though to the U.S. strategic misperception. (Black and white production in 1970 was $400 million.)

A brief comparison of the U.S. and Japanese price-experience curves for

---

[c]Though our discussion is restricted to monochrome television, color TV followed a similar competitive development. Initial Japanese current average wholesale prices in 1962 were high compared to U.S. prices ($500 versus $350 a set), and Japanese sets were smaller. Extraordinary domestic demand growth after 1965, however, brought costs and prices down rapidly. Production grew from 98,000 units in 1965 to 6.4 million units in 1970 (a growth of 196 percent *per annum* versus 41.0 percent for the United States), but only 16 percent were exported in 1970. The value of 1970 production was $1.9 billion. Failure to participate in this growth market not only created formidable international competitors but was also a sizeable lost market opportunity. With the examples of transistor radios, monochrome TV, and stereo equipment as guides, there seems little reason for U.S. misperception; yet, it did occur again.

monochrome television in Figure 2-4 and of price trends over time in Figure 2-5 indicate the United States maintained a large cost-price advantage before 1957. Still, there were no exports to the Japanese market despite its rapid growth. Just how rapidly production grew compared to the U.S. is documented in Table 2-4. Japanese producers between 1954 and 1970 accumulated experience at 61 percent p.a. versus 8 percent in the U.S. The result of this large differential accumulation rate was inevitable. A differential accumulation rate of 53 percent p.a. more than exceeded what could be permitted by a 1 to 2 percent inflation differential, and absolute cost advantage at a fixed exchange rate was gained quickly (Table 2-4). Yet, this was based on domestic market growth. Exports did not start until Japanese domestic prices were below U.S. prices, and penetration of the U.S. market did not occur until the price differential was substantial and third country export experience had been developed (Table 2-5).

This was a typical "follower" scenario of competitive development. But as the economics of monochrome production have shifted in turn from Japan to countries like Taiwan and Korea, the Japanese managerial response has differed from U.S. experience. In response to the emergence of competitors in the LDCs, the belated move of American companies offshore, and their own changing production economics, Hitachi, Toshiba, Matsushita and Sanyo all have established monochrome television plants in Taiwan or Korea. Unlike U.S. producers, though, they are not supplying their own domestic market in Japan but are using or are planning to use these sources to supply markets worldwide (United States, the LDCs, etc.). In this approach they remain one-step ahead of U.S. producers who produce only for the U.S. market; U.S. manufacturers will thus lose relative cost position due to their smaller volume and experience growth at the new location. Competitive initiative in television would seem to have passed from the U.S. innovators to the Japanese followers.

Japanese Competition in the 1970s

Any effort to project the competitive interaction between the economies of Japan and the United States over this decade encounters the customary hazards of prediction. Some of the factors that will determine the direction of Japan's economy are quite predictable, population size and rate of population increase for example. Some of the factors, the proportion of personal consumption to gross national expenditure for example, show rather long trend lines that seem unlikely to change abruptly. And yet, of course, any prediction is subject to the unpredictable—a Near East crisis that cuts off energy supplies, a shift in world power relations that changes Japanese policy in a direction discontinuous from the present.

Given the hazards of prediction, it remains useful to examine those facts that have a high degree of predictability, consider their implications for economic

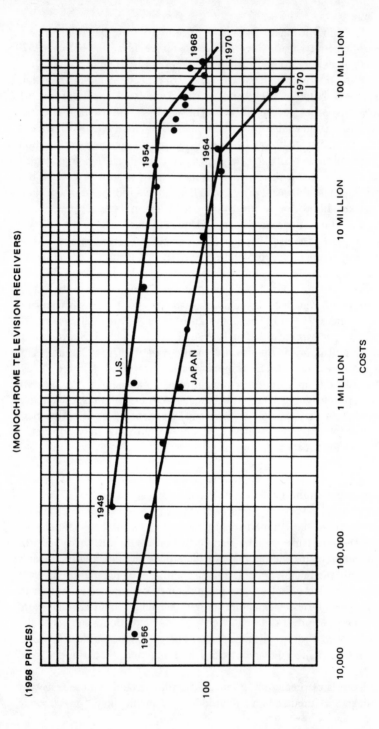

Figure 2-4. Real Wholesale Prices against Accumulated Production of Monochrome Television in the United States and Japan.

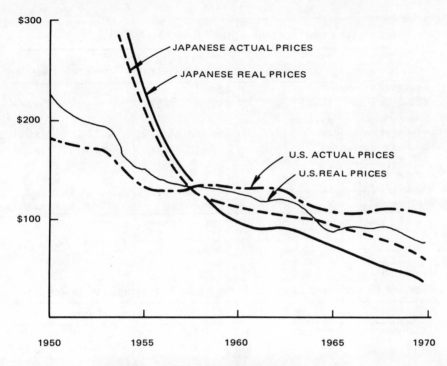

Figure 2-5. Prices against Time (Monochrome TV)

growth and policy, and review their impact on the economic interaction of Japan with the world. In selecting the facts that seem especially relevant for this exercise, and to array them systematically, we propose to examine in turn some main trends in three key areas—human resources, financial resources, and technology. An examination of these leads to conclusions not only about broad economic policy but also to some specific conclusions about the industries and product areas in which Japanese effort is likely to be focused. Finally, some general predictions about the rate and nature of growth can be outlined along with a view of the factors upon which this growth depends.

Human Resources in the 1970s

A first fact about Japan in the 1970s is that the population will increase slowly, about 1 percent per year, and this population will be slowly aging in conse-

Table 2-4
Monochrome Television Cost Competition: 1954-70, 1965-70

	United States		Japan	
	1954-70	(1965-70)	1954-70	(1965-70)
Real annual accumulation rate	8.6%	(4.6%)	61.0%	(14.2%)
Real annual growth rate	-2.9%	(-12.0%)	29.0%	(8.4%)
Annual price decline in constant dollars or yen (75% curve)	3.6%	(1.9%)	25.6%	(6.0%)
Inflation rate per annum	2.6%	(4.0%)	3.8%	(4.7%)
Annual change in costs in current dollars	-1.0%	(+2.1%)	-21.8%	(-1.3%)
Competitor's cost advantage per annum			+20.8%	(+3.4%)

Note: Exchange rate fixed at Y360 = $1.00 through the period.

Table 2-5
Japanese Production and Exports: Monochrome Television (1,000 Units)

	1955	1960	1963	1965	1967	1969	1970
Production	137	3,552	4,878	4,060	5,681	7,284	6,089
Exports	–	45	686	1,414	1,922	3,286	3,715
% U.S.	–	18%	66%	75%	68%	70%	66%
E/P	–	1%	14%	35%	34%	45%	61%

quence of a low birth rate over the past decade or two. This means of course a reduced number of entrants to the labor force (the number of entrants peaked several years ago) with a resulting labor shortage in the sense of a slow rate of increase. While this does not mean a labor shortage in an absolute sense—that depends on capital investment and off-shore investment policies as well as on total numbers of workers—it does mean that the size of the labor force is one constraint on the nature of the economy.

At the same time, Japan's labor force is experiencing a very rapid rise in its level of education. By the mid-'70s, a quarter of the work force will be college graduated, and new entrants will virtually all have graduated from higher schools. The labor force is now probably on average the best educated in the world. This further increase in educational level leads to a need for and capability of more sophisticated employment than is now the case. Japanese companies have already had experience with an unwillingness on the part of higher school graduated employees to accept the kind of menial or brutally repetitive tasks that are offered for example on an auto assembly line. They have been trained to expect more interesting work and have a capacity for it.

Along with a reduction in the numbers of workers entering the work force, and a sharp increase in their level of education, will go a considerable rise in wage rates. Japanese wage rates have been increasing recently about 15 percent per year, that is, doubling each five years. (Note that since productivity has been rising equally rapidly, labor *costs* have not increased despite these increases in wage rates. The contrast with the British and U.S. experience over the same time could hardly be more sharp.) Whether this high rate of increase continues, and the 1971-72 reduction in growth rates will no doubt result in some slackening of the rate of wage increase, it can only be expected that wage levels will continue to rise rapidly.

In the case of Germany's rapid growth, subject to much the same kinds of pressures in terms of labor force, the solution was the large-scale importation of labor from such less-developed areas as Southern Italy, Spain, Greece, Yugoslavia, and Turkey. Large-scale immigration into Japan is politically and psychologically most unlikely indeed. The alternative is to move the jobs to the lower-rate labor supply. This will mean (as it already has begun to mean) the establishment of facilities offshore in Taiwan, Korea, and Hong Kong where well-disciplined, inexpensive labor is available in considerable volume.

Trade policy becomes important at this point. Japan needs to find imports from the areas which have less expensive labor that is willing to carry out the labor-intensive manufacturing tasks. By exporting capital and importing product, the trade relationship with these less-developed countries is aided. More important, as noted earlier, Japan is now devoted to a trade policy by which tariffs are kept low on low technology products, and quantitative restrictions are confined to high technology products. That is, domestic producers in labor-intensive, low-technology sectors are being exposed to maximum import competition in such industries as textiles. (Japan has the lowest textile tariffs of any OECD member.) Further, Japan is a high-cost producer of foodstuffs, with an uneconomic concentration of labor in agriculture. Again, imports are the solution both to high domestic costs and to high consumer prices. But this import competition means the shift of the economy, and therefore of the labor force, out of agriculture and the labor-intensive sectors, and makes the labor supply available to the more capital-intensive, high-technology sectors.

The pattern of human resources in the economy then is of a slowly growing labor force, with rapidly increasing skills, and rapidly rising wage levels. The static alternative under these conditions is labor shortage, increasing labor costs, and increasing labor unrest. The dynamic alternative is pressure on the labor-intensive sectors of the economy, displacement of the domestic labor force into higher skill, capital intensive sectors, and a rapid export of capital to move offshore the low-technology, labor-intensive industries to less developed countries. Present Japanese government policy is most explicitly directed to the dynamic alternative.

Financial Resources in the 1970s

What are the high-probability characteristics of the 1970s regarding deployment of Japan's financial resources? We have discussed above the characteristic sourcing of industrial investment funds, and the impact of high use of debt on corporate growth and on pricing. There has been a long-term decline in the importance of the capital market as a source of industrial investment funds, from 36 percent of the total in 1957, to 29 percent in 1963 to only 18 percent in 1969. In parallel, private financial institutions have been the source of 48 percent of investment funds in 1957 and 68 percent in 1969. Even assuming this long-term trend were over the 1970s to be slowed, then stopped, then reversed (and the Fuji Bank for one sees no such reversal in its forecasts), it is clear that through this decade bank borrowings will remain the predominant source of funding.

This brings with it continued commercial bank influence over corporate investment decisions, and a continuation of strong government influence through the Bank of Japan on these decisions. Further, the present pattern of pricing behavior and the pressure of companies to operate at full capacity are likely to remain major factors in Japanese competitive behavior over the decade.

Another long-term trend with critical bearing on the issue of the deployment of financial resources is the fact that personal consumption as a percentage of gross national expenditure has been declining for a long time. Personal consumption was 66 percent of total expenditure in 1953, 56 percent in 1963, and 51 percent in 1969. Despite the fact that taxes (as one measure of government expenditure) account for a very low proportion of GNP, there has been a steady decline in proportion of personal consumption over this period and again, as with sourcing of investment funds, it is difficult to see an abrupt stop and then reversal of this trend line.

It needs to be further noted that over this period from 1953 to 1969, the increase in percentage of gross national expenditure was in the area of private capital formation, reflecting the very high and very rapidly increasing rate of expenditure in capital goods and equipment. Government expenditures over the period as a percentage of the total were nearly constant.

This pattern of expenditure indicates the considerable demand that has built up for expenditures in the government sector—the need for investment in the whole gamut of infrastructure, social overhead needs, from harbor, road, railroad, waterworks, and sewage disposal investment to improvements in schools, hospitals, and social security programs. The 1972 policy reflects both the opportunity and the prospect of a shift in the direction of investment. As the growth of the economy slowed through 1971 and into 1972, and as in consequence private capital investment was held back, demand reflation has been sought through a sharp, 20 percent increase in the national budget, largely in the social overhead category of investment. Looking forward into the 1970s, it seems reasonable to suppose that increases in national expenditure will take place largely in the public sector, with continued high, but proportionately not increasing, investment in the private capital sector.

This probable pattern indicates increased government investment, and with it of course increased government influence over the direction of the Japanese economy. It needs also to be observed that this investment is likely over time to bring about a gradual decline in productivity increases and hence some slowing in the growth rate of the total economy. However, this is likely to be a long-run, gradual effect. In the shorter run, given long underinvestment in the infrastructure, government investment in distribution facilities for example could well provide higher productivity increases than the investment of similar amounts by private industry.

If these are indeed the likely central facts about financial resources in the 1970s, one must conclude that the basic patterns of government-business interaction are likely to remain in full force, that the role of banks in the private sector of the economy is unlikely to change, and that the principal change will be the diversion of resources made available by declining personal consumption into increased government expenditure. This will in time begin to slow the growth rate, but in the short run will have positive consequences for economic growth.

Technology in the 1970s

By the end of the 1960s, Japanese industry rather clearly had reached technological parity with competitors in other developed economies. This had been accomplished largely through the massive importation of technology from all over the world, at a cost far below that required if independent development had been undertaken. (The cumulative total cost to Japan of all technology imported from 1950 to 1971 is about $3 billion, about one-tenth of current annual U.S. expenditure in research and development.)

Clearly Japanese industry must increase its level of investment in research and development. In fact that investment is now at or above Western European levels in terms of amounts, and considerably greater in terms of numbers of personnel deployed. Further, while research expenditure in the West is largely through governmental channels, and has been for a long time (about two-thirds of the total in France, Britain and the United States), most of the expenditure in Japan is by businesses (about two-thirds of the total for the past fifteen years). Thus the Japanese effort is considerable and is much more tightly focused in the commercial area.

Still, this must be considered a question area for Japan in the 1970s. The education level in Japan is high, much higher at all social levels than Western Europe, although lagging still the United States in university graduates. R&D

investment is high, but again lags the United States at least in total sums expended. Can Japan achieve the needed results in terms of technological development necessary to continue rapid growth? The answer must be that no one can know since there is no historical record against which to examine the question. This might prove a real and substantial obstacle to a continuation of Japan's competitive success. But there is no more basis for a pessimistic answer than an optimistic one—whatever one's definition in this case of optimism or pessimism.

Japan's Focus in the 1970s

With this brief scan of the three areas critical to economic performance, and mindful of such issues in Japan as pollution control, energy costs, and trade relations, what do these facts lead to in viewing Japan as a competitor economy in the 1970s?

Continuing Shift to Higher Technology Industries. The entire thrust of the Japanese economy in the 1970s will be to add more value to imports, to reduce thereby import dependence, and in sequence to lessen export dependence. (A MITI official in private conversation in late 1971 observed, "We have been importing pollution and exporting clean air. We will in the future import pig iron, and export air frames.")

Massive Offshore Investment. Japan has quite ample foreign reserves to finance large-scale foreign investment. Japan has the same incentive to invest offshore as did U.S. companies in the 1950s and 1960s—rising protectionism in export markets and high domestic labor factor costs. Further, offshore investment in the processing of raw materials such as wood fiber and iron ore is pollution-controlling and energy conservative. Offshore investment in labor-intensive operations not only lowers labor costs but relieves domestic pressures on the labor force. Offshore investment in marketing facilities helps to secure and expand export trade positions already established. In sum, a major phenomenon in the 1970s will almost certainly be massive investment by Japanese firms in such countries as Australia, Brazil, Indonesia, and the United States.

The whole complex of factors that is likely to influence Japan in the 1970s comes into play in the basic strategy for the nation's economy of moving as rapidly as possible to capital-intensive, high-technology industries, and away from labor-intensive, low-technology industries. The changing nature of Japan's labor force, the continued high availability of investment funds, the domestic requirement for limits on energy demand and for pollution control, the tensions surrounding Japan's trade relations—all these and more press the nation to a program of steadily displacing its industrial focus away from the low-growth, low-technology, labor-intensive sectors into those industries that offer relief to these problems. What might these be? In what businesses is Japanese competition likely to intensify in the 1970s? We suggest that they might include the following areas of high Japanese growth:

- High R&D sectors, e.g., computers, electric autos, atomic energy and by-products, advanced circuitry, fine chemicals, synthetic paper, industrial robots.
- Systems sectors, e.g., communications equipment, business machines, automated freight warehousing and transport, numerically controlled production systems, prefabricated housing, centralized heating air-conditioning.
- Software, e.g., data storage, information retrieval, home electronic entertainment.
- Fashion, e.g., apparel, furniture, clothing and cosmetic design.

These are suggestive, rather than definitive, of course, but an examination of the issues confronting Japan, as well as the opportunities, suggests that these are the likely directions of further effort. And in most of these Japan will continue to confront the United States in the thrust of its economic effort as it has in the 1960s.

This appears the likely pattern of development over the decade. Its consequences if effectuated will include the following:

- Continued high growth, 10 percent real increase in GNP per annum.
- Steady yen revaluation against the dollar—perhaps two-three percent per year if inflation rates are comparable in the two countries.
- World's most free-trading nation.
- Massive overseas investment, similar to the United States in the 1950s and 1960s.

The key questions that arise regarding the probabilities of this pattern working out are:

- Can Japan manage in domestic political terms the continuing shift of resources to high-growth, high-capital investment, high-technology sectors?
- Can Japan manage successfully very high levels of overseas capital investment?
- Can Japan manage its increasing R&D investment to reduce dependence on imported technology?

Assuming Japan manages to deal with these problems of resource allocation, overseas investment management and R&D productivity, it is clear that the

United States and Japan will be in continued competition in key product areas, with resulting continued tension in the relationship through the period. The further prediction may then be offered that through the decade Japan will seek steadily to effect a disengagement from its very deep commitment to the United States, and search actively for viable alternatives to the United States in both the economic and security areas.

Notes

1. John C. Renner, Director, Office of International Trade, U.S. Department of State; speeches on January 30, 1971, to the "Foreign Policy Conference," sponsored by the Dayton Council on World Affairs; and on March 23, 1971, to the American Management Association, New York, New York.

2. The Boston Consulting Group, PERSPECTIVES ON EXPERIENCE. Boston, 1972.

3

Japan's Balance of Payments and Its Changing Role in the World Economy

Patricia Hagan Kuwayama

Introduction

After attaining one of the world's largest Gross National Products, and a living standard comparing well with many Western European countries, Japan has again astonished the world by experiencing balance-of-payments surpluses which are so large as to disturb the world economic equilibrium. This has provided one more forceful demonstration of Japan's new importance as a major economic power. Since 1968—the same year which marked the one hundredth anniversary of the Meiji Restoration and the beginning of Japan's industrialization effort—the Japanese balance of payments has undergone a fundamental change, from a condition of worrisome periodic deficit to one of chronic and ever-increasing surplus. This change has freed Japan from an external constraint which dominated economic policy-making for a century: the need to make sure that increased import requirements attending each spurt of growth would not exceed foreign exchange earnings from exporting. At the same time, it has brought a new set of problems to Japan and to the nations dealing with it.

Paralleling the change in Japan's international status has been the transformation in its relationship with the United States. For years following the end of World War II, Japan depended heavily on American military procurements, loans and investments to pay for the chronic excess of its imports over its exports in trade with the United States and other countries. Now Japan has found itself running large surpluses in its trade with the United States, at the same time that the United States is faced with an unaccustomed deficit in its overall trade.

The present chapter is an attempt to understand what this change in its balance of payments may mean for Japan and the United States and the world as a whole during the decade of the 1970s. It begins by discussing the role played by the balance of payments in Japan's growth until now and the economic policies which have been developed in response to the "old" balance-of-payments problem. It relates the emergence of the new surplus disequilibrium after 1968, and the response to this situation by Japan's leadership, to this historical

The opinions expressed in this chapter are those of the author, and are not to be attributed to the Federal Reserve Bank of New York. In addition to the other members of the Committee for Economic Policy Studies, thanks are due to Dr. Eleanor Hadley of the U.S. Tariff Commission for her helpful comments on an earlier draft.

51

context. It then briefly reviews the events of 1971, which were in part a consequence of the failure of Japan's response to satisfy its trading partners, and in particular to satisfy the United States. Attention is finally turned to the outlook for the future, now that the unilateral American actions in 1971 have forced Japan to revalue the yen by 17 percent and have also led to changes in the world economic order which will affect the future of all countries' trade. In this new order, the question remains: what kind of equilibrium will Japan achieve in its external payments during the decade of the 1970s, and what will be its consequences? The answer depends, of course, on the approach taken by Japan's leaders, as well as on many other unknown conditions. Nevertheless, it is possible to foresee that the compatibility of Japan's economic aims with those of other countries, including the United States, may still be a problem by 1980, assuming that these aims themselves will not be radically changed. While this conflict of objectives will probably not again approach the explosive level which it reached in 1970 and 1971, it may continue to be a source of friction between Japan and its allies in the coming years.

Balance-of-Payments Problems and Policies before 1968

The Balance-of-Payments Constraint on Growth

The Japanese have always tended to regard their country's lack of essential natural resources as an Achilles' heel, a weakness which could topple the entire industrial structure if outside conditions ever turned unfavorable. Japan's historical and geographical isolation from other countries has added to its sense of disadvantage in international relations, by creating the self-image of a people hopelessly behind the West in scientific and technical development, and also one inept in the linguistic and other requirements for dealing with foreigners. This sense of disadvantage has remained strong even after many of the reasons for it have disappeared, and Japanese people are still inclined to view their dependence on international trade as a special weakness against which they must protect themselves in unusual ways.

After the end of World War II, it was again Japan's lack of resources that kept most observers from being optimistic about its industrial recovery—and from even imagining the possibility that it might grow into a major economic power. The import requirements for such growth seemed simply too great. In fact import requirements did act as the immediate constraint on growth until the late 1960s, as the economy bumped into a balance-of-payments "ceiling" with each boom in the domestic economy. The location of this ceiling was clearly much higher than the pessimists had anticipated, however, and it allowed the Japanese economy to expand at unheard-of rates throughout the 1950s and 1960s. During this period Japan was still dependent on imports from advanced Western countries for the new productive technologies introduced, for sophisticated machinery and other capital goods which it was not yet able to produce itself, for indispensable industrial raw materials of which there was little or no domestic supply, and also for important primary agricultural products.[a]

In aggregate value, imports tended to exceed the exports which Japan was able to sell abroad, so that until the mid-1960s the trade balance was in deficit more often than it was in surplus. Figure 3-1 illustrates the postwar history of the trade balance, as well as the overall balance of private current transactions and of official settlements.[b] Imports of current services were always larger than exports of these services (excluding government transactions, primarily receipts from the United States related to its military establishment in Japan), making the total deficit in current private transactions even larger than the trade deficit. The largest deficit item in the services account was always payments for shipping and insurance required for Japan's merchandise trade with foreign countries. In addition, interest and dividend payments to overseas investors, and fees for patent royalties and management services were always a source of net payments abroad.

This tendency toward deficit in private current transactions did not always mean a loss of foreign exchange reserves, since the residents of other countries—including those of the United States—were generally willing to supply credit in the form of loans and investments to Japan, and since the requirements of the American defense establishment in Japan, particularly during the Korean and Vietnamese wars, also provided foreign exchange beyond that earned from merchandise exports. Nevertheless, as Table 3-1 shows, Japan's foreign exchange reserves were subject to severe fluctuations which at times brought them down to less than the value of three months' imports.

The sharp cyclical changes in the balance of payments bore a close relationship to fluctuations in domestic business conditions, a circumstance which led the Japanese to consider themselves unduly dependent upon world market conditions. Each time the economy began expanding rapidly, imports—particularly in the volatile category of investment goods—shot up and exportable goods were drawn into domestic uses, producing a deterioration in the trade balance and eventually a drain on external reserves. Since (as Table 3-1 shows) these reserves were never large compared with Japan's annual imports, the drain could not be allowed to continue long. In the context of the economic policies followed by Japan, which are discussed below, this meant that the domestic

---

[a]The case of rice, of which Japan has piled up immense surpluses, is a well-known exception. This has been the result of a protective system under which Japanese producers receive, and Japanese consumers pay, more than twice the world price for rice.

[b]Balance-of-payments statistics for Japan used throughout this article are, except where otherwise noted, derived from the Bank of Japan's *Balance of Payments of Japan*, an annual publication from 1954 to 1965, and its *Balance of Payments Monthly*, published from April 1966 to the present.

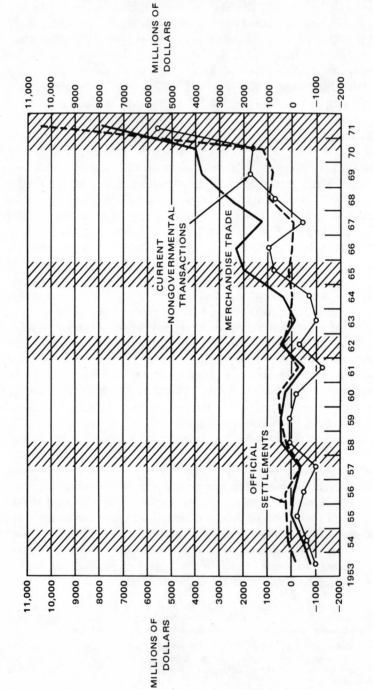

Figure 3-1. Balance of Payments of Japan, 1953-1971. Sources: The Bank of Japan, *Balance of Payments of Japan* and *Balance of Payments Monthly*; Economic Planning Agency, *Economic Statistics*, vol. 14 (April 1971), IMF, *International Financial Statistics*.

Table 3-1
Japan's International Reserves (Value in Millions of Dollars)

Year	Official Holdings of Gold and Convertible Foreign Exchange[a]	Annual Merchandise Imports[b]	Reserves as a Percentage of Imports
1953	892	2,410	37.0
1954	930	2,399	38.8
1955	1,076	2,471	43.6
1956	1,270	3,230	39.3
1957	828	4,284	19.3
1958	1,032	3,033	34.0
1959	1,446	3,599	40.2
1960	1,949	4,491	43.4
1961	1,666	5,810	28.7
1962	2,022	5,637	35.9
1963	2,058	6,736	30.6
1964	2,019	7,938	25.4
1965	2,152	8,169	26.3
1966	2,119	9,523	22.3
1967	2,030	11,663	17.4
1968	2,906	12,987	22.4
1969	3,654	15,024	24.3
1970	4,840	18,881	25.6
1971	15,360	19,695	78.0

[a]Holdings as of December 31, reported by the International Monetary Fund.
[b]Customs clearance basis, including cost of freight and insurance.
Sources: International Monetary Fund, *International Financial Statistics* (Supplement 1971 and March 1972); Bank of Japan, *Economic Statistics Annual* (1970), and *Balance of Payments Monthly* (January 1972).

boom had to be checked after each time the balance of payments went into deficit. This action, which was repeated in 1953, 1957, 1961 and 1964, eventually was reflected in reduced imports and an intensified export effort by Japanese firms, thus bringing the payments balance back into surplus.

The Balance of Payments with the United States

Japan's dealings with the United States have always accounted for a significant proportion of its overall international payments, and they have played a particularly crucial role in the period following World War II. In merchandise trade the United States has been Japan's largest partner by far throughout the postwar years and remains so today. The American share of Japanese exports has gradually increased since the war, from 22 percent in 1950 to 31 percent in 1970 and 1971.[1] The prominence of the United States as an import supplier to Japan has moved in the opposite direction, declining from 43 percent in 1950 to a (still impressive) 25 percent share in 1971. Imports from the United States exceeded exports to it in every year until 1965, when the balance was finally reversed as the result of long-term trends in export and import trade. The size of the imbalance has always been subject to strong cyclical fluctuations, particularly since capital and consumer durable goods form a large part of each country's exports to the other.[2]

Trade in services (excluding military procurements and other expenditures by the American government and military personnel in Japan) was the source of an additional deficit in Japan's current transactions with the United States. The largest payments were for transportation and insurance in connection with the trade between the two countries—a business which both countries (and also third countries) shared, but more of which was handled by American shippers than Japanese—and for interest payments, investment income, royalties, and other fees. American corporations have generally developed closer relations with their Japanese counterparts than have those of any other Western country, and they have collected a major part of the fees for investment and management-related services imported into Japan.

The deficit in private current transactions averaged about $300 million each year from 1951 through 1965, but it was more than offset by expenditures of the American government and servicemen in Japan. This spending ranged from a high of around $800 million in 1953, when American requirements for the Korean War were at a peak, to a low of about $350 million in 1964, before Vietnam spending became large. In 1971 it amounted to around $600 million. Japan's overall current account with the United States, including these government expenditures along with private transactions, has almost always been in net surplus. There have also been moderate net inflows to Japan on capital account resulting from loans and investments by American banks, corporations, and individuals. In aggregate, therefore, transactions with the United States have been a source of net foreign exchange earnings for Japan, even in the years when its deficit in trade with the United States was substantial.

The Balance of Payments and Economic Policy

Concern with the balance-of-payments constraint has strongly influenced economic policy-making in Japan throughout modern history. The growth-promoting strategies which Professor Rosovsky mentions in Chapter 1 are all aimed at least partly at encouraging the substitution of domestic production for imports and fostering the development of export industries. Specific incentives such as tax exemptions and special trade-financing facilities have also been used to encourage exports, but the long-range industrial planning strategies favoring development of industries which the government regarded as potential exporters have probably been more important.

Japan's policy with regard to the international exchange of capital has also been determined mainly by its concern with its balance-of-payments deficit problem, and with maintaining its independence of foreign influence. Loans and investments abroad by Japanese residents have been closely guided by the authorities and have been allowed for the most part only when they contributed to the long-run solution of what Japan considered its fundamental balance-of-payments problem: the securing of dependable sources of supply for raw materials and other vital goods which cannot be produced at home. Overseas borrowing by Japanese firms has been held down also, so as to protect the monetary authorities' control over credit supply and hence their ability to regulate the domestic economy. This, and also the severe limitations placed on direct investments by foreign corporations in Japan, is motivated in addition by the desire to prevent foreign companies from playing too large a part in Japan's economic system, whose order they are thought likely to disturb.

Anticyclical policy, even more than growth policy, has been dominated in the postwar period by balance-of-payments considerations. When the yen parity was set at 360 per dollar in 1949, and for many years afterward, it was widely thought to be overvalued. Nevertheless the Japanese, taking an orthodox view of foreign-exchange-rate policy, have never considered changing the parity to be an appropriate means for correcting balance-of-payments imbalance so long as any other choice existed. The Japanese were also unwilling to depend on capital flows from abroad to finance current deficits, for reasons which have already been mentioned. The result has been the pattern described above, in which the monetary authorities responded with restrictive measures each time the business boom produced a balance-of-payments crisis, and this in turn put a quick end to the domestic expansion. The balance of payments was undoubtedly not the only reason for anticyclical measures undertaken by the Japanese authorities, but the timing of these adjustments was usually justified in terms of external considerations. The idea, that adjustments in domestic economic activity are the appropriate response to balance of payments disequilibria, has thus been accepted as public policy in Japan at a time when it enjoyed little popularity in other industrial countries. One reason for this difference was undoubtedly that the Japanese financial structure, in which the major firms depend heavily on the large city banks for funds, and these in turn are closely guided by the monetary authorities, is more conducive to the success of such an adjustment policy than are those of most Western countries.[3]

The New Situation: The Balance of Payments after 1968

The Emergence of the Surplus Disequilibrium

The 1966-67 economic boom seemed at first to follow the pattern established in previous postwar business cycles. The balance of payments dipped into deficit in 1967, leading the monetary authorities to adopt some restraining measures during the final quarter of the year. The outcome was different this time, however, as exports spurted ahead eliminating the external deficit within two quarters, while there was virtually no interruption of the domestic expansion. Monetary policy was relaxed after mid-1968, and the boom continued into late 1969 when restrictive economic policies were adopted in order to curb accelerating price inflation. This was the first time in the postwar period that such tightening was undertaken while the balance of payments was in comfortable surplus.

The OECD, in its annual economic review of Japan in 1969, identified the 1968-69 improvement in the balance of payments as of a more permanent character than those of previous cycles, and said that Japan was now experiencing "the problems of surplus countries trying to avoid undue strains on international liquidity."[4] The evidence for this conclusion was ample. Japan's balance of trade, though it turned down sharply during the 1966-67 boom, remained in substantial surplus for both years as can be seen from Table 3-2. In fact, the last time a trade deficit was experienced for an entire year was in 1963. The current account showed a deficit in 1967, but not as large as in previous cycles, and Japan added almost $1 billion to its foreign exchange reserves—an increase of nearly one-third—between 1964 and 1968.

Table 3-2
Japan's Balance of Payments in the 1960s (in Billions of U.S. Dollars)

	1961	1962	1963	1964	1965	1966	1967	1968	1969	1970	1971
Exports (f.o.b.)	4.1	4.9	5.4	6.7	8.3	9.6	10.2	12.8	15.7	19.0	23.7
Imports (f.o.b.)	4.7	4.5	5.6	6.3	6.4	7.4	9.1	10.2	12.0	15.0	15.8
Trade Balance	−0.6	0.4	−0.2	0.4	1.9	2.3	1.2	2.5	3.7	4.0	7.9
Invisibles	−0.4	−0.4	−0.6	−0.9	−1.0	−1.0	−1.4	−1.5	−1.6	−2.0	−2.0
Current Account Balance	−1.0	0.0	−0.8	−0.5	0.9	1.3	−0.2	1.0	2.1	2.0	5.9
Net Long-Term Capital Balance	0.0	0.2	0.5	0.1	−0.4	−0.8	−0.8	−0.2	−0.2	−1.6	−1.2
Basic Balance	−1.0	0.1	−0.3	−0.4	0.5	0.4	−1.0	0.8	2.0	0.4	4.7

Source: Bank of Japan, *Balance of Payments Monthly*, no. 42 (January 1970) and no. 66 (January, 1972) pp. 1-2, table 1.

Underlying these balance-of-payments developments was the fact that Japan's exports for years had been growing at a faster rate than its imports. During the entire period from 1953, when the postwar recovery was more or less completed, to 1970, the average annual rate of increase in exports (measured in current prices) was slightly over 17 percent, while imports grew about 13 percent on average. This has been an outcome of the successful growth strategies already referred to which aimed at encouraging export growth and reducing import dependence. Long-run technological trends, tending to reduce industrial requirements for imported raw materials, seem to have more than balanced the effect of the gradual relaxation of official import controls. As a result imports have grown slightly more slowly than total output since the mid-1950s, lowering their proportion in total national expenditures from around 10 percent to between 7 and 8 percent.[c] Exports, on the other hand, have grown slightly faster than GNP as Japanese industry has been able to achieve competitive efficiency in the production of goods for which expanding world markets existed.[d]

In addition to these developments in merchandise trade, changes had occurred which limited the growth of Japan's deficit in payments for services, adding to the tendency toward surplus on overall current account. One of these was that the domestic shipping industry, aided by government subsidies, took over the transportation of an increasing share of Japan's trade. The deficit for freight and insurance, although it continued to be the largest part of the overall service deficit, thus grew much more slowly than did Japan's total trade. Another influence was that Japan began to change from a borrowing to a lending nation in the international context, and as a result Japanese corporations' receipts from investing activities abroad grew faster than their payments for foreign borrowing.

The Japanese leadership was of course aware that the continuation of these trends, which had been observed for many years, must eventually transform Japan's traditional balance-of-payments deficit into a surplus. Nevertheless, it seemed to many—both inside and outside Japan—that it was premature in 1969 to accept the OECD's conclusion as established after only a year or so of experience with external surplus. These doubts were eliminated when the surplus on current account rose from $1 billion in 1968 to $2 billion in 1969 and 1970, and then increased again to almost $6 billion in 1971—when the coincidence of an economic slowdown in Japan with inflationary conditions in the United States and elsewhere added a strong cyclical element to the secular trend.

By 1971 it was clear to everyone that Japan's balance-of-payments surplus was not merely a brief respite from the pressure of its old deficit problem. It was

---

[c]This refers to the proportion of merchandise imports alone (valued f.o.b., i.e., excluding freight and insurance charges) in national expenditures. This proportion for all imports, of both goods and services, has been between 10 and 12 percent for most of the same period.

[d]All of these comparisons are in current prices. The growth of both exports and imports has been faster than that of GNP when measured in real terms, as Professor Sato shows in Chapter 4.

a fundamentally new problem, and one which urgently required corrective action. From Japan's own point of view, it meant a waste of precious resources in the piling up of foreign exchange reserves, resources which were badly needed for improving social services and social overhead capital at home. For the world as a whole, the continued imbalance of Japan's international payments indicated a failure of the international adjustment mechanism. In particular, it contributed to doubts about the U.S. dollar and about the viability of an international monetary system which was based on the dollar as a reserve currency.

About $3 billion of Japan's $5 billion current-account surplus during the years 1968-70 was accounted for (according to Japanese statistics) by its surplus in current transactions with the United States. According to American statistics, the deficit of the United States in its merchandise trade with Japan alone amounted to $3.2 billion in 1971, more than the overall U.S. trade deficit of about $2.9 billion for that year. Looking at figures like these, Americans tended to attribute much of their own balance-of-payments difficulty to the change in their economic relationship with Japan. And in the end it was America's action to meet its own crisis which dictated the timing, if not the fact, of Japan's revaluation of the yen.[5]

The Response of Japanese Economic Policy

Before the Nixon administration acted in August 1971, Japan had responded to its new balance-of-payments situation with a variety of moves to relax restrictions on importing and on international capital movements, and to reduce special incentives for exporting by Japanese producers. Quantitative import quotas, which at the end of 1968 applied to 121 different BTN categories, were reduced to 60 by the middle of 1971—as compared with 70 in France and 38 in Germany.[6] The schedule for completion of Japan's Kennedy-Round tariff cuts was advanced from January 1972 to April 1971, and the average tariff rate on industrial imports was thus reduced to about 10 percent, comparable with 11 percent for the United States and 7 percent for the European Economic Community.[7] With respect to both tariffs and quotas, therefore, Japan's protectionist barriers in 1971 had been brought more or less into line with those of major Western industrial countries. Official control over all sizeable direct investments and loans by Japanese firms in foreign countries was maintained, but it was applied more and more liberally so that the amount of such investment went from less than $1 billion in 1967 to $2.3 billion in 1971. These same years also saw four rounds of a "capital-decontrol" program designed to allow more direct and portfolio investment by foreigners in Japan, but the resulting inflows were not large enough to offset the increase in Japanese investments abroad. On a net basis, therefore, long-term capital outflows rose to $1.6 billion in 1970, and $1.2 billion in 1971.[e]

Interest rates on the Bank of Japan's loans for short-term export financing, which previously had been offered at preferentially low rates, were raised so as to be as costly as discounts of prime domestic commercial bills. Also before late 1971, Japan had 264 cases (including duplicate requests by different countries) of 4-digit BTN items to which it was applying "voluntary" export control at the request of importing countries, of which 51 were at the request of the United States.[8]

These measures, while important, did not have sufficient immediate effect to prevent continued growth of the balance-of-payments surplus in 1970 and 1971. In May of 1971 worldwide currency speculation brought very large inflows of short-term capital to Japan, which after the floating of the German mark was the leading surplus nation still holding to its old exchange rate. This, and continued political pressure from the United States and elsewhere, led the government to announce in June an "Eight-Point Program" of projected measures to reduce Japan's balance-of-payments surplus with the world as a whole and with the United States in particular.

The eight points included: (1) further removal of import quotas (the number of which was reduced to 40 in September 1971, and to 33 by early 1972), (2) preferential tariffs for imports from less developed countries (which were enacted on a quota-limited basis in August 1971), (3) additional reductions in tariffs (a few of which have been lowered beyond the Kennedy-Round levels—strategic items being computers, film, and machine tools), (4) liberalization of capital movements, including allowing Japanese residents to purchase foreign stocks in appreciable amounts for the first time (a change which was instituted in July 1971) and relaxed rules governing foreign lending and the holding of foreign currency balances by Japanese banks and firms (introduced in a series of steps which had begun before June 1971 and continued into 1972), (5) reduction of certain nontariff trade barriers, such as the 40 percent excise tax on large automobiles particularly resented by American car manufacturers (which was done in March 1972), (6) increased aid to less developed countries, (7) ending preferential financing of exports (carried out in August 1971) and of special tax benefits for exporters (partly done for the 1971 fiscal year, and to be completed in fiscal 1972), and also establishing of new "orderly marketing"

---

[e]The decline from 1970 to 1971 was due to large foreign purchases of Japanese securities. These have been a volatile item in the "long-term" capital balance, responding sensitively to short-run changes in Japanese and foreign stock-market conditions as well as to currency speculation. In May of 1971 the Japanese authorities put a stop to most of this speculative inflow by prohibiting foreigners from purchasing unlisted Japanese bonds. When securities investments are excluded, the total of net long-term capital outflows from Japan increases quite steadily from $0.9 billion in 1967 to $1.9 billion in 1971.

programs to prevent disruptive export growth in specific markets, (the first of which was applied to some electronics items in April 1972), and (8) monetary and fiscal policies designed to stimulate the domestic economy.[9]

The Question of Yen Revaluation

The "Eight Points" represented, in the main, the speeding up of existing long-term Japanese policies for liberalizing trade, capital, and foreign exchange movements. When the possibility of a yen revaluation as a means of aiding this adjustment was suggested, Japanese leaders usually responded that the dismantling of their complicated system of controls—built to handle the "old" balance-of-payments deficit problem—must logically come first. In addition to this liberalization process, the official view held that changes in domestic resource allocation would bring about a large part of the adjustment required to correct the external disequilibrium, as had happened in all of the previous postwar balance-of-payments crisis. Just as they had taken external deficit in the past as a sign that the domestic economy was exceeding its natural limits and must be adjusted accordingly, the Japanese viewed their new surplus problem as an indication of the need for certain domestic adjustments rather than—as many outsiders saw it—a problem of the yen's valuation relative to other currencies. Parity change was clearly viewed as a last resort, and one which they hoped would prove unnecessary once the other adjustments had had their effect.

In defending their position, that the yen was not undervalued in the context of expected changes in policies and conditions, the Japanese pointed to their growing shortage of labor, the closing of their technological "gap" with Western countries, and other changes which suggest a slower export growth and a more rapid increase of import requirements in the next decade than were experienced in the last. They also emphasized the urgent requirements for housing, sanitation, environmental protection and other types of social overhead capital, needs which had been seriously neglected in the rush to increase industrial capacity and exports in the previous two decades.[f] As Japan now turned its attention to meeting these domestic requirements, it was felt, the recent tendency toward growing trade surpluses would end, since this effort would divert resources away from private manufacturing investment and channel them into uses, both public and private, which do not directly increase exporting capacity. In addition, Japan considered that its readiness to accept the responsibilities of a capital-exporting nation, and increase its economic aid to developing areas, made the continuation of a moderate surplus in its current transactions with other countries a sustainable, and not a disequilibrating, situation for the coming years.

---

[f]For a fuller discussion of these problems, see Chapter 1.

In spite of these arguments, it seemed clear in mid-1971, when the Eight-Point Program was announced, that the measures proposed by the Japanese government would not bring about a reduction in the surplus on the scale or with the rapidity that was required. Some of the measures, including those for liberalizing imports, might take years before their effects were fully realized. Exchange control relaxations, like the freeing of Japanese stock purchases overseas, would have no effect at all so long as the speculative mood of 1971 persisted, since the likelihood of a yen revaluation outweighed any possible advantages of such investment in the short run. Perhaps the most important part of the Eight-Point Program was its fiscal policy, but this was clearly a long-run rather than a short-run proposition. Marked increases in housing, environmental improvement, and other social-overhead expenditures had been visible in the government budgets of the last few years, and this trend would be accelerated under the new program. However, radical actions like increasing the share of taxation in the national income—a ratio which has been kept at a relatively low 20 percent level since the late 1950s by means of annual tax-rate reductions—were not mentioned, and changes of this order would seem to be required for any resource-reallocation plan strong enough to have immediate effects on the payments balance.

In spite of the government's resistance, therefore, yen revaluation appeared inevitable to most people in Japan and elsewhere by mid-1971. A survey of Japanese business and other leaders in July 1971 reported that over half of those questioned considered the yen to be undervalued. When asked about the timing of revaluation, assuming that it was to occur, fewer than 20 percent thought that the action would be delayed past 1972.[10] Most did expect it to be delayed until late in 1972, however, apparently believing that the Japanese authorities would wait until the domestic economy had recovered from its 1970-71 slowdown before subjecting it to the difficulties of revaluation. Because of extensive exchange controls, the Japanese authorities were able to hold the volume of foreign exchange inflows to a level which did not impair their control of the domestic money supply, in spite of persistent speculation that the yen would be revalued. Table 3-3 compares monthly foreign exchange inflows in 1971 with other sources of change in the domestic monetary base.[g] It is noticeable that

---

[g]As can be seen in Table 3-3, the Japanese authorities were also able to offset the more than $4 billion inflow in August by the traditional means of reducing Bank of Japan lending to commercial banks. However, any future disturbance of this kind would likely be a different story, since the amount of these outstanding credits was contracted so much, in the course of these adjustments in 1971, that by December they amounted to only 624 billion yen (about $2 billion) as compared with 2,247 billion yen at the end of 1970. The amount by which the central bank can further reduce the volume of this lending would clearly offer only limited leverage, if there should again be a need to offset large external increases in the other parts of the base. These claims on the banks, which in December 1970 accounted for 36 percent of the reserve money base, fell to 9 percent in December 1971, at the same time that foreign assets of the monetary authorities grew from 26 to 67 percent. Thus, while Japan was able to survive the turmoil of 1971 without seriously modifying its monetary

Table 3-3

Sources of Change in the Monetary Base

(Monthly Changes during 1971, in Billions of Yen)

	Total Reserve Money	Sources of Reserve Money Monetary Authorities'			
		Foreign Assets	Net Claims on Government	Claims on Banks	Other Assets (net)
January	−794.5	48.0	−992.0	177.7	−28.2
February	137.9	120.8	39.4	−57.0	34.7
March	261.3	212.4	−539.0	268.3	319.6
April	−172.4	115.1	247.7	−222.5	−312.7
May	−98.4	409.7	−585.2	−137.7	214.8
June	328.8	245.9	123.0	−152.5	112.4
July	−2.1	118.2	−43.3	−48.4	−28.6
August	21.2	1651.2	−432.9	−786.4	−453.1
September	105.5	313.2	−8.6	−275.5	76.4
October	72.9	257.0	−18.6	−214.4	−96.9
November	180.7	265.7	316.3	−90.9	−310.4
December	1048.5	−573.1	659.7	−83.5	1045.4

Source: Bank of Japan, *Economic Statistics Monthly*, February 1972, pp. 15-16, table 4, "Monetary Survey."

even in May, the month of 1971's first worldwide currency crisis, the 1.4 billion dollar inflow (equivalent to almost 500 billion yen) was able to be offset using the traditional monetary control instrument, changes in central bank credit to the banking system. The ease with which the domestic monetary impact of the May crisis was contained in Japan contrasts with the experience of Germany and other European countries, which were forced to close their exchange markets to stem massive inflows which could not be absorbed by conventional means.

Consideration of domestic economic problems alone thus made it seem that the Japanese were not under overwhelming pressure to revalue, particularly while the business cycle was in a phase that required expansionary economic policies rather than restraint. International pressure was more urgent, however, and it was this which finally dictated yen revaluation during 1971. The Nixon administration suspended the convertibility of the dollar into gold and temporarily imposed a 10 percent surcharge on all dutiable American imports, in an

---

institutions, the cumulative effect of these adjustments has been more profound, and is likely to require new instruments to be developed in the future. (Data from Bank of Japan, *Economic Statistics Annual*, 1970 edition, p. 14, Table 8, and *Economic Statistics Monthly*, February 1972, p. 16, Table 4.) For a description of the operation of monetary policy in the past, see the references cited in note 3 of this chapter.

attempt to force a number of its trading partners—but most particularly Japan—to undertake sizable revaluations immediately. Japan was forced to abandon its defense of the yen parity, although it resisted until August 27, nearly two weeks after all the other major trading partners of the United States had floated their currencies. Months of negotiations followed, during which the Japanese leadership insisted it could revalue the yen only as part of an overall realignment of world currencies, since it felt that the American crisis was a problem of the dollar and not primarily one of the yen. A multilateral agreement was reached late in the year, and on December 20 a new official rate of 308 yen per U.S. dollar became effective, representing an increase of 16.88 percent in the yen's value relative to the dollar.

The Prospect

Japan's Balance of Payments in the 1970s

Table 3-6 (on page 70) outlines what may happen to the Japanese balance of payments during the 1970s if there is no further revaluation of the yen during that time. The projections are based on a set of simple assumptions which are outlined below. The outlook could easily be changed by another change in the parity, or by unpredictable developments in world trade, the domestic Japanese economy, or government policy. Nevertheless, the projections help in the evaluation of Japan's present situation by showing what could develop under one set of plausible circumstances.

Exports. The rate of growth of Japanese exports is taken to depend mainly on (1) the growth of world trade and (2) changes in the prices of Japanese exports relative to those of competing products. During the second half of the 1960s, Japan's export volume grew about 2 percent for every 1 percent increase in the volume of world trade—that is, the elasticity of world demand for these exports (in real terms), with respect to total imports of the rest of the world, was about 2. The independent increase in real exports due to a 1 percent reduction in their relative prices was also about 2 percent.[h] Japanese exporters are likely to

---

[h]These estimates are based on my own regression analysis of the dependence of Japanese export volume on the ratio of Japanese export prices to competing foreign prices and the level of world imports, using quarterly data from the 1960s. Numerous other estimates exist of aggregate trade relations for Japan, and most give roughly similar results, though precise elasticity estimates often vary with the period, the use of quarterly or annual data and other differences in specification. These simple macroeconomic equations of course provide only a rough indication of the underlying elasticities because (among other reasons) the presence during the 1960s of strong trends in both relative prices and world trade—in both cases favorable to Japanese export growth—makes it difficult to identify the separate influence of the two factors.

increase their share of world trade at a much slower rate in coming years, since the scope for breaking into important new product fields, and also for expanding the Japanese share in principal regional markets, has to a large extent been exhausted by the rapid growth of the last two decades.[i] The world-trade elasticity of Japanese export demand is therefore assumed in the projections to decline gradually after the next year or so, to 1.4 by the end of the decade.

The total volume of world imports grew slightly more than 7 percent annually, on average, during the fifteen years 1955-70, and during the last five years of this period the rate rose to about 9 percent. The conditions which led to this more rapid growth between 1965 and 1970, particularly the inflationary expansion of the U.S. economy, are not expected to continue in the 1970s. The projections below therefore assume that world trade will grow about 7 percent per annum (in real terms) after 1972, a rate which is slightly less than that of the 1955-70 period, but which still implies some increase in the ratio of international trade to world output as a whole.[j]

The initial change in export sales resulting from the yen's revaluation in December 1971 is expected to be completed in the course of 1972 and 1973. Since a number of other countries also revalued in 1971, the increase in the cost of the yen, for the foreigners who buy Japanese exports, is not everywhere as great as 16.88 percent. When the average change in the yen's value relative to each currency is weighted by the importance of each country in Japan's export markets the outcome is about a 15.5 percent revaluation—that is, Japanese exports whose yen prices have not changed are on average 15.5 percent more expensive than they were before relative to the domestic products available to consumers in Japan's overseas markets. There are two main reasons for expecting that Japanese export prices will rise less than 15.5 percent. One relatively small factor is that the effect of revaluation in reducing the cost of imported industrial materials may allow Japanese producers to lower their yen prices somewhat. Since imported inputs worth about 6.5 yen are required for each 100 yen of manufacturing production in Japan,[11] this factor might lower the rate of export price increase to 14.5 percent. More important is that some domestic producers, especially in the modern sectors, may be able to absorb a significant part of the revaluation in lowered profit margins. This will enable the more efficient exporters to retain most of their current overseas business, though its growth may be seriously affected in the next few years. About three-quarters of Japanese exports before revaluation were products of high-technology industries such as machinery, metal products and chemicals, and about one-quarter were of less sophisticated goods—food, materials, and light manufactures.[12] Assuming

---

[i]This problem is treated at length in Professor Sato's chapter.

[j]See Professor Sato's chapter for more regional detail. He projects growth of real imports at 6.7 percent for developed areas, 8 percent for the Middle East, and 5 percent in other less developed areas. World trade data for the 1955-70 period are from his chapter and the IMF's *International Financial Statistics* (monthly-various issues).

that producers in the less sophisticated industries have small profit margins and will not lower their yen prices at all, but that exporters of sophisticated products will hold their foreign-price increases to about half of the amount of the revaluation, the result would be an average increase of export prices of about 9 percent. Using the previously mentioned price-elasticity of 2, this would mean about an 18 percent reduction in the volume of annual exports, of which it may be assumed two-thirds will occur in 1972, and one-third in 1973.

Japanese export prices have been quite stable in comparison with prices of foreign goods through the past two decades, and this has been a source of competitive advantage for Japanese exporters. This advantage is not expected to continue in the future because the special conditions which allowed the extraordinary productivity increases of the 1950s and 1960s no longer exist.[k] The projections therefore assume that Japanese export prices will increase at about the same rate as those of competing countries.

Table 3-4 below summarizes the assumptions used in projecting the growth of Japanese exports in the 1970s. As the reader will see, the implication of these assumptions is that Japanese export growth will continue once the revaluation impact is absorbed, at rates of 10 to 11 percent annually in real terms, and 13 to 14 percent in dollar terms, through the latter part of the 1970s.

Imports. The growth of imports is taken to depend on (1) the growth of industrial production in Japan, (2) changes in the prices of imported goods relative to import-competing domestic products, and (3) government measures to liberalize or actively encourage imports. The last factor is arbitrarily assumed to add about 3 percentage points to import growth (in real terms) in 1972, and about 1 percent in each of the following four years.

Time-series analysis of the experience of the 1960s indicates that the elasticity of imports with respect to Japanese manufacturing production is close to 1—that is, a 1 percent increase in output leads to about a 1 percent increase in imports. Measured changes in the relative price of imports have not seemed to exert a significant influence on import volume in the past. This may change, now that most quantitative restrictions on imports have been removed. However, since Japanese imports are mainly comprised of industrial supplies and food products, the demand for them will probably continue to be relatively insensitive to price changes.[l] In the projections below, it is assumed that the price elasticity of imports will be about 0.5 through the 1970s.

The pattern of domestic economic growth assumed is that the rate of increase in real GNP will be close to 10 percent annually for a few years following the

---

[k]See Professor Rosovsky's Chapter 1 for a detailed discussion of the reasons for this.

[l]The proportion of food and industrial materials and supplies was 85 percent in 1970 (MOF, op. cit., p. 68, Table 4). These remarks assume that this will not change radically in the next several years. Some considerations bearing on this important assumption are discussed below.

Table 3-4
Determination of Projected Japanese Export Growth (Percentage per Annum)

	1972	1973	1974-76	1977-80
1. World Trade Growth				
Assumed annual growth rate (real terms)	5	7	7	7
Assumed world-trade elasticity of Japanese export demand	2	2	1.6	1.4
Contribution to export growth (real terms)	10	14	11	10
2. Relative Price Change				
Change, due to 1971 revaluation, in relative (foreign-currency) prices of Japanese exports	9	0	0	0
Difference between domestic and foreign wholesale price inflation	0	0	0	0
Assumed price-elasticity of exports	-2			
Contribution to export growth (real terms)	-12	-6	0	0
3. Total Growth in Real Exports (sum of 1. and 2. above)	-2	8	11	10
4. Assumed Annual Rise in Japanese (Yen) Export Prices	-5.5	3	3	3
5. Increase in Yen Value of Exports	-7.5	11	14	13
6. Increase in Dollar Value of Exports	9	11	14	13

expected recovery during 1972, and after that will decline, coming down to 8 percent by the last few years of the decade.[m] More of the increase in GNP will be concentrated in nonmanufacturing activity, such as construction and government and other services, than has been true in the past, but manufacturing production is still assumed to grow about 2 percentage points faster than GNP.

The effect of the revaluations carried out at the end of 1971 is to lower the price of imported products, relative to Japanese goods, an average of 13.5 percent.[n] Assuming that foreign suppliers do not raise the prices they receive for

[m]The reader may wish to compare this with the GNP growth projections of Professor Rosovsky and Professor Sato. The former uses an average of 6.5 percent for the entire period from now to 1990, with the rate declining from about 8 to 4 percent during that interval. The latter projects 8 percent average growth for the 1970s; the average for the decade implied by my assumptions would also be 8 percent.

[n]This, similarly to the 15.5 percent mentioned above for export prices, is based on a computation of the average change in the value of each currency relative to the yen, weighted by the importance of each country in Japan's 1970 import trade.

goods sent to Japan, application of the 0.5 price elasticity mentioned above would imply an increase in import volume of almost 7 percent, which it can be supposed will take place during 1972 and 1973. Unlike the situation with export prices, domestic prices of import-competing goods—especially agricultural products, industrial materials and labor-intensive light manufactures—can be expected to rise much faster in Japan than the 3 percent annual increase projected for world export prices, and this will provide an additional stimulus to imports.

Table 3-5 summarizes the assumptions used in forecasting import growth during the 1970s. The implied average growth rate for imports from 1972 to

Table 3-5
Determination of Projected Japanese Import Growth (Percentage per Annum)

	1972	1973	1974-76	1977-80
1. Industrial Production Growth Assumed annual growth rate	7	12	11	10
Assumed output elasticity of imports	1	1	1	1
Contribution to import growth (real terms)	7	12	11	10
2. Relative Price Change Difference between inflation rate for domestic import-competitive products and for world exports	1	3	3	2
Changes due to 1971 revaluation in relative (yen) prices of imported goods	-13.5			
Assumed price elasticity of imports	0.5	0.5	0.5	0.5
Contribution to import growth (real terms)	5	4	1.5	1
3. Official Import-Encouraging Policies	3	1	1	0
4. Total Growth in Real Imports (Sum of 1., 2. and 3. above)	15	17	13.5	11
5. Increase in Yen Value of Imports	4.5	20	16.5	14
6. Assumed Annual Rise in Dollar Prices of Imports	4	3	3	3
7. Increase in Dollar Value of Imports[a] (Sum of 4. and 6. above)	19	20	16.5	14

[a]The 19% increase in dollar value for 1972 is about 1% more than the increase in yen value (4.5%) plus the rise in the value of yen in the "average" foreign currency used in Japanese imports (13.5%), because some of these currencies were revalued relative to the dollar as well.

1980 is about 13 percent per annum in real terms, and about 16 percent in dollar terms.

The Trade Account. As Table 3-6 shows, the assumptions outlined above imply a moderate reduction in Japan's annual trade surplus after the 1971 revaluation to a level of $7 billion in 1972 and $6 billion in 1973, and a gradual increase after that to about $9 billion in 1980. The 1971 revaluation has been taken to cause an 18 percent reduction in annual export volume, and a 7 percent increase in annual imports in the years after 1972, which would imply a cut of more than $6 billion in each year's trade surplus measured in terms of 1971 prices. But since the currency realignment also means an increase of about 10 percent in the dollar prices of Japanese exports, while the effect on import prices would be much smaller,[o] the impact of revaluation on the dollar balance of Japan's international payments comes to about $4 billion per year based on 1972-73 trade levels. While this would be a substantial reduction, the remaining Japanese trade surplus is also very large.

One noticeable consequence of these hypotheses is that they do not involve an increase in the quantitative importance of international trade in the Japanese

Table 3-6

A Balance-of-Payments Projection for Japan in the 1970s (Billions of Current Dollars)[a]

	1971[b]	1972	1973	1974	1975	1976	1977	1978	1979	1980
Exports	23.7	25.8	28.6	32.6	37.2	42.4	47.9	54.1	61.1	69.1
Imports	15.8	18.7	22.5	26.2	30.5	35.5	40.5	46.2	52.6	60.0
Trade Balance	7.9	7.1	6.1	6.4	6.7	6.9	7.4	7.9	8.5	9.1
Invisibles	-2.0	-1.9	-1.8	-1.8	-1.8	-1.8	-1.8	-1.8	-1.8	-1.8
Current Account Balance	5.9	5.2	4.3	4.6	4.9	5.1	5.6	6.1	6.7	7.3
Memorandum: Current Account Surplus as % of GNP	2.7	1.9	1.4	1.3	1.2	1.1	1.1	1.0	1.0	1.0

[a]These projections are based on an assumption that the yen parity will remain at 308 per U.S. dollar in order to assess the tenability of such a situation. All values are based on the yen/dollar parity in effect at the time, so that part of the changes in 1971 and 1972 reflect the change in dollar valuation of the yen, as well as effects of this change on the real trade flows.

[b]Figures for 1971 are actual totals (reported in the Bank of Japan's *Balance of Payments Monthly*, January 1972, p. 1, table 1).

---

[o]Import prices were assumed to be unchanged in terms of suppliers' currencies. Since these were revalued on average (weighted by the geographical distribution of Japan's imports) about 1 percent relative to the U.S. dollar, this means that Japan's import prices would also rise about 1 percent in dollar terms overall. (See note to Table 3-5.)

economy. The proportion of imports or exports of goods and services in the total Gross National Product has remained in the neighborhood of 10 to 12 percent throughout the years since 1955. In 1970 the proportion was about 11 percent for imports and 12 percent for exports, and the projections above would imply about the same ratios for 1980. This trade/GNP ratio is much smaller than it was in the prewar Japanese economy, and it is also smaller than those of other leading industrialized countries except the United States.

The fact that this ratio has been projected here to stay low throughout the present decade is due mainly to the assumptions made about Japanese imports—that they will continue to be mainly of industrial supplies and food products, although the importance of capital and nonfood consumer goods imports may increase somewhat, and that neither rising domestic prices nor official liberalization policy will cause massive increases in imports in any particular year, though both will add to the growth rate. The appropriateness of these assumptions depends sensitively on one's judgment of the role which official protection plays in the Japanese economy. Bringing down the rate of dependence on world trade seems to have been one of the objectives of postwar growth policy, and therefore the characteristic of a low import-to-GNP ratio may be regarded as at least in part a result of the success of this policy.

Now that Japan can afford a greater dependence on imports, however, it does not necessarily follow that the ratio will increase sharply once official controls and other import-discouraging policies are ended. The view is often expressed that Japanese imports have failed to respond to liberalization of formal barriers like quotas and tariffs because of remaining informal policies, perhaps the most frequently mentioned being "administrative guidance" of purchases by major Japanese corporations. How widespread and important such informal barriers are is an empirical question which is difficult to answer.[p] In the absence of strong evidence that this is a major influence, however, it seems possible to explain the continued low import ratio mainly on the basis of the historical fact that Japanese manufacturing industries are by now at least roughly competitive with imports in most important lines of production, combined with the geographical isolation which makes transportation cost a more significant consideration in Japan than in most other industrialized economies. If this is correct, it may mean that the present small proportion of international trade in the economy is a more or less permanent characteristic.

Invisible Trade. The projections of Table 3-6 assume that imports and exports of transportation services and insurance will grow along with the volume of

---

[p]Professor Kiyoshi Kojima's recent survey *Nontariff Barriers to Japan's Trade*, (Tokyo, Japan Economic Research Center, December 1971) provides a general impression that nontariff restrictions—including administrative guidance—are not a much greater influence on imports in Japan than they are in other developed countries (although he argues strongly that further reduction and rationalization of these barriers is nevertheless needed).

Japanese merchandise trade as they have in the past, registering a deficit which increases about $20 million for each $1 billion increase in either imports or exports. Net payments for foreign travel, fees and gifts have also tended to increase each year in the past and in all probability will continue to do so. The net inflow from government transactions will decline if the United States government succeeds in reducing its own balance-of-payments outflow in connection with the defense establishment in Japan, by shifting more of this fiscal burden to the Japanese authorities. All of these trends in travel, fees, gifts, and government transactions together have been assumed to increase Japan's annual deficit in invisible trade by $100 million in each year from 1972 to 1980.

Counterbalancing these tendencies toward increased net spending for imported services will be a rapid growth in income received from Japanese investments abroad. Each year's surplus in current transactions implies a net increase in foreign assets held by Japanese, which will in turn lead to increased earnings in subsequent years. On the assumption that Japan will avoid further large accumulations of official foreign exchange reserves, it is expected that most of the assets acquired will be private long-term loans and investments. Based on past experience, a rough rule has been applied that annual earning (as reported in Japan's balance of payments) will grow about $6 million following each $100 million increase in net external assets held by Japanese.q Combined with the assumptions about trade and other invisible payments, this would mean that the balance of interest receipts and payments would change from a deficit ($209 million in 1970) to a surplus of $2 to $3 billion dollars by 1980. This would just about balance the other expected changes in the invisibles deficit, leaving it close to $2 billion throughout the decade.

The Problem of International Equilibrium

Prospects for Basic Balance in the 1970s. The outcome projected for the current account as a whole, described in Table 3-6, is that it would continue in surplus throughout the 1970s. Under the conditions assumed, the size of this surplus would decline from its 1971 level of $6 billion to about $4.5 billion in 1973, but then increase again gradually, exceeding $7 billion by 1980.

It is possible that current surpluses of this magnitude could be accompanied by net long-term capital outflows of about equal size, and thus lead to no sizable addition to Japanese foreign exchange reserves over the coming years. This would involve about doubling the current rate of capital exporting, which has

---

qThis rate of return of course depends on the composition of growth in assets, both those held overseas by Japanese residents and those owned in Japan by foreigners. Some of the factors influencing this composition are discussed below. The presumption here is that an increase in the proportion of direct investments—whose rate of return (in terms of balance-of-payments reports) is usually higher than that of loans—will about balance the expected increase in low-interest lending to less developed areas by Japan.

already been subject to rapid increases in recent years. Nevertheless it might possibly be regarded as a satisfactory equilibrium from the Japanese point of view.

Japan has not published any official balance-of-payments target. However in the "New Economic and Social Development Plan" which it presented in 1970, the government projected that the current account surplus would equal about 1 percent of GNP by 1975, a ratio which it seemed to regard as acceptable and which it expected to be about balanced by projected long-term capital outflows.[13] If this 1 percent surplus in current transactions, financed by long-term capital outflows, is taken as Japan's own definition of external equilibrium, the above projections imply that the target may be met—with present exchange rates—by the late 1970s. Even so, it is not at all clear that current account surpluses of the size implied—which would add up to nearly $50 billion in the rest of the decade—would be acceptable to the rest of the world. This would depend on a number of things, including the geographical distribution of the surplus and the nature of the aid and other capital outflows which Japan is willing to offer in exchange.

The "equilibrium" described would be a precarious one, even from the Japanese point of view, since even a temporary change in the assumed conditions could at one point or another add a billion dollars or more to the surplus and bring about renewed pressure for yen revaluation. In particular, if the domestic economy does not recover as quickly as has been supposed in 1972—as a result of a failure in business psychology, inadequate governmental enforcement of the policies expressed in the Eight-Point Program, a slump in world trade, or any number of other possible influences—the resulting depression in imports could mean an even larger trade and current-account surplus than was experienced in 1971 and lead to strong pressure for another yen revaluation by late 1972 or 1973.

If there is a second, smaller revaluation, it will substantially reduce the size of the surpluses projected above and therefore mitigate the adjustment problem for Japan and the world economy. It is not likely that such a parity change would eliminate the surplus, however, and it is reasonable to expect that Japan will remain in the position of an important surplus country through most of the present decade.[r]

The Problem of Global Balance. The reasoning above leads to the conclusion that Japan may be able to maintain a basic international balance (of current and long-term capital transactions) during the 1970s without a further change in the yen parity. Even if a continued large Japanese trade surplus does not create

---

[r]On the basis of the same assumptions about price-response that were used above, an additional 10 percent yen revaluation at the end of 1972 would be expected to lower the annual current-account surplus in the neighborhood of $2.5 billion in 1973, and by larger amounts in later years. A 5 percent revaluation would reduce it half as much.

difficulties from a national point of view, however, it may lead to international conflict if it is not consistent with what other countries expect or hope to achieve in their own external balances. If Japan is to earn a surplus in its current transactions with the rest of the world, some other countries are going to have to experience corresponding deficits.[s] It is important, therefore, to consider the implications of Japan's payments prospect from a global, as well as national, point of view.

It has been presumed that the surplus in Japan's current account will be balanced in the main by long-term lending overseas.[t] Much of this increased capital outflow will be to less developed countries, which in 1970 received about two-thirds of Japan's foreign loans and almost half of its overseas investment. These countries will presumably be willing to accept an increased flow of capital from Japan, at least if Japan makes promised changes in the nature of the capital being supplied. A great deal of attention has been paid to the fact that Japanese aid to underdeveloped areas reached 0.93 percent of GNP in 1970, close to the 1 percent target which it had set itself for 1975. However, well over half of Japan's lending to these countries is in the form of export credits, and in other respects also Japan's aid falls below the standards that have been set by the OECD's Development Assistance Committee and those achieved by other members.[14] Japanese officials have repeatedly stressed the need to improve the quality of Japanese aid, by increasing the proportion of direct government assistance, reducing that of export-tied loans, lowering interest rates and channeling more

---

[s]These deficits of course, will not necessarily be in direct trade with Japan. It may be worth emphasizing the distinction between the problem being raised here, of global consistency among different countries' *overall* balance-of-payments aims, and the much less significant matter (although it sometimes receives considerable attention) of bilateral payments balance among individual countries. Thus, for example, the fact that Japan imports more from Australia than it exports is not inconsistent with Japan's earning a surplus in overall trade or with Australia's being in deficit, but a conflict does result if all countries try to be in overall surplus at the same time.

[t]There have been newspaper reports that Japanese officials are interested in establishing a yen settlement area in Southeast Asia, by encouraging more use of yen in these countries' trade and capital transactions with Japan, most of which are now settled in U.S. dollars. (*Journal of Commerce* (New York), January 4, 1972, "Japan Seeks New Settlement Role for Yen".) Such a development would require the relaxation of controls on international short-term capital movements, and on domestic interest rates, since those engaged in international trade must be able to borrow, lend and hold yen at internationally competitive rates if they are to use it as a normal means of settlement. In theory, the development of such an international capital market in Tokyo could provide an additional counter to Japan's expected current-account earnings, in the form of short-term lending by Japanese banks and firms overseas, particularly in Southeast Asia. But the presence of at least latent speculative pressure on the yen is likely to make such a plan unworkable for the time being. So long as Japan is in chronic surplus on current account, there will always appear to be some likelihood of further revaluation, and virtually no probability of devaluation, so that any liberalization of Japanese exchange controls is likely to lead both Japanese and foreigners to add to their yen asset positions—i.e., to short-term inflows to Japan instead of outflows. This is likely to dissuade the Japanese from undertaking the decontrol measures that would be required for the creation of a "yen bloc," no matter how much they may favor the idea in theory.

funds through international agencies. Rapid progress in this will be one requirement for foreign acceptance of Japan's new international role as a trade-surplus, capital-exporting nation.

In order to assess the feasibility of Japan's balancing a large current surplus by exports of capital to less developed areas, it is necessary to consider also the balance-of-payments expectations of other developed countries. Except for the United States, most of the other OECD countries have experienced substantial balance-of-payments surpluses in recent years. At least some of these countries expect to continue their surpluses, financed by aid and private investments overseas, and there seem to be no obvious candidates for the role of a large-scale deficit country among the OECD group. The United States, as part of its "New Economic Policy," announced in 1971 an objective of reversing its trade deficit, and achieving a surplus in current transactions by 1973 or 1974 of $9 billion—enough to continue its current level of aid and private long-term capital outflows to LDCs, cover expected short-term outflows and yield some overall surplus as a margin of safety. If the United States were to achieve this target in 1974, and Japan were to run the $4.6 billion surplus projected above, there would have to be almost a 50 percent increase—from about $9.5 to $13.5 billion—in the level of capital outflow from OECD to non-OECD countries between 1970 and 1974, assuming that the other developed countries' surplus is reduced to zero by the dollar devaluation.[15] This is unlikely to be acceptable to the recipient countries, many of which are already trying to reduce their dependence on foreign investments and loans.

An alternative assumption, which underlies the American target, is that the $9 billion surplus will be achieved entirely through changes in American trade with other developed countries. According to the OECD estimate, this would require a reduction of the total current surplus of other OECD countries—including Japan—to $2 billion in 1974. This surely will not be achieved if Japan is in $4.5 billion surplus during that year.

It seems inevitable, therefore, that some or all of these expectations will be disappointed. The United States target, which involves a $13 billion "swing" from the overall deficit which by its own projection is expected in 1972, is ambitious to say the least. With respect to Japan's part of U.S. trade, American officials have said that achievement of the U.S. goal requires a reversal of the deficit in trade with Japan.[16] The prospect for such a bilateral balance between the United States and Japan is considered in the following section.

The Bilateral Balance Between Japan and the United States. The growth of Japan's trade with the United States is likely to follow a pattern similar to that of its overall trade, with Japanese imports growing considerably faster than its exports over the next several years. American exports to Japan may benefit particularly from the yen's revaluation, since almost 30 percent of them are of relatively price-sensitive machinery and other capital goods. Nonfood consumer products, now a very small import category in Japan (6 percent of imports from the United States in 1971) are another price-sensitive area in which American exporters may be able to do relatively well. Food exports, which accounted for 21 percent of the total in 1971, will be less affected by the price change, but they may benefit over the period as a whole from increasing liberalization of agricultural imports into Japan. The remainder of American exports to Japan are mainly industrial materials and supplies (41 percent in 1971) and their growth will tend to follow the pace of the Japanese economy as a whole.[17]

On the other side of the balance, there is some evidence that American imports from Japan are more price-sensitive than Japanese exports to other areas.[u] Revaluation may therefore substantially dampen the growth of this trade. Japanese producers are still strong competitors in some of the most dynamic American markets, however, and their exports are likely to continue increasing at a healthy rate. On the basis of the optimistic assumptions that (1) the growth rate of U.S. exports to Japan will each year be 2 percentage points faster, and (2) that of U.S. imports from Japan will be 2 percentage points slower, than the rates that have been projected for overall Japanese trade, the American trade deficit with Japan would become smaller each year, but it would nevertheless remain substantial until 1980. Net American earnings in service transactions with Japan can be expected to continue growing along with the trade between the two countries (since the overseas investments from which Japan is projected to earn its interest-income surplus are likely to be concentrated mainly in areas outside the United States). Thus Japan's current account with the United States will be substantially smaller than its trade surplus, and might even turn into a deficit by 1980. In the meantime, however, Japan's net earnings from current transactions would, under these hypothetical conditions, continue to be quite large for the next few years.

A continued Japanese current-account surplus of several billion dollars thus seems likely to conflict with the balance-of-payments aims of other countries. Not all of these countries' expectations can be realized, and the United States' target in particular seems unlikely to be achieved as quickly as desired. In this situation, a continued large imbalance in bilateral trade between the United States and Japan is likely to add to tensions between the two governments. The American government has often tended to look at its balance-of-payments problem in a bilateral manner, deducing from the large part of the overall deficit attributable to Japanese trade that what is needed is a strong campaign to

---

[u]My regression estimates of aggregate demand relations for Japanese exports to the United States have yielded a significantly higher estimated price elasticity than that for all Japanese exports. These aggregate measurements should only be taken as a rough indication of the average degree of price-response, since an accurate estimate would require detailed commodity-level study of specific markets.

persuade the Japanese to import more from, and export less to, the United States. There are some benefits to be gained this way, and insofar as it induces Japan to speed up its import-liberalization program the benefits will be felt by Japanese consumers as well as foreign exporters. But policies aimed only at such bilateral adjustments will not reverse the past trends in American and Japanese trade, which are mainly due to the fact that Japan's producers have increased their efficiency more rapidly than their American counterparts. A fundamental improvement in the U.S. balance of trade—with Japan or with other countries—will only result from overall economic policies which succeed in improving the competitiveness of American goods in all markets, both domestic and foreign.

Conclusions

It seems highly probable that Japan will be living with its "new" balance-of-payments problem throughout the decade of the 1970s. If reorientation of the Japanese economy to the new situation continues at the pace established so far, and no further change is made in the yen parity, the surplus in current international transactions is likely to stay large during all of these years. Japan might be able to balance such excess earnings in current transactions with increased long-term capital outflows, and thus avoid adding to its already large foreign exchange reserves. Even so a continuing annual surplus of several billion dollars is likely to cause friction between Japan and its trading partners, since other developed countries may expect to increase their capital exports at the same time, and the underdeveloped world cannot bear the greatly increased burden of debt which this combination implies. Thus Japan may be forced to adopt more radical import-encouraging and export-discouraging policies—including further exchange-rate changes—in order to bring its surplus down to a level which will be accepted as "reasonable" from an international, as well as a national, point of view.

The positive aspects of the new situation are surely more important than the frictions, however. While the difficulties of Japan's relationships with its less developed neighbors are not to be minimized, the fact that Japan—a non-Western country with its own recent experience of modernization—now has the means to offer aid to these countries' industrialization effort can only be regarded as a favorable development. On the domestic side, the change in Japan's balance-of-payments position frees it to use resources in building up its social capital, and to launch a serious attack on its mammoth problems of urban congestion and environmental deterioration. Perhaps we will see a sequel in the next few years to the "Income-Doubling Plan" of the 1960s, which will change our ideas of what can be done in these areas as much as Japan's earlier performance changed our ideas about economic development.

Notes

1. Historical data on the geographical distribution of Japan's trade (customs-clearance basis, with imports valued c.i.f.) are found in the Bank of Japan's ECONOMIC STATISTICS ANNUAL (1970 edition, pp. 235-38, Table 132), and current data in its ECONOMIC STATISTICS MONTHLY or its BALANCE OF PAYMENTS MONTHLY (January 1972 edition, pp. 15-22, Tables 4 and 5).

2. This discussion of the Japanese-United States payments balance is based on Japanese balance-of-payments statistics. Because of differences in timing and definitions, these are not exactly the same as the American statistics covering the same transactions, although basic trends are reflected similarly in both sets of reports. Except where noted otherwise, statistics used in this article on the bilateral trade balance (using "balance-of-payments" base figures, with imports valued f.o.b.) are from the Bank of Japan's BALANCE OF PAYMENTS MONTHLY, the table entitled "Regional Balance of Payments Summary" (in the January 1972 issue, Table 12, pp. 65-68, contains figures for 1970). Corresponding American statistics would be found in the U.S. Department of Commerce, SURVEY OF CURRENT BUSINESS (e.g., March 1972 edition, pp. 54-56, Table 9, "U.S. International Transactions by Area," and Table 10, "Summary of Known Current and Long-Term Capital Transactions, by Area").

3. See Hugh T. Patrick, MONETARY POLICY AND CENTRAL BANKING IN CONTEMPORARY JAPAN (University of Bombay Press, 1962), and "Cyclical Instability and Fiscal-Monetary Policy in Postwar Japan," in THE STATE AND ECONOMIC ENTERPRISE IN JAPAN, ed. by William W. Lockwood (Princeton University Press, 1965), also Michael W. Keran, "Monetary Policy and the Business Cycle in Postwar Japan," in VARIETIES OF MONETARY EXPERIENCE, ed. by David Meiselman (University of Chicago Press, 1970).

4. Organization for Economic Cooperation and Development, OECD ECONOMIC SURVEYS: JAPAN (1969), especially pp. 5 and 39 ff.

5. For further discussion of the political-economic argument between the two countries, see Professor Hunsberger's Chapter 5 in this study and Martin Bronfenbrenner, "A Japanese-American Trade War?" in QUARTERLY REVIEW OF ECONOMICS AND BUSINESS, 11, no. 3 (Autumn 1971).

6. JAPAN ECONOMIC JOURNAL (Tokyo), April 27, 1971, p. 1. This number refers to "residual" import quotas which Japan is obliged to remove eventually under GATT. Like other countries, Japan restricts a number of items which are exempted by GATT; when these are included the total number of "unliberalized" items comes to 164 at end-1968 and 103 at end-1970. (Most of the exempted items are drugs, arms, gold, and other commodities whose trade all countries control, although a few—e.g., rice and other state-traded agricultural goods, some aircraft and computer items—can be considered protective in effect.)

7. This refers to a simple average of post-Kennedy Round tariffs on all

dutiable industrial imports including raw materials, semimanufactures and manufactures. On manufactures alone, the rates are 11.5 percent for Japan, 13 percent for the United States and 8 percent for the EC. When weighted by the importance of individual BTN commodities in world trade, the ranking changes to (for all industrial imports): 10 percent for Japan, 7 percent for the United States and 6 percent for the EC. Numbers are based on a recent GATT study, BASIC DOCUMENTATION FOR TARIFF STUDY (Geneva, 1970), as reported in EUROPEAN COMMUNITY BACKGROUND INFORMATION, no. 3, February 15, 1972 (Washington, D.C. European Community Information Service).

8. Kiyoshi Kojima, NONTARIFF BARRIERS TO JAPAN'S TRADE (Tokyo: The Japan Economic Research Center, 1971), p. 55.

9. THE JAPAN ECONOMIC JOURNAL (Tokyo), June 8, 1971, p. 1.

10. THE JAPAN ECONOMIC JOURNAL, 9, no. 445 (Tokyo: July 6, 1971), p. 2. The Survey was conducted by the Japan Economic Research Center in cooperation with the Japanese daily newspaper, the NIHON KEIZAI SHINBUN.

11. This is based on the Japanese Input-Output Table for 1965 (Bank of Japan, ECONOMIC STATISTICS ANNUAL, 1970, p. 292).

12. Ministry of Finance, THE SUMMARY REPORT TRADE OF JAPAN (Tokyo, Japan Tariff Association, monthly), 1970 No. 12, Page 70, Table 5 (Part 2).

13. OECD, OECD ECONOMIC SURVEY: JAPAN (Paris, 1970), pp. 32 ff.

14. Organization for Economic Cooperation and Development, DEVELOPMENT ASSISTANCE: 1971 REVIEW (Paris: OECD, 1971).

15. OECD ECONOMIC OUTLOOK, 10 (December 1971), pp. 10 ff.

16. Treasury Secretary Connally's statement to this effect was reported in the NEW YORK TIMES of November 12, 1971, p. 71, and was subsequently repeated by other officials.

17. U.S. Census Bureau, HIGHLIGHTS OF EXPORTS AND IMPORTS (FT-990), December 1971, Table E-7, pages 60-67.

4

Japan's Foreign Trade—Retrospect and Prospect

Kazuo Sato

It is needless to emphasize the overwhelmingly important position that foreign trade has occupied in Japan's modern economic growth of the past hundred years. It will continue to play as important a role as ever in the decades to come. This role will be examined in this chapter. I shall first review the contribution of foreign trade to Japan's growth and its structural change from 1955 to 1971. In this connection, I may remind the reader that Japan regained its prewar levels of consumption and production by 1954 and followed its booming growth path during the next fifteen years. Its rapid growth of aggregate output was accompanied by even faster growth of its export volume. This expansion, however, brought certain frictions in the international market. The examination of Japan's trade prospects in the seventies will start from this point.

A review of Japan's trade is given in the first section. On the basis of the past trends, an attempt is made to project world trade and Japan's share in it at 1980. The projection of world trade is presented in the second section, and Japan's trade prospects are evaluated in the third section. Its main objective is to ascertain what sort of adjustment Japan has to make in order to expand its exports in the anticipated milieu of the international economy if Japan is to maintain its growth at a reasonable rate over the decade of the 1970s. The discussion is summarized in the last section.

Review of Japan's Trade, 1955-71

General Trends

From 1955 to 1971, commodity exports and imports expanded roughly *pari passu* with GNP in current value. The average annual growth rates were about 14 to 16 percent as shown in Table 4-1. Exports and imports were roughly 9 to 10 percent of GNP.[a] Like other industrial nations, Japan experienced persistent rises in domestic prices (measured by the GNP deflator and the consumer price

---

[a]What is important from the balance-of-payments point of view is the current-account balance of goods and services including factor income. Exports and imports on the current account were roughly in balance if the entire period is taken as a whole. Their shares in GNP remained at about 10 to 12 percent.

81

Table 4-1
Japan's GNP and Commodity Exports (f.o.b.) and Imports (c.i.f.)

	(A) Growth Rates (%)								
	In Current Prices			In Constant Prices[a]			Deflators		
Period	GNP	Exports	Imports	GNP	Exports	Imports	GNP	Exports	Imports
1955-60	12.6	15.0	12.7	8.9	15.4	13.8	3.2	-.3	-1.0
1960-65	15.5	15.8	12.7	10.1	15.5	12.6	4.9	.3	.1
1965-70	17.3	18.0	18.2	12.1	15.6	16.2	4.7	1.6	1.8
1970-71	10.7	20.8	1.5	6.1	19.1	.5	4.4	1.4	1.0
1955-71	14.9	16.6	13.7	10.1	15.7	13.4	4.3	.7	.3

	(B) Percentage Shares in GNP (Current Prices)[b]			
Period	Exports		Imports	
1956-60	9.3	(11.8)	11.2	(11.7)
1961-65	8.4	(10.1)	9.9	(10.6)
1966-70	9.4	(11.1)	9.4	(10.2)
1971	10.7	(12.6)	8.8	(9.9)
1956-71	9.1	(11.1)	10.1	(10.8)

[a]In 1965 prices.

[b]Numbers in parentheses are the shares of foreign trade of goods and factor and nonfactor services on the current account of the balance of payments as recorded in national accounts statistics.

Source: Economic Planning Agency (Japan), *Annual Report on National Income Statistics*; Bureau of Statistics, Office of the Prime Minister (Japan), *Japan Statistical Yearbook* and *Monthly Statistics of Japan*; Bank of Japan, *Economic Statistics Monthly*.

index) exceeding changes in export and import prices by considerable margins. Thus when measured in constant prices, exports and imports grew at much faster rates than GNP. Foreign trade expanded at an average annual rate of 13 to 16 percent, while GNP registered an average increase of about 10 percent over the period under survey. The inflationary pressure on domestic prices came mainly from rises in service prices and in prices of products of small enterprises due largely to wage increases beyond their productivity advances. A reflection of this is the incessant rise in the consumer price index. In contrast, the wholesale price index of manufactured goods was relatively stable.[b] The export price index was similarly stable (except in the very recent years) because Japanese exports consist mainly of manufactured goods.

[b]In fact, the sharp rise in this index over the latter half of the sixties was due to a large increase in prices of small-firm products. The Bank of Japan wholesale price index of manufactures was 109.6 in 1970 relative to 1965. That of large-enterprise products stood at 104.6 whereas that of small-enterprise products was 122.9. In 1971 the former fell slightly but the latter inched upwards (103.0 vs 124.2).

The balance of payments was a main constraint on economic growth in Japan until 1965. There were periodic recurrences of growth cycles—troughs being 1954, 1958, 1962, and 1965. The general mechanism was that rapid growth generates import surpluses, which lead to monetary stringency and slackens the pace of growth temporarily (from 10 to 5 percent) until the balance of payments is again favorably restored. Since the recession of 1965, almost chronic export surpluses had been maintained on the current account. The removal of this major growth constraint enabled Japan to sustain unprecedentedly high growth of GNP, which averaged 12 percent per annum, uninterrupted for five years until 1971.

The extraordinary half decade helped to permeate strong optimism and complacency throughout the nation including the government as symbolized in popular catch-phrases like the twenty-first century being Japan's century. Further, it was argued that the balance of payments problem was finally eliminated as a serious constraint on growth. However, while Japan's exchange reserves increased at rapid rates, the international currency system faced a serious imbalance. Strong international pressures were exerted upon Japan to take necessary measures to help to restore the balance. For fear of its depressing effect on Japan's exports, the Japanese government resisted the pressure for exchange revaluation until the last moment.

In 1971 economic growth finally came to a slowdown. GNP growth was reduced to 6 percent. Commodity imports hardly increased in response. However, commodity exports registered a more than 20 percent increase in value, partially the result of a strong export drive by Japanese business to offset the slack in domestic demand. The net outcome was a huge export surplus, which amounted to more than 4 billion dollars. It accounts for more than a half of the surplus on the overall balance of payments, which was 7.7 billion dollars. In the meantime, Japan amassed gold and foreign exchange reserves. The increase was 10.8 billion dollars—from 4.4 at the end of 1970 to 15.2 billion dollars at the end of 1971. As contracts for exports were made before the currency revaluation, customs clearance statistics show continued expansion of exports into 1972 while imports remain stagnant. The resulting accumulation of foreign exchanges (16.7 billion dollars as of the end of March 1972) is giving Japanese business and government the scare of another revaluation of the yen. However, the adverse effect of the revaluation upon exports remains to be seen.

It was fortunate for Japan that world trade in manufactures was extremely buoyant over the period under survey, amounting to 10 percent growth in current value. Japan's exports of manufactures expanded at the annual average rate of 16 percent at the same time. Accordingly, Japan's share of world markets increased. However, as Japan's exports had been heavily concentrated in a few regions, the United States and South East Asia in particular, there had been an especially large increase in Japan's shares in these regions' imports over the past decade and a half. This rapid expansion of trade in limited areas led to the revival of a protectionist mood in the United States against foreign imports which directly competed with domestic industries and to an increased resentment and fear in South East Asia of the threat of Japan's economic domination.

Structure of Commodity Exports

Composition of Japan's Exports by Commodity Groups. Japan's commodity exports were traditionally concentrated on manufactured goods. This concentration was intensified in the past sixteen years as seen in Table 4-2. Primary exports decreased from 13 percent of the total value in 1955 to 5 percent in 1971. Among manufactured exports, machinery and transport equipment increased the fastest, reflecting Japan's increasing specialization in heavy industries. Their share increased from 12 percent to 44 percent. On the other hand, textile products, which had long been the main staple of Japan's exports, lost their dominant position. Their share fell from 37 percent to 9 percent. This shift

Table 4-2
Composition of Japan's Commodity Exports (f.o.b.), 1955-70 (Percentage)

SITC[a]	1955	1960	1965	1970	1971
0 + 1 Food	6.7	6.7	4.1	3.4	2.8
2 + 4 Crude materials	5.7	3.8	3.0	1.8	1.9
3 Mineral fuels	.3	.4	.4	.2	.3
0~4 Primary Goods	12.7	10.9	7.5	5.4	5.0
5 Chemicals	4.7	4.2	6.5	6.4	6.2
7 Machinery and transport equipment of which:	12.2	23.2	31.2	40.5	44.2
radio receivers	.4	3.6	2.6	3.6	3.3
motor vehicles	.3	1.9	2.8	6.9	10.0
vessels	3.9	7.1	8.4	7.3	7.8
6 + 8 Other manufactured goods of which:	69.7	61.8	54.3	46.9	43.8
textiles	37.3	30.1	18.7	9.0	8.6
metal and metal products	19.2	14.0	20.3	19.7	19.0
nonmetallic mineral products	4.6	4.2	3.1	1.9	1.6
5~8 Manufactured goods	85.6	89.1	92.0	93.8	94.2
0~9 Total	100.0	100.0	100.0	100.0	100.0

[a]Standard International Trade Classification. See the appendix for explanation.
Source: U.N., *Monthly Bulletin of Statistics*; Bureau of Statistics, Office of the Prime Minister (Japan), *Japan Statistical Yearbook* and *Monthly Statistics of Japan*.

in commodity composition reflects not only changes in domestic industrial structure but also changes in patterns of demand and supply of manufactured goods in the world. Demand for capital goods had been rising rapidly over the period under survey, while demand for products of light industry, in particular textiles, had been relatively slack. Moreover, developing countries have begun to establish their own light industry and to engage in import substitution and export promotion programs.

Direction of Japan's Exports. There were also significant changes in the direction of Japan's exports as shown in Table 4-3. Reflecting the fact that trade of developed countries increased rapidly while trade of developing countries grew relatively sluggishly, the share of developing areas in Japan's exports declined from 58 percent to 40 percent in 1971. At the same time, that of developed economies increased from 39 percent to 55 percent. Thus the relative importance of developed and developing areas was reversed. For individual regions, the notable change is a sharp decline in the share of developing Asia and an equally sharp increase in the share of the United States. Centrally planned economies expanded their share from the miniscule 2 percent to 5 percent.

Table 4-3
Direction of Japan's Exports, f.o.b. (Percentage)

Region[a]	1955	1970	1971
Developed market economies	39.3	54.6	54.8
United States	22.6	31.2	31.7
Canada	2.3	2.9	3.7
European Community	4.0	6.7	6.8
Other Europe	5.7	8.3	7.3
Oceania and South Africa	4.6	5.3	5.3
Developing market economies	57.7	40.0	40.3
Latin America	9.0	5.7	6.2
Africa	8.5	5.5	6.7
Middle East	4.1	2.8	2.9
Asia	35.8	25.4	24.0
Others	.5	.6	.5
Centrally planned economies	1.9	5.4	4.8
Europe and the USSR	.5	2.3	2.3
Asia	1.4	3.1	2.5
Total	100.0	100.0	100.0

[a]For the classification of regions, see the appendix.

Source: U.N., *Monthly Bulletin of Statistics*, June 1972; UNCTAD, *Handbook of International Trade and Development Statistics*, 1972 (New York, 1972).

Table 4-4

Average and Marginal Shares[a] of Japan's Exports of Manufactures in Imports of Various Regions, 1955, 1962, and 1970 (Percentage)

Region	Chemicals (SITC 5)				
	average shares			marg. shares	
				1955- 1962	1962- 1970
	1955	1962	1970	1962	1970
Developed market economies	.7	1.4	3.2	2.5	4.2
United States	2.1	6.0	12.9	14.7	17.4
Canada	.4	.6	1.7	1.0	2.9
European Community	.5	1.4	2.1	2.0	2.7
Other Europe	.4	.5	1.7	.6	2.4
Oceania and South Africa	1.4	3.4	9.7	6.7	15.1
Developing market economies	3.5	7.1	11.1	14.4	14.6
Latin America	.8	1.5	3.2	3.2	4.4
Africa	.0	.4	1.2	1.6	1.9
Middle East	.0	.5	2.2	.9	3.2
Asia	10.0	20.0	29.8	38.6	39.5
Centrally planned economies	.5	1.9	9.7	-.7	14.2
Europe and USSR	.0	.7	3.1	1.2	4.6
Asia	1.6	10.0	42.6	-33.3	56.3
World	2.0	3.2	5.6	4.6	7.3

[a]Average shares are percentage shares of Japan's exports to a particular region in the latter's total imports (f.o.b.) from the world. Marginal shares from 1955 to 1962 and from 1962 to 1970 are percentage shares of changes in Japan's exports to a particular region in changes in the latter's imports (f.o.b.) from the world in each of the subperiods.

Japan's Market Share in World Trade. Japan's penetration into the world market significantly altered its market shares in various regional markets. Table 4-4 tells this story vividly by showing changes in Japan's shares for 1955, 1962, and 1970 with respect to three major categories of manufactured goods—chemicals, machinery and transport equipment, and other manufactured goods. The table shows the average shares of Japan's exports to a particular region in the latter's total imports (f.o.b.) at these three years and the marginal shares from 1955 to 1962 and from 1962 to 1970. Marginal shares are the ratios of changes in Japan's exports to a particular region to changes in the region's total imports in each of the subperiods. Particularly high shares (above, say, 20 percent) are observed for the United States (machinery and transport equipment, other manufactured goods), Oceania and South Africa (other manufactured goods), developing Asia (all categories), mainland China (all categories), developing Africa (machinery and transport equipment),[c] Middle East (other manufactured

[c]This, however, is largely due to exports of ships to Liberia, with which many foreign-owned vessels are registered.

Machinery and Transport Equipment (SITC 7)					Other Manufactured Goods (SITC 6 + 8)					All Manufactures (SITC 5~8)				
average shares			marg. shares		average shares			marg. shares		average shares			marg. shares	
			1955-	1962-				1955-	1962-				1955-	1962-
1955	1962	1970	1962	1970	1955	1962	1970	1962	1970	1955	1962	1970	1962	1970
2.6	2.6	7.4	4.2	9.6	3.6	6.4	7.8	10.8	8.6	2.4	4.4	7.1	6.8	8.6
3.7	12.9	20.9	16.4	22.4	9.7	18.8	23.7	35.2	26.7	8.4	16.6	21.9	26.7	24.1
.1	.7	3.9	2.4	5.5	2.9	6.5	10.1	19.4	14.0	1.3	3.8	5.7	11.5	7.5
.1	.7	2.1	1.0	2.8	.9	1.6	2.3	2.3	2.6	.6	1.2	2.2	1.7	2.7
.8	2.2	5.5	3.3	7.8	1.2	1.9	3.0	3.1	3.7	1.0	1.9	3.9	2.9	5.3
.2	2.1	10.2	12.0	15.1	5.6	12.5	20.2	-235.0	29.7	3.0	6.9	13.8	40.8	19.3
3.7	8.2	16.6	15.5	23.6	12.5	15.3	22.0	29.1	29.7	8.0	11.0	17.7	18.7	24.5
1.5	4.2	7.1	10.7	9.6	7.4	8.3	12.4	100.0	15.7	3.8	5.1	8.9	10.4	10.9
4.1	4.4	16.6	5.3	23.6	5.9	9.5	8.6	53.3	7.5	4.6	6.4	11.9	15.9	16.6
3.6	3.4	7.1	5.9	9.0	11.7	11.1	16.7	10.0	22.4	6.8	6.8	10.3	6.9	12.8
8.3	17.9	33.3	27.1	48.1	24.2	28.5	40.3	33.8	55.2	17.1	22.1	35.9	30.5	50.0
.1	2.0	2.5	3.8	2.8	.9	1.9	6.5	2.6	12.3	.8	1.9	4.9	3.5	7.5
.0	2.0	1.3	3.5	.7	.7	1.4	3.2	1.7	5.7	.3	1.7	2.2	2.4	2.8
.5	1.0	12.1	.0	23.7	1.4	12.5	25.0	4.4	44.9	2.5	7.3	30.4	-1.5	38.9
1.5	3.8	8.7	6.3	11.7	5.8	7.6	10.0	10.8	11.8	3.8	5.6	9.0	8.0	11.3

Source: U.N., *Monthly Bulletin of Statistics*, July 1972; UNCTAD, *Handbook of International Trade and Development Statistics*, 1972.

goods). In contrast, Japan's infiltration was of a limited scope in Europe, both Western and Eastern, and Canada. In these areas, Japanese products are not too well known, protection against them stronger, or Japan's sales efforts less enthusiastic, even though overall trade expanded at high rates in these regions.

The concentration of Japan's efforts of export promotion in a few regions raised Japan's marginal shares of these markets. But the marginal rates of 30 to 50 percent, observed in developing Asia, were bound to create economic and political frictions of considerable magnitude with importing countries. Though it is a perfectly rational economic behavior that exporters directed their sales to those areas which require the least cost, any excess in that direction is to give rise to unfavorable consequences.

Table 4-5 shows average shares of Japan's exports in total imports, as well as those of Japan's imports in total exports, of each country in developing Asia, Oceania, and South Africa. One can readily see the importance of Japan as a major supplier of manufactured goods in these countries.[d] These ratios indicate

[d]Note that these refer to all imports. If restricted to trade of manufactured goods, Japan's shares must be considerably raised.

Table 4-5

Japan's Shares in Total Trade of Developing Asia, Oceania, and South Africa: 1971 (Millions of Dollars)

Country	Imports (f.o.b.)			Exports (f.o.b.)		
	total[a]	from Japan	%	total	to Japan[b]	%
Korea	2155	856	40	1068	207	19
Taiwan[c]	1501	923	61	1907	216	11
Hong Kong	3008	787	26	2832	74	3
Thailand	1153	445	39	834	174	21
Singapore	2545	508	20	1755	86	5
Malaysia	1371	204	15	1720	281	16
Philippines	1183	465	39	1103	388	35
Indonesia[c]	1049	453	43	1180	645	55
India	2234	209	9	2101	284	14
Pakistan	825	113	14	666	44	7
Burma	85	59	69	124	13	11
Subtotal	17109	5022	29	15293	2412	16
Developing Asia, Total	21020	5763	27	15810	2570	16
South Africa	4039	413	10	2186	255	12
Australia	4633	719	16	5084	1374	27
New Zealand	1187	129	11	1364	127	9

[a]Except for South Africa and Australia, figures are obtained as 0.90 times total imports (c.i.f.).

[b]Figures are obtained as 0.755 times imports (c.i.f.) into Japan. The ratio is that of the f.o.b. figure to the c.i.f. figure.

[c]Total imports and exports: provisional figures.

Source: U.N., *Monthly Bulletin of Statistics*, June 1972; Bank of Japan, *Economic Statistics Monthly*.

how difficult it will be to expand Japan's market shares in many of these countries. It is noted that among leading industrial exporters (United States, France, West Germany, Italy, and the United Kingdom), Japan has the least even geographic distribution of export markets.[1]

A related phenomenon is Japan's increasing shares in exports of individual commodities. Japan has assumed a leading position among industrial exporters in the world markets of a few commodities. In certain lines like pearls, binoculars, radios, two-wheeled vehicles, TVs, and tape recorders, Japan has become the largest exporter in the world.[e]

[e]A number of industries which are heavily dependent on exports are small-firm industries. For example, in the binocular industry, 73 percent of output was produced by establishments with less than 300 employees and 87 percent was exported in 1969.

Factors that Contributed to Japan's Rapid Export Growth—Relative Stability of Export Prices. Japan's unit value index of manufactured exports showed an absolute decline from mid-fifties to mid-sixties due to large productivity advances in the manufacturing sector and to the relative weakness of primary prices in the world market through most of the period under survey. As export prices of other industrial economies edged upward, Japan's export prices fell more in relative terms as seen in Table 4-6. The recent few years, 1968-71 (up to August 1971), witnessed a sharp rise in Japan's export prices, but because the world prices showed a comparable increase, the international competitiveness of Japanese exports was not impaired. However, the price factor does not seem to be quantitatively the predominant one that accounts for Japan's export expansion.[f]

Undervalued Yen. The exchange rate was fixed at one dollar to 360 yen for the past two decades until 1971. Even though the rate initially put Japan at a disadvantage in the world market, the scale was turned for Japan in the course of time because of the factor mentioned above.[g]

Nonprice Competition. Intensive sales efforts by export firms (with heavy competition among themselves, sometimes blamed as excessive competition), fast delivery, trade credits, and other services offered to foreign importers are strong elements of nonprice competition,[h] without which Japanese exports would have been unable to record such a rapid increase, though it is difficult to assess the effect of this factor quantitatively.

Quality Change and New Goods. By far, the most dynamic factor in Japan's export expansion in this period must be the quality change of existing goods and the introduction of new goods. Indeed, the remarkable advances in Japan's productivity have been accomplished not only by improving techniques of production to produce old goods but more significantly by bettering their quality or introducing entirely new goods. This influenced both domestic and foreign demand.

---

[f]Most econometric studies of Japanese exports find that the price elasticity of world demand for Japan's exports is about −2. That is, if Japan's export price index relative to that of world trade declines by 1 percent, Japan's export volume will increase by 2 percent. Table 5-6 shows that Japan's relative price declined by 17.5 percent from 1955 to 1971. This price decrease accounts for an expansion of Japan's export quantum by 47 percent. But Japan's export volume increased by 11.0 times from 1955 to 1971. This shows that the price factor is only a partial explanatory variable. $11.0 \div 1.47 = 7.5$ may be compared with the expansion of world manufacturing exports, 3.6; the difference between the two should be attributed to other factors.

[g]Interestingly, however, the purchasing power parity of the yen/dollar continued to rise at the same time. Prices of those goods and services which do not enter into international trade (e.g., local food produce, rent) increased relatively faster in Japan.

[h]In this connection, one may compare Japan's efficient and streamlined trading company system in the export market and its antiquated distribution system in the domestic market.

Table 4-6

Exports of Manufactures, Japan and the Total of Major Industrial Countries, 1955-71[a]

Year	Unit Value Index[b]			Quantum Index[b]		Value of Exports (Billions of Dollars)		
	total	Japan	Japan/total %	total	Japan	total	Japan	Japan/total %
1955	92	105	114	60	34	35.62	1.75	4.9
1956	95	108	114	66	41	40.68	2.18	5.4
1957	98	112	114	70	46	44.71	2.54	5.7
1958	97	107	110	69	48	43.88	2.52	5.7
1959	96	107	111	75	57	47.02	3.04	6.5
1960	98	109	111	84	67	54.02	3.62	6.7
1961	99	105	106	87	73	56.54	3.76	6.7
1962	99	102	103	93	87	60.34	4.39	7.3
1963	100	100	100	100	100	65.21	4.95	7.6
1964	101	99	98	113	124	74.34	6.07	8.2
1965	103	98	94	124	161	83.27	7.83	9.4
1966	106	97	91	135	188	93.12	9.05	9.7
1967	107	101	94	143	196	99.75	9.76	9.8
1968	107	101	94	165	243	114.81	12.19	10.6
1969	110	106	96	187	286	134.59	14.97	11.1
1970	117	112	96	203	327	155.00	18.12	11.7
1971	124	116	94	217	375	175.49	22.22	12.7

[a]Belgium-Luxembourg, Canada, France, Federal Republic of Germany, Italy, Japan, Netherlands, Sweden, Switzerland, United Kingdom, United States.
[b]1963-100.
Source: U.S., *Monthly Bulletin of Statistics* and *Statistical Yearbook*.

On the domestic side, there had been marked changes in consumer tastes from traditional to modern goods in the period under survey. Starting from transistor radios, TVs, refrigerators, and vacuum cleaners, and more recently to air conditioners and automobiles, consumer acquisition of new durable goods continued with great bounds. This sort of change was very significant through the 1960s. The same had been true of producer durables. Strong domestic demand for new or better-quality goods provided a firm basis for improving the quality of export goods. Japanese goods, which were once synonymous with slipshod workmanship and unabashed imitation of foreign goods, have wiped off their prewar ill fame. The superb performance of Japan's exports had been supported by a strong domestic base.

There is a well-documented theory of the product cycle in international trade. A new manufactured commodity is first produced and exported by the most advanced economy. Other late comers follow it and even replace it in the world market as they cut the cost of production when they accumulate experiences. Finally, they too are to be replaced by later comers. For many new goods (particularly, consumer electronics), Japan had the advantage as one of the first to produce them on a mass scale. For more established goods (e.g., automobiles, ships, and iron and steel), Japan benefited from being a late comer, which enabled it to build new facilities embodying the newest technology.[i]

Structure of Imports

After World War II, various import restrictions sheltered the Japanese economy from foreign competition, but they were largely lifted in the course of the 1960s. Commodities under import quota were reduced from 466 in 1962 to 118 in 1969, which were further cut to 40 in the fall of 1971 and to 33 in April 1972.[j] This is comparable to many Western European countries.[k] Also, along with other advanced nations, Japan grants nonreciprocal, nondiscriminatory trade preferences to exports of less developed countries.

Composition of Commodity Imports. Japan's commodity imports also experienced significant change in composition over the same period. Table 4-7 shows that while imports of food and crude materials had their shares decreased, imports of petroleum, machinery, and other manufactured goods increased their shares. Nonfuel primary imports reduced the share from 76 percent of total imports in 1955 to 47 percent in 1971, while fuel imports expanded the share from 12 to 24 percent. Manufactures raised the share from 12 to 28 percent.

Foodstuffs. The reduced share of food imports can be attributed to the persistent decline of the proportion of food expenditure in total consumption or the Engel coefficient. National income statistics reveal that this coefficient was 52.0 percent in 1955, 44.0 percent in 1960, 38.7 percent in 1965, and 35.3 percent in 1970. With the continued rise in per capita income, this downward trend will continue for some time since the ratio is still higher than other

---

[i]Through the 1960s, cotton textiles and toys were in the declining phase, iron and steel in the peak phase, and ships, automobiles, TVs, and optical instruments in the rising phase of the product cycle. See Chapters 8 and 9 for the significant role that the government's "administrative guidance" played in realigning industrial structure so as to adapt the economy to changing patterns of internal and external demand.

[j]Nine are industrial goods—mainly electronic computers and parts. The remaining twenty-four are agricultural commodities including rice, wheat, beef, cheese, and citrus fruits. The Japanese government announced that this list would remain in force until 1975 when necessary adjustments are expected to be completed in agriculture.

[k]As of March 1971, the number was 70 in France, 38 in West Germany, and 25 in the United Kingdom, while it was 80 in Japan.

Table 4-7
Composition of Japan's Commodity Imports (c.i.f.), 1955-70 (Percentage)

SITC	1955	1960	1965	1970	1971
0 + 1 Food	25.3	12.2	18.0	13.6	14.8
of which:					
rice	7.9	.4	1.8	.0	.0
wheat	6.7	3.9	3.0	1.7	1.7
maize	1.0	1.8	2.8	1.6	1.8
sugar	4.6	3.5	1.9	1.5	1.6
2 + 4 Crude materials	51.1	49.2	39.4	35.4	32.5
of which:					
textile fibres	23.7	17.0	10.4	5.1	4.9
metalliferous ores and scraps	7.5	8.2	12.5	14.3	12.8
3 Mineral fuels	11.7	16.5	19.9	20.6	24.1
0~4 Primary Goods	88.1	77.9	77.3	69.6	71.4
5 Chemicals	4.6	5.9	5.0	5.3	5.1
7 Machinery and transport equipment	5.4	9.0	8.7	11.3	11.3
6 + 8 Other manufactured goods	1.9	7.0	8.8	13.2	11.5
of which:					
iron and steel	.4	2.0	1.7	1.5	.6
non-ferrous metals	.9	2.3	3.0	5.0	3.6
textile yarn and fabrics	.3	.4	.6	1.7	n.a.
5~8 Manufactured Goods	11.9	21.9	22.5	29.8	27.9
0~9 Total	100.0	100.0	100.0	100.0	100.0

Source: Bureau of Statistics, Office of the Prime Minister (Japan), *Japan Statistical Yearbook* and *Monthly Statistics of Japan.*

developed countries, for example, 18.0 percent in the United States, 19.3 percent in Canada, 30.8 percent in the European Community, and 29.2 percent in other Western Europe in 1969. The relative reduction in domestic demand for food is especially marked for rice consumption. With the government's price-support program, chronic surplus arose in rice production. This had given very little scope to importing rice from South East Asia, where the rice yields have been rising much in recent years.[1] Consumer demand patterns have been shifting from traditional foodstuffs to Western-type food. The import content of food expenditure rose from 7 percent in 1960 to 16 percent in 1969 and the trade liberalization may expand it still further, particularly because Japan's per capita

---

[1]As percent of total supplies (domestic production and net imports), rice imports decreased from 7 percent in the 1950s to 3 percent in the 1960s. By 1970, this ratio declined to 0.1 percent.

food imports are still only one-third of that of West Germany and the United Kingdom. Such instances are noted in the explosive expansion of consumption of imported instant coffees, bananas, lemons, honeys, and others after import restrictions were removed in the 1960s.

Crude and Processed Materials. The share of imports of crude materials fell very significantly from one-half in 1955 to one-third in 1971. This decline is largely attributable to an even greater decline in the share of imported textile fibers. At the same time, imports of mineral ores increased their share. Along with this, imports of semiprocessed goods (e.g., textile yarn and fabrics, iron and steel, and nonferrous metals) increased their share very much (the category of other manufactured goods consists mainly of these semi-processed goods). Taken together, industrial materials were about one-half of Japan's imports in the period under survey, though the share tended to decline.

Shift of imports from unprocessed to processed materials was observed also in other industrial countries at this time. Japan, however, remains inclined to purchase more unprocessed materials.[m] For materials as a whole, the import dependency ratio, that is, the ratio of imports to total supplies, increased from 80 percent to 90 percent over the 1960s. Indeed, the ratio was 100 percent for a few key materials such as aluminum and nickel. In spite of material-saving technical change and of the shift of industrial composition toward products with more processing and less material content (e.g., machinery), consumption of raw materials increased relative to GNP. It is expected that this trend will continue and that Japan's dependence on foreign supplies will increase even more.

Fuels. Imports of petroleum expanded rapidly over this period due mainly to the shift from coal to oil as the primary energy source and to the rapid motorization. 99 percent of petroleum consumed in Japan has to be imported and fuel imports will continue to rise rapidly.[n]

Manufactured Goods. Imports of machinery and transport equipment as well as those of chemicals maintained a fairly stable share in total imports over the 1960s. Imports of other manufactured goods increased their share substantially. As noted above, this was largely due to increased imports of semiprocessed goods. Japan's imports of finished consumer goods occupied only a small fraction of total imports.[o] However, Japan's rising consumption level may direct consumer demand toward imports of finished consumer goods.[p]

---

[m]Of imported materials (excluding food and fuels), 70 percent was unprocessed in 1969. The proportion was about one-third in West Germany and the United Kingdom. Similarly, the proportion of mineral ores in imports of mineral ores and concentrates was about two-thirds in Japan while it was one-fourth in the United States and Western Europe.

[n]The sharp expansion of the share in 1971 is due partially to the rise in fuel import prices (by some 14 percent more than the average import price index).

[o]These goods are classified mainly in SITC 8 (miscellaneous manufactured articles). This category has been about 20 percent of imports of other manufactured goods (SITC 6+8).

[p]So far, high custom duties on these goods discouraged demand for them.

Japan's Bilateral Balances of Trade by Region

The rapid change in Japan's trade structure resulted in persistent imbalance between Japan's exports to and imports from various regions of the world. Table 4-8 shows this for 1969 and 1971. Throughout the period under study, Japan maintained large export surplus with developing Asia. In fact, as a proportion of Japan's exports to this region, the surplus increased over time (from 30 percent in 1960 to 41 percent in 1971). This is because Japan's demand for nonfuel primary goods, which developing Asia exports, increased at a rate much less than the latter's demand for Japan's manufactured exports. In contrast, Japan kept huge import surplus with Middle East oil countries. Japan used to maintain import surplus with the United States, but the balance was turned in the latter half of the 1960s. Japan keeps export surplus with Western Europe, in this case because this region does not specialize in exports of industrial materials that Japan wished to purchase. The story is reversed with Oceania; which sold more goods, 80 percent of which were primary, than they bought from Japan. The same is true about Eastern Europe and the USSR. The particularly large trade gap with developing Asia was partially financed by Japan's economic aid, a significant portion of which is export credits. But the persistence of trade imbalance in various regions led to serious political problems on the international level, notwithstanding economists' emphasis on the unimportance of bilateral balances. In many cases, this resulted in discrimination against Japanese exports.

A Projection of World Trade to 1980

We shall now attempt to examine the prospects of Japan's trade in the 1970s in the light of what happened over the past decade and a half. We are interested primarily in ascertaining the direction of change that Japan's trade is required to take. Japan's trade prospects can be meaningfully evaluated only within the framework of world trade. Therefore, the first task in this exercise is a projection of world trade up to 1980 from the base of 1971.

It is needless to emphasize that, just as in any exercise of this kind, the present one is based on a number of ifs. This is particularly so at this time when there is a great deal of uncertainties in future developments in international trading and monetary systems. Nevertheless, projections are necessary if we want to indicate the order of magnitude of the adjustment that Japan must make. As time and resources are limited, I have had to resort to a short-cut method in this exercise though with a considerable factual basis. As the method is fully explained in the appendix to this chapter, I shall give only a rough explanation below just to give a general idea to the reader.

From the nature of the problem, we regard world trade as being demand-

Table 4-8
Japan's Trade Balance by Region, 1969 and 1971 (Millions of Dollars)

Region[a]	1969 Exports (f.o.b.)	Imports (c.i.f.)	Difference	Aid	1971 Exports (f.o.b.)	Imports (c.i.f.)	Difference
Developed market economies	8393	8016	377		13053	10278	2775
United States	4958	4090	868		7495	4978	2517
Canada	481	669	-188		876	1004	-128
European Community	968	820	148		1635	1138	497
Other Europe	1077	654	423		1788	925	863
Oceania	631	1485	-852		847	1914	-1067
South Africa	278	298	-20		412	319	93
Developing market economies	6888	6263	625	1092	9818	8490	1328
Latin America	944	1162	-219	77	1597	1339	258
Africa	875	684	191	56	1650	676	974
b	(408)		(-276)		(670)		(-6)
Middle East	559	1931	-1371	109	696	2927	-2231
c		(63)	(-496)			(n.a.)	(n.a.)
Asia	4448	2381	2067	848	5763	3404	2359
Centrally planned economies	764	848	-84		1148	944	204
USSR	268	462	-194		377	496	-119
China	391	235	156		578	323	255
Total	15990	15023	976		24019	19712	4307

aRegional classifications are somewhat different from other tables.
bExcluding exports of ships to Liberia.
cExcluding imports of petroleum.
Source: MITI (Japan), *White Paper on International Trade*, 1971; Prime Minister's Office, *Monthly Statistics of Japan*; Bank of Japan, *Economic Statistics Monthly*.

determined. In other words, we start from projecting import demand. My projection begins by extrapolating the f.o.b. values of total commodity imports of various regions of the world in 1980. In this extrapolation, I assume that the growth rate of real national output will follow more or less its past trend and import demand is related to it in one way or another in each of the major regions under consideration. In this connection, we may observe an empirical finding that the growth rate of gross domestic or national product shows considerable decade-to-decade variations in individual countries but that such variations are greatly reduced when countries are grouped together. For instance, the average annual growth rates in the 1950s and the 1960s were 4.1 percent and 4.9 percent in developed areas and 4.7 percent and 5.2 percent in developing areas. Not only are they relatively stable but also the direction of change is largely predictable. I assume that, for developed countries (excluding Japan), GNP will continue to grow in the 1970s at a rate comparable to that in the 1960s.[q] The same assumption is made for developing areas. To simplify, the growth rate of GNP is assumed to be 7.5 percent per annum in the Middle East and 4.5 percent per annum in all other developing regions.[r]

In order to project the volume of commodity imports, a certain relation must be postulated between GNP and imports. A conventional procedure is to assume that demand for imports is determined by real GNP and the price level of imports relative to the domestic price level. The former is represented by the income elasticity, showing what percentage change in imports would result when GNP changes by 1 percent. The latter is given by the price elasticity, which is negative. If the income elasticity is one and the price elasticity minus one, the current-value share of imports in GNP will remain unchanged. We make this assumption for imports of developed areas. In the past decade and a half, there was a small increase in the share of trade in GNP in developed areas as a whole (see Table 4-9). We assume that the share will stabilize during the next ten years. However, real exports and imports of goods and services expanded at rates (about 8 percent per annum) above GNP (less than 5 percent per annum) in developed areas. The divergence between real and nominal rates is due to much less increases of export and import prices than those of domestic prices. The differential was 2.0 percent per annum for export prices and 2.3 percent for import prices. The persistent differential between export price and domestic price changes was due mainly to sectoral differentials in productivity change. The rise in import prices was less than that in export prices, partly because of the weakness of prices of primary commodities exported by developing coun-

---

[q]OECD projected potential growth of the combined real national product of the OECD areas to be a little over 5 percent per annum in the 1970s. See OECD, *The Outlook for Economic Growth* (Paris, 1970). Also see projections for Western and Eastern Europe in ECE (UN), *Economic Survey of Europe in 1969*, part I (New York, 1969).

[r]The United Nations Second Development Decade target for 1970-1980 is annual growth of above 6 percent. See U.N., *International Development Strategy* (New York, 1970).

Table 4-9

Growth Rates of GNP and Foreign Trade of OECD Countries, 1955-69, Percentage

	In Constant 1963 Prices	In Current Prices and Exchange Rates	Price Change
GNP	4.7	7.6	2.8
Private consumption	4.4	7.0	2.5
Government consumption	3.6	8.4	4.6
Gross domestic fixed capital formation	6.4	9.0	2.4
Exports of goods and services	7.9	8.8	.8
Imports of goods and services	8.2	8.7	.5

Source: OECD, *National Accounts of OECD Countries, 1953-1969* (Paris, 1971).

tries. I assume that the gap between domestic and import price changes will remain the same through the 1970s as in the past. If we assume that GNP will grow at $100a$ percent and the GNP deflator relative to the import price index will increase at $100b$ percent, total real imports will grow at $100(a+b+ab)$ percent under our assumptions. b is the price-change gap noted above. If b is greater than assumed above, world imports will grow faster than my projection indicates.[s] This method is applied to most of the developed regions.

As for developing regions, GNP data have not been compiled in a comparable form so that we cannot follow the procedure adopted for the developed regions. Imports increased at rates roughly comparable to GNP growth in developing areas in the past decade and a half except in Asia where growth of imports surpassed that of GNP considerably. For developing areas as a whole, GNP increased at 5.0 percent per annum from 1955 to 1970 while real imports expanded at 5.2 percent. I assume that, just as I have assumed for GNP, real imports will grow at 7.5 percent in the Middle East and 5 percent in all other developing regions.[t,u]

[s]The recent change in international currency valuation will make imports cheaper in those countries whose currencies were revalued and dearer in those countries whose currencies were devalued. This will be translated as an increase in b in the former and a decrease in the latter. A rough adjustment of b is made on this account. See the appendix.

[t]The United Nations Second Development Decade target is 7 percent growth for imports and exports.

[u]For the developing areas, a more reasonable procedure (which has been frequently employed) may have been to start with projections of their exports, add foreign aid and other capital inflows and subtract interest payments on foreign debt. These will give their capacity to import.

To complete the projection of world imports, we must say something about those of centrally planned economies. Centrally planned economies continued to expand their participation in world trade over the past two decades. The East-West trade is a little over one-third of total trade of centrally planned economies now—a considerable increase from one-fourth in the latter half of the 1950s.[v] Eastern Europe and the USSR increased their imports (in current value) by 13.3 percent per annum in the 1950s and 8.6 percent per annum in the 1960s. Their national plans for the first half of the 1970s, however, provide for more modest 7 percent annual growth of foreign trade.[2] I have therefore assumed that their imports will grow at 8 percent per annum through the 1970s. Trade of Asian socialist economies suffered a setback early in the 1960s due to unfavorable developments in domestic economic conditions. But since then it has recovered. Their imports (in current value) registered an average annual growth rate of 9.1 percent from 1962 to 1971. It seems that the annual growth rate of 8 percent is more or less what one may expect for the 1970s.

Japan's imports are projected by the same method as the one used for developed areas. We have to make first an hypothetical assumption on its GNP growth rate. The above-ten-percent growth of the 1960s is now generally believed to have passed. The high rate of growth in the decade that ended is attributed *inter alia* to the introduction of better techniques imported from abroad, especially the United States, and to the massive migration of labor from agriculture to industry which enabled the secondary and tertiary sectors to expand production without encountering the ceiling of full-employment labor supply. It is generally acknowledged that the era of easy importation of new techniques has come to an end. Japan must rely more and more on its own research and development activities in raising its productivity. At the same time, the share of agricultural employment in the labor force fell from 40 percent in 1955 to 15 percent by 1971. Value-added originating in agriculture and forestry declined in the meantime to 7 percent of total GNP. It is anticipated that the transfer of labor from rural to urban areas will encounter increasing difficulty, though this does not necessarily deny the existence of any slack in the labor market, particularly in small-scale enterprises. But these factors, along with other indicators like the increasing pollution and the overcrowding into metropolitan centers, suggest that Japan's growth will decelerate to some extent in the years to come. I tentatively set the growth rate of GNP at 8 percent per annum on average through the 1970s.[w]

The current-value share of commodity imports in GNP showed a slightly

---

[v]Imports of centrally planned economies from market economies were limited so far largely by their own capacity to export to the rest of the world. Much of their trade is on the basis of bilateral agreements.

[w]See Chapter 1 for assessment of Japan's future growth. Though the majority of Japanese opinion seems to accept the deceleration thesis, it is not without dissension. For instance, in a very recent projection study for the Japan Economic Research Center, H. Kanamori and his associates assume 9.5 percent annual growth of GNP up to 1980.

declining trend over the past sixteen years as shown in Table 4-1. I assume that the share will stabilize at the 1970 level through the 1970s because the 1971 level is too low to be taken as the base. The recent revaluation of the yen makes imported goods cheaper.[x] This will induce the Japanese producers and consumers to step up their demand for foreign goods to keep this share stable. Together with liberalized trade and improved living standards, the share may possibly even increase as Japanese consumers are finally able to enjoy luxury goods of foreign make.

As other developed economies experienced, Japan's domestic prices rose much faster than import and export prices. From 1955 to 1971, the GNP deflator grew at an annual average rate of 4.6 percent relative to the import price index. This trend is assumed to continue. Taking account of the expected temporary fall of the import prices due to the revaluation of the yen, this rate is raised to 5.1 percent. With our assumption of a constant share of imports in GNP, we arrive at the import growth rate of 13.6 percent. This rate is applied to the 1971 level of imports after it is raised by 9 percent to adjust for the cyclically low import level of that year.

It is assumed that all countries will face the same average import prices. The total figures of commodity imports in 1980 are obtained by applying the assumed growth rates of imports to 1971 values. To allocate the total among major SITC commodity categories, I have calculated how a marginal dollar of imports in constant prices was divided among these categories between 1955-57 and 1968-70. These provide estimates of the marginal shares of individual commodity categories in total imports, which are then applied to the increment of total imports of 1980 over the base-year figure.

Table 4-10 reports the projection of imports (f.o.b.) for major regions of the world in 1980 in comparison to actual values of 1970 and 1971. In spite of large potential margins of error, I think that the rough figures of Table 4-10 represent broad trade structure in the decade hence. Table 4-11 shows changes in composition and growth rates of world imports by SITC groups. Trade in manufactures and fuel will be growing at about 8 percent per annum,[y] while trade in primary goods is expected to increase at about 6 percent per annum.

Trade Prospects of Japan up to 1980

I am now able to examine Japan's trade prospects up to 1980 within the framework of world trade. Consider first Japan's export requirement. If imports are to grow *pari passu* with GNP in current value, exports must grow at the same rate in current value, provided that trade is initially balanced. In the past, the GNP deflator increased at a rate 3.6 percent greater (per annum) than the export

[x]Over the half year since August 1971, the import price index (in yen) fell by 7 percent.
[y]From 1955 to 1971, total exports of manufactures by industrial economies grew at 8.3 percent per annum (see Table 4-6). Therefore, this projection is not unreasonable.

Table 4-10

Imports (F.O.B.) from World by Major Regions and by Major SITC Categories, 1970, 1971, and 1980, Projected (in Millions of Dollars)

Year	SITC	Developed Market Economies							Developing Market Economies					Centrally Planned Economies			World^b
		United States	Canada	European Community	Other Europe	Oceania & South Africa	Japan	Total^a	Latin America	Africa	Middle East	Asia	Total^a	Europe & USSR	Asia	Total^a	
1970	0+1	$5720	$1020	$12380	$7770	$390	$2140	$29570	$1910	$1610	$920	$2860	$9430	$3700	$500	$4190	$41430
	2+4	3360	760	10090	5880	420	5010	25620	950	520	335	1750	3570	3280	310	3590	32960
	3	3250	810	8520	5370	560	3050	21550	2200	660	485	1220	4630	1660	97	1760	28700
	5	1240	710	6280	4500	760	780	14360	2000	970	540	1610	5150	1730	340	2070	21840
	7	11580	5840	20130	15860	3760	1820	59430	6780	4520	2480	5250	19270	9440	730	10180	89570
	6+8	13440	2960	26780	17800	2530	2210	66160	4340	3370	1950	5380	15250	7730	840	8570	90300
	5~8	26260	9510	53190	38160	7050	4810	139950	12120	8860	4950	12240	39670	18900	1910	20820	201710
	0~8	38590	12100	84180	57180	8420	15010	216690	18180	11650	6710	18070	55300	27540	2817	30360	304800
	0~9	38970	12430	85080	58350	8580	15160	220030	18590	11890	7070	18610	57690	28630	2860	31490	311390
1971	0~9	44750	14670	94550	64560	9460	16750	245420	19760	13730	8530	21020	64580	31020	3010	34040	345320
	0+1	7900	1800	37100		500	7200	54700	3200	2600	1800	5100	12900	7100	1100	8200	75700
	2+4	4000	1300	26800		600	16300	49200	1500	1000	800	2800	6100	5000	800	5700	61000
	3	5400	1500	30300		900	12300	50400	4200	1200	1000	2100	8600	3100	200	3300	62300
	5	2300	1400	26400		1600	2900	34900	3800	2200	1500	3300	10800	4200	800	5000	50700
1980	7	23600	12100	82000		6900	6500	132000	10800	8500	6100	9800	35700	22700	1500	24200	191900
	6+8	24400	5200	101300		3900	8400	144100	6500	5300	4300	8700	25200	17500	1700	19200	188500
	5~8	50300	18600	209800		12400	16800	311000	21100	16100	11900	21700	71600	44500	3900	48400	431000
	0~8	67600	23100	304000		14400	53600	465200	30000	20900	15500	31700	99200	59700	5900	65600	630000
	0~9	68200	23800	308300		14700	54100	471600	30700	21300	16400	32600	102200	62000	6000	68000	641800

aIncluding some areas not shown explicitly.

bIncluding figures unallocated among regions.

Source: For 1970 and 1971, U.N., *Monthly Bulletin of Statistics*, April, June, and July 1972.

Table 4-11
Change of World Imports from 1970 to 1980, (Percentage)

SITC	Commodity Composition of Imports		Growth Rates of Imports
	1970	1980	1970-80
0 + 1	13.3	11.8	6.2
2 + 4	10.6	9.5	6.3
3	9.2	9.7	8.1
5	7.0	7.9	8.8
7	28.8	29.9	7.9
6 + 8	29.0	29.4	7.6
5~8	64.8	67.2	7.9
0~9	100.0	100.0	6.4

Source: Table 4-10.

price index. It is very likely that a differential of this magnitude will persist. The service sector will continue to lag behind the goods sector in productivity improvements so that the general price level will continue to rise relative to the price level of commodities, though the assumed declined in GNP growth implies that overall productivity will increase less rapidly than in the 1960s and as a consequence the sectoral productivity differential may not widen at the past trend. Provided that the productivity change keeps the same difference for the time being as in the past, real exports must expand at about 12 percent per annum.[z]

In projecting Japan's export requirement, I begin from the 1971 level of exports. There was a large export surplus in 1971. Exports of goods and services were some 27 percent above actual imports and 17 percent above normal imports (which were assumed to be 9 percent above actual imports). Hence, as we start from the 1971 level, we lower the required growth rate of exports to 10.0 percent per annum. For the time being, we disregard the effect of the currency revaluation and apply ten percent growth to Japan's exports of manufactures.

To expand Japan's exports faster than world imports, Japan must continue to increase its world market share. To consider its feasibility, I have first computed the prospective level of Japan's exports of manufactures in 1980 when Japan maintains its marginal market shares of 1962 to 1970 in the 1970s (see Table 4-4). The results are summarized in Table 4-13. The growth rate is 6.5 percent

[z]There are empirical relations that make these crude projections reasonable. From the volume indices of GNP, manufacturing production, exports and imports that are given in Table 4-12, we can compute their elasticities with respect to GNP. They indicate percentage changes of these variables in response to a 1 percent change in GNP. When GNP grows at 8 percent per annum, manufacturing production will grow at 11.5 percent, exports at 12.5 percent, and imports at 11.1 percent.

Table 4-12

Volume Indices of Production in Japan, 1965 = 100

Year	GNP	Manufacturing	Exports	Imports
1955	40.6	26.1	22.6	28.1
1971	187.6	229.6	236.0	227.9
1971 / 1955	4.61	8.80	10.44	8.11
GNP elasticity	1.00	1.42	1.53	1.37

Source: Bureau of Statistics, Office of the Prime Minister (Japan), *Japan Statistical Yearbook* and *Monthly Statistics of Japan.*

Table 4-13

Exports of Manufactures (F.O.B.) from Japan, 1970, 1971, and 1980 (Projected)[a]

Region	Exports in Billions of Dollars			Average Shares, %	
	1970 (Actual)	1971 (Actual)	1980 (Projected)	1970 (Actual)	1980 (Projected)
World	$18.1	$22.2	$39.0	9.0	9.4
Developed market economies	10.0	12.4	21.7	7.1	7.4
United States	5.8	7.3	11.6	21.9	23.0
Canada	.5	.8	1.2	5.7	6.5
Western Europe	2.7	3.1	6.9	2.9	3.3
Oceania and South Africa	1.0	1.2	2.0	13.8	15.8
Developing market economies	7.0	8.9	14.7	17.7	14.8
Latin America	1.1	1.4	1.9	8.9	9.0
Africa	1.0	1.6	2.2	11.9	13.5
Middle East	.5	.7	1.4	10.3	11.8
Asia	4.4	5.2	9.0	35.9	41.7
Centrally planned economies	1.0	1.1	2.6	4.9	3.9
Europe and USSR	.4	.5	1.2	2.2	2.7
Asia	.6	.6	1.4	30.4	35.0

[a]Projected on the assumption that the marginal shares of 1962-70 apply.

per annum from 1971 to 1980, which is one percentage point below the growth rate of world imports of manufactures. This is because the largest importers of Japan's manufactures, namely the United States and South East Asia, are assumed to be increasing their demand for imports at a rate substantially below the world average.

Table 4-14 shows that 74 percent of Japan's required exports can be sold without altering its marginal market shares of the 1960s. The remaining 26 percent must be absorbed by expanding its market shares.

So far, I have not taken into account the effect of currency revaluation. It does two things. One, the yen is now exchanged for a larger amount of foreign currencies. This reduces the export requirement. However, as Japanese goods become more expensive in foreign currency, it becomes more difficult to maintain the present marginal shares in foreign markets. This means that the figures in row (2) and (3) of Table 4-14 must both be reduced. If the price elasticity of Japanese exports is in fact minus two, (3) may be more affected than (2). Qualitatively speaking, then, the relation of Table 4-14 suffices to make our point. It is presumable that any further international currency adjustments would be in the direction of upward revisions of the yen, making the expansion of Japanese exports more difficult.

A simple arithmetic shows that if Japan is to sell all the excess of the export requirement in its traditional markets—the United States and South East Asia—Japan's average shares must be raised from the present 29 percent to 47 percent, implying a marginal share of two-thirds. From 1955 to 1971 Japan could maintain a much higher growth rate of exports than total world trade by selling heavily in the United States and South East Asia. We have seen various factors that made this direction of action feasible over the period. However, by the beginning of the 1970s Japan strained the tension in international relations by following this direction. Any significant expansion of Japan's exports in the United States and South East Asia beyond the shares that were already achieved seems likely to encounter more and more resistance, particularly in view of Japan's heavy export surpluses with these regions, which have become a major debating issue in international politics.

Heavy concentration of Japanese exports in particular markets and particular commodities is liable to give rise to strong frictions and disruptions in importing countries' economic conditions. The past decade witnessed the revival of a strong protectionist mood in the United States against Japan's expansion of sales in such products as textiles, iron and steel, and consumer electronics. Also, it is doubtful whether Japan can continue to supply 50 percent of some manufactured imports into South East Asia because many of them are those intended for import substitution. A few countries, namely Taiwan, Korea, and Hong Kong, already established a firm base of light industry and have been competing with

Table 4-14
Japan's Export Requirement in 1980

	Billions of 1971 Dollars	%
(1) Japan's exports (f.o.b.) of manufactures, 1971 (actual)	$22.2	42
(2) Japan's export requirement of manufactures, 1980 (projected with annual growth of 10.0%)	52.4	100
(3) Japan's exports of manufactures, 1980, on the assumption of constant marginal shares of 1962-70 maintained through the 1970s	39.0	74
(4) Excess of the export requirement that must be absorbed by increased market shares = (2)–(3)	13.4	26

Japan in its traditional markets, that is, the United States and South East Asia. China (mainland) will make its appearance on the stage, too. More and more developing countries will become strong competitors to Japan in the world market through their comparative advantage of abundant labor supply. They will import less and export more of light industry products. This means that Japan has to anticipate the need of shifts away from light manufactures in which it has been losing competitiveness. Moreover, such shifts are necessary to promote economic development in less developed countries.

In any case, the figures given in Table 4-14 reveal that most of the remaining one-quarter of the export requirement may have to be sold in areas in which Japan's sales have been small or negligible, though there may be still some room for expanding trade in markets where Japan is well established, in particular Oceania which may be brought closer to Japan through the loosening of its ties with the United Kingdom. But by and large Japan must expand its sales areas.[aa]

This change of direction of exports no doubt requires substantial new efforts by Japanese exporters. Japan has been unable or unwilling to go into these markets before for a number of reasons such as discriminatory restrictions (for

[aa]In his public lecture in Tokyo in October 20, 1971, Paul Samuelson called Japan's growth an "export-preserved miracle," remarking on the strategic role of exports in sustaining rapid growth of the Japanese economy over the past decades, and made a point that the world economy would be unable to absorb exports from Japan that continue to expand more rapidly than world trade. Hisao Kanamori of the Economic Planning Agency argues against this thesis, noting that Japan's share in world trade is still modest. However, he does not look at the present structure of importing propensities of the world economy. His own trade projections imply increasingly heavier concentration of Japan's exports in its traditional markets. See H. Kanamori, "Nihon Boeki no Shinro" [The Future Course of Japan's Trade], *Keizai Hyoron*, 20 (December 1971), 6-17. There are a few other trade projections along more or less the same lines.

instance, in Western Europe which keeps heavy nontariff barriers on Japanese exports), institutional arrangements not preferred by Japanese business, political instability, geographical distance and climatic difficulty, language and cultural barriers, and high cost of sales efforts. These barriers must now be overcome. The difficulty cannot be underestimated. For instance, the European Community is a potentially attractive market with its rapid trade expansion and high income. However, it is also well known that it is essentially inward-looking as any customs union is. Further, there is a strong, traditional undercurrent of fear and suspicion among European business toward Japan's powerful international competitiveness. As Japanese exporters begin (and are already beginning) to expand their Western European markets, it seems that they must expect some strong resistance from European business. Further, unless Japan's import structure shifts substantially toward final consumer goods, the bilateral balance of trade will be adverse to Western Europe. This will add to European's wariness of trade with Japan.

A hope may be raised about Japan's exports to centrally planned economies. Both Japanese government and business express their keenness in promoting trade with them. However, as far as regular trade is concerned, one should not expect too much in this quarter. My projection shows an annual growth rate of 9 percent for manufactured imports into Eastern Europe and the USSR. Japan's share in them is only 2 percent. This may lead one to hope for fairly rapid expansion of Japan's export by expanding this share. However, some 70 percent of their trade is within themselves. Their national plans suggest that this ratio may even rise in the future. Further, longer trade experiences of countries of Western Europe put them at advantage over Japan. Hence, Japan's expansion of trade with them does not seem to be too easy at present.

It is possible, however, that developmental efforts in these countries open up a new vista. For instance, in its Five-Year Plan of 1971-75, the USSR officially expresses its keenness on developing natural resources and establishing the industrial complex in Siberia. A cooperative program has been developed for Japan's participation. But it seems that there is a high degree of international competition here, and it is not quite certain that Japan can get a lion's share. As for China (mainland), I have assumed 8 percent annual growth of imports and very high marginal shares for Japan's exports in them. Unless China is going to increase its GNP more rapidly, to expand its trade share more, or to shift imports from food to manufactures, it is not very likely that Japan can expand its exports to China much more than projected here. Further, there has been a chronic problem of Japan's export surplus with China, which may have to be solved.

Serious concern is placed on "orderly marketing" in current discussions of trade problems. That is, Japan should avoid disrupting foreign markets by an abrupt increase in exports to a particular market, especially by way of dumping. It seems that orderly marketing has become everybody's concern. European business and government have been very vocal about it in particular reference to Japan's impending export drive into Europe. Japanese business and government also set up special committees in order to study the subject. However, if the excess is to be absorbed, rapid expansion of Japanese exports is inevitable in some new markets, whether Europe or elsewhere. It will inevitably conflict with the norm of orderly marketing.

So far, we have looked at Japan's export requirement. It is already obvious that Japan will continue to expand its role as a major importer in the world and will exert an increasingly important influence on the world market. My projection gives Japan's imports as percentage of world trade as reported in Table 4-15. If the past trend persists, one-quarter of crude materials and one-fifth of petroleum that enter into international trade will be purchased by Japan in 1980. Japan will become a dominant importer of a number of strategic materials. When Japan's demand for raw materials expands to such a gigantic proportion, it will be a serious problem for Japan to secure stable raw materials supplies at stable prices especially because important mineral materials, for example, copper, nickel, aluminum, and crude petroleum, are under tight international oligopoly control. There are already complaints that Japan's voracious appetite for primary goods raised the world prices of certain goods in recent years. The question is as to whether primary-producing countries are willing to expand supplies to meet Japan's demand because these economies wish to industrialize rather than to remain primary producers,[bb] even though various arrangements are being made with them to develop raw material resources.

Table 4-15
Shares of Japan's Imports in World Trade (Percentage)

SITC		1960	1970	1980
0 + 1	Food	2.3	5.2	9.5
2 + 4	Crude materials	8.7	15.2	26.8
3	Mineral fuels	4.2	10.6	19.8
5	Chemicals	3.2	3.6	5.8
7	Machinery and transport equipment	1.2	2.0	3.4
6 + 8	Other manufactured goods	0.8	2.4	4.4
0~8	Total	3.0	4.9	8.5

Source: Table 4-10 and U.N., *Monthly Bulletin of Statistics.*

bbTable 4-11 shows that demand for nonfuel primary products may increase at around six percent per annum (5.4 percent if Japan's demand is excluded). On the other hand, from 1958 to 1969, nonfuel primary production expanded at an average annual rate of 3.8 percent. This rate probably does not change much in the 1970s. Then, there is a clear conflict between prospective demand and supply.

Concluding Remarks

I have reviewed Japan's trade experience from 1955 to 1971 and examined its trade prospects up to 1980 in the light of my review. It is observed that Japan will face serious problems if it is to maintain the balance of trade equilibrium while sustaining a rate of output growth surpassing the rates of other economies even though lower than the past trend rate.

The rapid growth of the Japanese economy in the past two decades has been made feasible under circumstances exceptionally favorable to Japan. Japan was able to expand its exports of manufactures because the world trade exhibited a very strong expansionary trend after World War II. At the same time, the pressure from imports was weak because of soft price trends of primary commodities. Foreign trade, however, remained a key cyclical factor circumscribing fluctuations in Japan's economic growth except for a brief episode of the past few years. It will continue to play as significant a role in influencing Japan's overall growth in the 1970s. However, there is a great difference between the 1960s and the 1970s. Japan has grown with great strides in the 1960s and has become a major economic figure in the world. What it does will have greater impacts on the world economy henceforth and vice versa.

We have assumed that Japan can maintain its growth above other developed economies through the 1970s though not at the spectacular rate of the 1960s. However, even that reduced growth is still likely to bring about a considerable strain in the world market if Japan tries to stick with its familiar areas because Japanese exports must grow at a higher rate than the world market will expand.

Where can Japan find markets for sales expansion? A few regions—the United States and South East Asia—have been buying Japanese goods in increasingly larger amounts in the past two decades. Various frictions that had already arisen in the course of the 1960s suggest the inadvisability of unchecked expansion of Japan's sales in these areas even if Japan may be able to keep its competitiveness. It is estimated that maintaining the present shares in various regions of the world will leave a little above one-quarter of Japan's export requirement unfilled. It requires Japan to diversify its markets as much as its competitors have been doing. Such areas are Western and Eastern Europe, the USSR, Latin America, Africa, and mainland China. Since most of these markets have been entrenched with well-established trade connections with leading exporting countries, this is not an easy task if Japan's competitiveness should be weakened.

As for composition of export goods, the trend away from light manufactures must and will continue. With increasing sophistication of technology, Japan should concentrate more and more on exporting products embodying advanced technology, leaving the production and exportation of textiles and other less sophisticated and labor-intensive goods to developing nations.[cc] Since trade

---

[cc]As Dr. Krause's Chapter 6 notes, Japanese direct overseas investment has been in these lines as well as in development of raw material supplies abroad.

among developed nations is largely in differentiated manufactured goods, Japan should go into diversifying products to expand its exports in these countries. At the same time, it means that production by inefficient small firms, which very often dominate exports of light manufactures, must now be modernized.

As for imports, Japan will become a leading importer of raw and processed materials in the world market. Demand for petroleum will also increase rapidly. In view of Japan's heavy dependence on imported materials, it is imperative for Japan to take measures to ensure uninterrupted supplies of these materials. In this connection, a further shift from raw to more processed materials in imports will adapt the Japanese economy to anticipated changes in world production structure.

Appendix: Technical Notes on Projections of Trade up to 1980

This appendix explains the method and assumptions employed in making projections of trade up to 1980.

Classifications.[a]

Regions. The following regions are distinguished:

Developed market economies:
    United States
    Canada
    European Community (Belgium-Luxembourg, France, Federal Republic of Germany, Italy, Netherlands)
    Other Europe (all Western European countries excluding those of the European Community and including Turkey and Yugoslavia)
    Oceania and South Africa (Australia, New Zealand, and South Africa)
    Japan
    Others (not elsewhere specified, including Israel)
Developing market economies:
    Latin America
    Africa (excluding South Africa)
    Middle East
    Asia (excluding the Middle East and Japan)
    Others (mainly islands in the Pacific)
Centrally planned economies:
    Europe and the USSR (excluding Yugoslavia)
    Asia (China, Mongolia, North Korea, North Viet Nam).

Commodity Groups. The following commodity groups are distinguished:

SITC (Standard International Trade Classification)
0+1   Food, beverages, and tobacco
2+4   Crude materials (excluding fuels) and oils and fats
3   Mineral fuels and related materials
5   Chemicals
7   Machinery and transport equipment
6+8   Other manufactured goods (SITC 6 is manufactured goods classified by

---

[a]The classifications below are those adopted by the United Nations Statistical Office.

material, consisting of leather, rubber, wood, paper and pulp, textile yarn and fabrics, nonmetallic mineral products, silver, platinum, and jewelry, iron and steel, nonferrous metals, and other manufactures of metals. SITC 8 is miscellaneous manufactured articles, consisting of prefabricated buildings, furniture, travel goods, clothing, footwear, scientific instruments, photographic equipment, and other miscellaneous articles.)

9   Commodities and transactions not elsewhere specified.

Projections

General Procedure. Based on the 1955-70 trends in growth of real output and commodity imports, certain rates of growth are assumed for total commodity imports of each region over the decade of the 1970s as summarized in Table 4A-1. These rates are applied to the 1971 figures given in Table 4-10 in the text in order to obtain total commodity imports in 1980. These projected figures are in 1971 dollars.

Total imports are then broken down into SITC categories[b] by applying the marginal shares of respective categories in total imports, both expressed in 1970 prices, computed between 1955-57 and 1968-70. They are obtained by dividing the increase in sectoral real imports from 1955-57 to 1968-70 by the increase in total imports (SITC 0 to 8) over the same period. Table 4A-2 shows these marginal shares and the elasticities, which are obtained by dividing the marginal shares by the corresponding 1968-70 average shares. (Since price indices are not available for centrally planned economies, ratios are computed in current value for them.)

Regional Specifications

Developed Market Economies. In developed economies, except for South Africa, Australia, and New Zealand, the shares of imports and exports in GNP tended to increase somewhat over the period under survey when measured in current prices. Real imports and exports, however, grew much faster than real GNP. This means that the domestic price level rose at a faster rate than the export and import price indices. It is assumed that this increase in the shares of foreign trade in GNP will stop and they will remain stable in the next ten years. Then, the growth of real imports or exports will be equal to the growth rate of real GNP plus the growth rate of the GNP deflator minus the growth rate of the import or export price indices. Table 4A-3 gives the past relations.

Specific assumptions adopted in projecting total imports are as follows:

---

[b]First, total imports are separated into SITC 0~8 and 9 by applying the proportion of 1970.

Table 4A-1
Growth Rates of GDP and Commodity Imports (Percentage)

Region	Actual Growth (1955-70)			Assumed Growth (1971-80)	
	g_y	g_{mp_m}	g_m	g_y	g_m
World	–	8.3	–	–	–
Developed market economies	4.4	9.0	8.3	–	–
United States	3.4	8.6	7.5	4.0	4.8
Canada	4.7	7.3	6.2	4.7	5.5
European Community	5.2	10.5	10.3	5.2	8.4
Other Europe	4.1	9.9	9.2	4.1	6.4
Oceania and South Africa	5.2	5.5	4.6	5.2	5.0
Japan	10.7	14.5	14.7	8.0	13.6
Developing market economies	5.0	5.7	5.2	–	–
Latin America	5.3	4.9	3.9	5.0	5.0
Africa	4.3	4.6	4.0	5.0	5.0
Middle East	7.4	7.9	7.4	7.5	7.5
Asia	4.6	6.3	6.2	5.0	5.0
Centrally planned economies	–	9.2	–	–	–
Europe and USSR	7.2	10.0	–	7.0	8.0
Asia	–	4.2	–	–	8.0

Legend: g growth rate, y GDP (real), m imports (real), p_m unit value of imports (in current dollars).

Source: Data on actual growth from UNCTAD, *Handbook of International Trade and Development Statistics*, 1969 and 1972 (New York, 1969 and 1972).

1. Except for Japan and the United States, the growth rate of GDP in the 1970s is assumed to be the same as the trend rate from 1955 to 1970. For Japan, it is assumed that the growth rate will be 8 percent per annum through the 1970s. For the United States, the growth rate is raised to 4.0 percent per annum.

2. As for the price trends, the same differentials as over the period under survey are assumed to continue into the 1970s. However, in order to account for the recent revaluation in currencies, an additional assumption is made that import prices expressed in domestic currency will fall in Japan, rise in the United States, and remain more or less unchanged in Western Europe. In other words, Western Europe is taken as the base of reference. The devaluation of the dollar raised the value of other currencies by 8.57 percent. Some European currencies were revalued more

Table 4A-2

Marginal Shares and Elasticites of Import Categories with Respect to Total Imports: 1955-57 to 1968-70

	Developed Market Economies					
SITC	United States	Canada	European Community	Other Europe	Oceania & South Africa	Japan
	Marginal Shares					
0+1	.074	.066	.123	.066	.021	.130
2+4	.022	.050	.075	.049	.033	.293
3	.073	.058	.103	.097	.058	.240
5	.037	.063	.092	.105	.145	.056
7	.415	.564	.261	.328	.519	.121
6+8	.378	.199	.346	.355	.224	.160
	Elasticities[a]					
0+1	.50	.87	.81	.46	.44	.90
2+4	.23	.86	.60	.46	.62	.87
3	.90	.89	1.01	1.02	.85	1.15
5	1.16	1.17	1.24	1.36	1.63	1.07
7	1.43	1.12	1.14	1.21	1.17	1.08
6+8	1.07	.82	1.09	1.15	.75	1.11

	Developing Market Economies				Centrally Planned Economies	
SITC	Latin America	Africa	Middle East	Asia	Europe & USSR	Asia
	Marginal Shares					
0+1	.109	.106	.102	.162	.106	.388
2+4	.046	.054	.052	.076	.052	.116
3	.166	.056	.061	.066	.045	−.010
5	.152	.133	.104	.121	.078	.196
7	.343	.436	.410	.333	.414	.116
6+8	.184	.214	.271	.242	.305	.194
	Elasticities[a]					
0+1	1.01	.78	.78	.95	.81	2.13
2+4	.91	1.25	1.04	.83	.44	.92
3	1.37	.91	.81	.96	.75	−.27
5	1.40	1.59	1.32	1.35	1.21	1.52
7	.92	1.16	1.11	1.15	1.19	.47
6+8	.55	.71	.91	.84	1.10	.69

[a]Marginal share ÷ average share, 1968-70.

Table 4A-3
Growth Rates of GNP, Exports, and Imports:[a] Developed Regions, 1955-69 (Percentage)

Region	g_x	g_{p_x/p_y}	g_{xp_x/p_y}	g_m	g_{p_m/p_y}	g_{mp_m/p_y}	g_y	Exports 1955	1969	Imports 1955	1969
United States	6.2	−1.1	5.0	7.2	−1.8	5.3	3.7	.049	.059	.046	.057
Canada	7.0	−1.2	5.8	6.1	− .8	5.3	4.5	.212	.248	.237	.262
European Community	9.5	−2.7	6.6	10.1	−3.0	6.9	5.3	.190	.229	.176	.217
Other Western Europe	6.0	−1.9	4.0	6.0	−2.2	3.7	3.8	.238	.241	.246	.241
Oceania and South Africa[b]	5.4	−1.9	3.4	5.0	−2.0	2.9	4.7	.220	.193	.230	.190
Japan[c]	14.6	−3.4	10.8	14.7	−4.5	9.7	10.1	.114	.126[d]	.105	.099[d]

Legend: g growth rate, x exports (real), m imports (real), y GNP (real), p price index.
[a]Exports and imports of goods and services.
[b]1955-68.
[c]1955-71.
[d]1971.
Source: OECD, *National Accounts of OECD Countries*; U.N., *Yearbook of National Accounts Statistics*; Economic Planning Agency (Japan), *Annual Report on National Income Statistics*.

than this. Assume that the average valuation increase was 10 percent. Then, in relation to average European currency, the dollar was depreciated by some 9 percent and the yen (revalued by 16.88 percent) appreciated by 6 percent. As we examine the year 1980, these valuation changes are added to the price trends of the United States and Japan. On the compound-rate basis, they are equivalent to 1.0 percent and −0.6 percent per annum.

3. The growth rate of real imports is derived from the formula (1 + the growth rate of real imports) = (1 + the growth rate of GDP) x (1 + the growth rate of p_m/p_y). This assumes that the income elasticity of imports is one and the price elasticity minus one.

4. In Australia, New Zealand, and South Africa, the shares of imports and exports in GNP continued to decline over the period under consideration. These countries are primary exporters and their export earnings determined their capacity to import. It is assumed that their real imports will grow at the past trend rate.

Developing Market Economies. Because of lack of comparable data, we cannot use the assumptions adopted for developed market economies. In developing areas, the growth rates of international trade were roughly commensurate with the growth rate of GDP. The growth rate of GDP, averaged for developing areas, showed a small improvement in the 1960s over the 1950s. See Table 4A-4. It is assumed that there will be no significant increase in their growth in the 1970s. The growth rate of imports will also remain about the same as that of GDP. To simplify, it is assumed that it is 5 percent for all developing regions except in the Middle East, for which it was set at 7.5 percent.

Centrally Planned Economies: Europe and the USSR. In socialist economies, foreign trade is part of national plans. As Table 4A-5 shows, plan targets were exceeded in the 5-year plans of 1966-70, partly because of price increases. In the 1971-75 plans, the growth of foreign trade is expected to decelerate somewhat. Considering this as well as the fact that imports grew a little above 8 percent per annum through the 1960s, it is assumed that imports will increase at 8 percent per annum up to 1980.

Centrally Planned Economies: Asia. Imports were constrained by exports and exports in turn by domestic production. Reflecting economic conditions at home, imports fluctuated. Value of imports (c.i.f.) started at $1.0 billion in 1950, reached the high of $2.3 billion in 1959, dropped to the low of $1.4 billion in 1962, and then shot up again to $3.1 billion in 1971. From 1962 to 1971, the average annual rate of expansion was 9.2 percent. We assume that the rate will be 8 percent per annum over the 1970s.

It may be estimated that imports were about 4 percent of GNP of the region. The region's dependence on trade with the rest of the world will presumably

Table 4A-4

Actual Growth of GDP and Commodity Imports, Developing Regions, 1950-60 (Percentage)

Region	1950-60			1960-70		
	g_y	g_{mp_m} [a]	g_m	g_y	g_{mp_m} [a]	g_m
Developing areas	4.7	5.6	4.5	5.2	6.4	5.4
Latin America	5.2	4.1	2.8	5.4	6.3	4.7
Africa	4.5	6.7	5.3	4.2	4.9	3.3
Middle East	6.9	8.9	7.8	7.7	8.0	6.8
Asia	4.1	5.6	5.2	4.9	6.6	6.4

[a]In current dollars.

Source: U.N., *Handbook of International Trade Statistics*, 1964; UNCTAD, *Handbook of International Trade and Development Statistics*, 1972.

Table 4A-5

Planned and Actual Growth Rates of Trade, Centrally Planned Economies, Europe and the USSR[a] (Percentage)

	1961-65 (Actual)	1966-70 (Plan)	1966-70 (Actual)	1970-71 (Plan)	1970-71 (Actual)	1971-75 (Plan)[b]
Exports	9.7	–	9.5	–	10.6	–
Imports	8.0	–	8.7	–	8.3	–
Turnover[c]	8.8	7.3	9.3	8.2	9.5	6.9
National income	6.0	6.6	7.3	6.5	–	–
Propensity[d]	1.5	–	1.3	1.3	–	–

[a]Bulgaria, Czechoslovakia, German Democratic Republic, Hungary, Poland, Romania, and the USSR.

[b]Average of Bulgaria, Hungary, Romania, and the USSR.

[c](Exports + imports)/2.

[d]Increase in turnover $\div$ increase in net material product.

Source: ECE (UN), *Economic Survey of Europe in 1970*, pt II (New York, 1971).

remain low for the time being. The 8 percent growth rate of imports implicitly assumes a small increase in this dependency.

The elasticities of sectional imports with respect to total imports show considerable differences from all other regions of the world. This must reflect special circumstances of the region. I have divided total imports of 1980 into components by applying the 1968-70 average shares.

Notes

1. See MITI, WHITE PAPER ON INTERNATIONAL TRADE, 1971 (Tokyo, 1971), p. 296.

2. Computed from ECE (UN), ECONOMIC SURVEY OF EUROPE IN 1970, part II (New York, 1971), p. 143.

5

Japan-United States Trade—Patterns, Relationships, Problems

Warren S. Hunsberger

Introduction: Surging, Unbalanced Trade Growth and Multiplying Problems

Commodity trade is the largest of the many links between the United States and Japan, the world's first and third most productive economies. The huge quantities of goods moving in both directions across the Pacific Ocean are essential to Japan. They are certainly very important, but probably not essential, for the United States. The value of these movements has grown almost explosively during the past two decades, but very unevenly, and now much more is coming into the United States than is going the other way. Continued upgrading in quality and advances in technology have changed radically the goods Japanese firms sell in the United States. There has been less change in the American primary products and manufactured goods going to Japan.

For Japan these developments represent phenomenal success in solving a basic problem: how a crowded island country poor in natural resources can find means to pay for the imports necessary to maintain a modern economy and support a modern and rising standard of living for its population. Trade with the United States does not, of course, constitute the whole answer to this Japanese problem. But commodity trade is the biggest component of Japan's balance of international payments, and the United States is a far larger factor than any other country in Japan's foreign trade.

Japan's trade success has two distinct aspects. The first is Japan's production "miracle," which provides goods of high quality in a range from tiny transistorized radios, television receivers and pocket-sized calculators, to steel, automobiles and mammoth ships, all at costs so low as to attract customers in large numbers. The second aspect is equally new and unexpected. It is the tolerance of the American market for an import surge of competitive manufactures such as the world has never seen before. Trade barriers there certainly are, and they have limited in various ways the flow of Japanese goods to the United States. But the barriers have not stopped this unprecedented surging movement, nor even perceptibly slowed it thus far, despite the effects on the flow of particular products.

Trade problems are not new in the Japan-United States relationship. Trade was the leading demand of the United States in sending Commodore Perry to

117

open Japan to international intercourse in the 1850s. Trade problems were an important element in the background to the Japanese attack on Pearl Harbor. Japan experienced severe losses when the American import market for Japanese silk collapsed after 1929. Then followed strong opposition in the United States (and elsewhere) to a rush of textiles and other cheap manufactured goods from Japan during the depression-ridden 1930s, Japanese resentment at the import restrictions imposed by the United States (and many other countries) against these Japanese goods, and in the summer of 1941 a freezing of Japanese assets abroad that effectively cut off many imports into Japan, including petroleum. Now a new period of tension has developed between Japan and the United States, and again trade issues are a major element causing strain.

During the Pacific War, it was the strangulation of trade through the sinking of Japanese ships that brought down the Japanese war economy before the first atomic bombs persuaded the Japanese government to surrender. After World War II, the United States took the lead in establishing international institutions and supporting policies that have fostered freer world trade and permitted Japan to achieve unprecedented success, not only in bilateral trade with the United States, but elsewhere as well.

For nearly two decades, imports from Japan have raised more often, more seriously and in more different ways than goods from any other country the question of how far the United States will go in accepting imports of competitive manufactured goods. Thus far the various quotas and other barriers that have been erected have not checked the tidal flow from Japan. In fact the inflationary boom in the United States, associated with the Vietnam War, accelerated the import inflow. Then the economic slowdown at the end of the 1960s, and the enlarged deficit in the balance of payments have caused more and more Americans to see the cause of their troubles in imports, especially imports from Japan. Still American inflation persisted, and the imports from Japan continued to rise, without any visible slowdown within six months after the Smithsonian Agreement of December 1971 had at long last changed the exchange rate for an overvalued dollar and an undervalued yen. Meanwhile, an economic slowdown in Japan at the beginning of the 1970s cut Japanese demand for imports, and American sales in Japan actually dropped from 1970 to 1971.

Thus a rising tide of American protectionism coincides with a massive import flow, the momentum of which contributes strongly to a growing trade and payments deficit in the United States and a simultaneously growing trade and payments surplus in Japan. On Capitol Hill, protectionist sentiment was reflected in the Burke-Hartke bill, which proposes quantitative controls, at least potentially, over all imports into the United States.

Clearly there are serious problems related to American trade with Japan.

Patterns and Trends in Trade Flows

Volume of Trade and Its Postwar Growth

The upsurge of United States trade with Japan in the postwar period shows clearly in Table 5-1, which also gives annual averages for 1934-36. From its very small postwar beginnings, this trade has grown phenomenally, to reach today's huge volume of over 11 billion dollars a year. The following average annual rates of growth for the two decades 1951-71 compare this growth with some other average annual growth rates for the same period:

	%
US exports to Japan	9.5
US imports from Japan	18.5
World trade	6.9
Total US trade	6.1
Total Japanese trade	12.9
Total Japanese exports	14.7
Total Japanese imports	11.4

The recent growth of United States exports to Japan has been substantially faster than the growth of total U.S. trade or total world trade, but only about half as fast as the growth of U.S. imports from Japan. These imports grew faster than anything else listed, including total Japanese exports and total Japanese imports. Imports from Japan have also grown more steadily than exports to Japan. The latter actually declined in 1971 and on several previous occasions when the Japanese economy experienced slowdowns.

Imports from Japan are a phenomenon indeed. The 1971 level of over $7 billion is nearly seven times the 1961 figure, and 24 percent above 1970. The actual *increase* in 1971, $1,386 million, is larger than *total* imports from Japan in 1961 or any earlier year.

Importance of the Trade for Each Country

The United States has been a leading trade partner of Japan ever since the opening of Japan to foreign trade in the 1850s. As a market for Japanese exports, the United States has usually been first, except during the period from 1931-45, when Japanese exports to occupied areas, especially China and Korea, exceeded sales in the United States. In recent years the United States market has taken a progressively rising share of Japan's exports. As a source of Japanese

Table 5-1

United States Balance of Trade with Japan, 1946-1971

	US Exports (F.O.B.) ($ Million)	US Imports (F.O.B.) ($ Million)	Balance of Trade ($ Million)	Exports as a %of Imports
1934-36 average	206	148	58	139
1946	102	81	21	126
1947	60	35	25	171
1948	325	63	262	516
1949	468	82	386	571
1950	418	182	236	230
1951	601	205	396	293
1952	633	229	404	276
1953	686	262	424	262
1954	693	279	414	248
1955	683	432	251	158
1956	998	558	440	179
1957	1,319	600	719	220
1958	987	666	321	148
1959	1,080	1,029	51	105
1960	1,452	1,149	303	126
1961	1,840	1,055	785	174
1962	1,574	1,358	216	116
1963	1,846	1,498	348	123
1964	2,018	1,768	250	114
1965	2,087	2,414	(−)327	86
1966	2,374	2,963	(−)589	80
1967	2,699	2,999	(−)300	90
1968	2,954	4,054	(−)1,100	73
1969	3,490	4,888	(−)1,398	71
1970	4,652	5,875	(−)1,223	79
1971	4,055	7,261	(−)3,206	56

Sources:

1934-36 average, 1946-1949: US Department of Commerce, Bureau of the Census, *Historical Statistics of the United States.* (Washington, D.C.: GPO, 1960), pp. 550, 552.

1950-1970: US Department of Commerce, Bureau of the Census, *Highlights of U.S. Export and Import Trade* (FT 990), various years.

1971: US Department of Commerce, Office of Business Economics, *Survey of Current Business*, March 1972, pp. S-21, S-22.

imports, the United States has not always been first, as Japan long sold more than it bought in the American market. During the occupation, by contrast, the great bulk of imports into Japan came from the United States. This predominant share has declined irregularly ever since, but the United States remains the leading source of Japan's imports as well as the largest market for Japan's exports. Table 5-2 shows details.

Japan's share of U.S. trade, on the other hand, has always been smaller. Before World War I Japan never accounted for as much as 5 percent of total U.S. trade. In the late 1920s silk movements boosted Japan's share of U.S. imports to almost 10 percent. In the mid-1930s when Japan's economic boom attracted large imports at a time of depression in U.S. and world trade, Japan for a while bought almost 10 percent of U.S. exports. Table 5-3 shows these shares. Then in the early years after World War II, because Japanese trade was very small in absolute value, it accounted for only a tiny share in total U.S. trade. In 1948 Japan took 2.6 percent of total U.S. exports, but provided only 0.9 percent of the substantially smaller value of U.S. imports. Substantial growth began in 1951, since then Japanese trade has become more and more prominent in United States statistics. Exports to Japan reached an all-time high in 1970 before dropping back in 1971 to a little over 9 percent of U.S. exports. Meanwhile, imports from Japan have climbed steeply and almost continuously, reaching nearly 16 percent of United States imports in 1971, more than double their share in 1960.

Table 5-2
United States Share of Japanese Foreign Trade, 1921-1971

	Japan's Exports (% of Total)	Japan's Imports
1921-30	35.0	23.7
1931-40	15.2	25.0
1945-50	22.6	65.5
1950	21.7	43.3
1955	22.7	31.3
1960	27.2	34.6
1965	29.3	29.0
1970	30.7	29.4
1971	31.2	25.3

Sources:

1950 and earlier years: W.S. Hunsberger, *Japan and the United States in World Trade.* (New York: Harper and Row, 1964), pp. 241, 184-85.

1955-70: Bank of Japan, *Economic Statistics Annual*, 1970, p. 237.

1971: Bank of Japan, *Economic Statistics Monthly*, March 1972, pp. 109, 110.

Table 5-3
Japan's Share of United States Foreign Trade, 1950-1971

	US Exports	US Imports
	(% of Total)	
1934-36 average	9.0	7.2
1950	4.1	2.1
1955	4.4	3.8
1960	7.1	7.8
1965	7.6	11.3
1970	10.8	14.7
1971	9.2	15.9

Sources:

1934-36 average: US Department of Commerce, Bureau of the Census, *Historical Statistics of the United States.* Washington, D.C.: GPO, 1960), pp. 550, 552.

Other years: US Department of Commerce, Bureau of the Census, *Highlights of U.S. Export and Import Trade* (FT 990), various years.

Reversal of the Trade Balance

Before the Great Depression, Japan consistently sold to the United States substantially more than it bought in this country. In the 1930s the balance shifted and Japan experienced substantial trade deficits, both with the United States and with the world outside of Japan's occupied areas. These deficits reappeared in exaggerated form after World War II, reflecting Japan's inability to export much in the face of domestic shortages, while United States aid made possible imports well beyond what Japanese exports paid for. The United States supplied most of Japan's imports but bought only a small fraction of what Japan succeeded in selling abroad.

Since 1950 the faster growth rate of Japan's exports as compared with imports has caused a progressive shift from the early deficit, until now there is an export surplus, both with the United States and with the world at large. Japanese exports have paid for the following percentages of imports:

	Trade with U.S.	Total Trade
1945-50	19	55
1951-55	36	67
1956-60	62	55
1961-65	78	87
1966-70	110	102
1971	151	122

In 1965, for the first time after World War II, Japan experienced an export surplus, both in its total trade with the world and also in its bilateral trade with the United States. These surpluses disappeared, then returned and grew. Still the cumulative total of Japanese exports from 1945 through 1971 came to only 95 percent of the cumulative total of imports. In the bilateral trade with the United States, exports cumulated to only 90 percent of imports.

Japanese vs. American Views of the
Trade Balance

The figures just cited on the trade balance are from Japanese sources. The view they give of the changing balance is usually accepted in Japan. But United States statistical practice is different and makes the balance look different to a degree that is sometimes significant. For example, both countries report deficits in their trade with each other in 1967. Table 5-1 above shows the balance from the American point of view, both in dollars and percentages.

The difference is that, whereas the United States reports both exports and imports at f.o.b. values (without shipping and related costs), Japan reports exports at f.o.b. values and imports at c.i.f. values (including freight and insurance). Thus both exports and imports in Japan are reported at their value at the Japanese end of their movement, whereas American statistics show both exports and imports at the port in the exporting country.

The reported movements from Japan to the United States look very much alike in the statistics of the two countries. The variation is about 1 percent for the total of all postwar movements through 1970. But total movements from the United States to Japan are reported by Japan as 17 percent more valuable than they appear in United States statistics, since only the Japanese figures include freight and insurance costs.

The difference usually causes no trouble to trained analysts in either country. But it seems that the attitudes both of the public and of political leaders are influenced to some extent by the trade figures as they are published. Thus nonspecialist Americans and Japanese approach the bilateral trade relationship with different presumptions, and even specialists do so to some extent. Here may lie one of the lesser and less obvious reasons why many Japanese were so slow to see in their recent export surpluses, both with the United States and with the world at large, a problem requiring prompt and decisive action.

The importance of the bilateral trade balance is once again a matter of policy disagreement with Japan. When the bilateral deficit was Japan's, particularly during the 1950s, Japanese tended to view the deficit as more serious than it seemed to some Americans. American officials from time to time pointed out the importance of nontrade items and multilateral settlements in Japan's overall balance of payments. Still, the disagreement was limited because Japan's basic problem of paying its way in the world economy was a matter of concern for American as well as Japanese policy, since the United States felt a strong interest in Japan's economic strength and political leanings.

Now the shoe is on the other foot and the bilateral deficit is American. Now Americans are so concerned about the trade deficit with Japan that American officials have said overall equilibrium in the U.S. balance of payments is impossible at the present level of bilateral trade deficit with Japan. In 1971 this bilateral deficit ($3.2 billion) was much larger than the U.S. worldwide trade deficit ($2.8 billion). Japanese observers could see the mounting deficit as mid-1971 passed. Other items than trade in the Japanese balance of payments did not prevent a large and growing surplus and rising foreign exchange reserves. Nor did nontrade items prevent a large and growing deficit in the American balance of payments. But most Japanese neither shared the degree of concern the Americans felt, nor even understood it. Some Japanese leaders reportedly saw the need for yen revaluation but were unable to get agreement for such action; shipbuilders and other exporters strongly opposed any increase in the exchange value of the yen. In addition, it is significant but not surprising that Japanese felt no sense of responsibility for the U.S. economy parallel to the sense Americans used to feel for the Japanese economy.

Thus the Japanese were psychologically unprepared for President Nixon's drastic moves of August 1971 and for the degree of pressure the United States government then exerted for substantial yen revaluation. Once the revaluation was accepted in the December Smithsonian Agreement, many Japanese seemed to hope that the storm had passed. American leaders, on the other hand, pressed hard the trade negotiations that were made a condition of American devaluation of the dollar. Negotiations with Japan continued in 1972, but the extent of further Japanese liberalization thus far achieved proved minor. American officials remained concerned about the bilateral trade deficit with Japan, and seem likely to continue so as long as the United States balance of payments continues to run a large deficit.

Commodities Moving to Japan

Primary Products. The United States sells to Japan large quantities of both primary commodities and manufactured goods and is Japan's largest supplier of each. At the same time Japan is the market for the largest share of American exports of a number of individual items, especially grains and raw materials. Table 5-4 presents statistics on the total trade in primary products for 1971 and on major groups and important individual commodities. The main commodities are food and animal feed, raw materials and fuels. Altogether, primary commodities made up 52 percent of total 1971 U.S. exports to Japan.

The overall quantitative importance of these primary movements was about

Table 5-4
United States Exports of Primary Products to Japan, 1971

Commodity Code and Name	Value ($ million)	Share of U.S. Exports to Japan (%)	Japan's Share of U.S. Exports to All Countries (%)	U.S. Share of Japan's Imports from All Countries (%)
0 Food and Live Animals	532	13.3	12.2	24.1
041 Wheat	152	3.8	15.1	52.3
044 Corn	148	3.7	19.8	54.3
042,045, other cereals, unmilled	75	1.9	17.3	38.7
1 Beverages and Tobacco	27	0.7	3.8	52.4
2 Crude Materials, Inedible	1,028	25.6	23.8	20.6
21 Hides and skins	52	1.3	26.1	64.8
221.4 Soybeans	311	7.8	23.5	91.0
24 Wood and lumber	283	7.1	58.7	26.9
242.2 Logs, softwood	234	5.8	88.6	55.5
243.2 Lumber, softwood	33	0.8	22.9	35.0
25 Pulps and waste paper	58	1.4	15.1	43.7
263 Raw cotton	126	3.1	21.1	24.4
28 Metalliferous ores and scrap	123	3.1	25.3	6.9
282 Iron and steel scrap	55	1.4	25.6	70.2
283 Nonferrous ores and concentrates	20	0.5	18.2	2.3
3 Mineral Fuels, Lubricants, etc.	447	11.1	29.9	13.1
321.4 Coal	353	8.8	39.1	51.1
332 Petroleum products	64	1.6	13.5	13.7
4 Oils and Fats, Animal and Vegetable	34	0.9	5.5	48.0
Total codes 0-4 ("Primary")	2,068	51.6	18.0	19.2

Note: Minor inconsistencies result from rounding.

Sources: Columns 1-3: U.S. Department of Commerce, Bureau of the Census, Exports, Commodity by Country, December 1971, FT 410-71-12, pp. 1-1 to 1-13; and U.S. Department of Commerce, National Technical Information Service, U.S. Exports, Schedule B Commodity Groupings, World Area, Country, and Method of Transportation, EM 450/455, pp. 540-51; Column 4: Calculated from Japan Tariff Association, Japan Exports and Imports '71.12.

equal for the trade of the two countries, accounting for 18 percent of United States exports in these categories and 19 percent of Japanese imports in these categories. But the importance of the movement of individual commodities was in many cases much higher for one country or the other. For the United States, Japan was the market for 89 percent of softwood log exports. Shares for other products included 39 percent for coal, 26 percent for hides and skins, as well as for iron and steel scrap, and 24 percent for soybeans. For Japan the high figures included 91 percent of imported soybeans coming from the United States, 70 percent of iron and steel scrap, 65 percent of hides and skins, 56 percent of softwood logs, 54 percent of corn, 52 percent of wheat and of beverages and tobacco, and 51 percent of coal.

Manufactures. Manufactured products, which made up 48 percent of 1971 United States exports to Japan, look very different to the two countries. Table 5-5 shows details for these categories. This trade made up only 6 percent of the huge American export business in these categories, but 41 percent of Japan's much smaller imports of these things. Only three subgroups shown saw Japan buy as much as 10 percent of American exports. For metalworking machinery the percentage was 14, for office machinery 11 percent. Within this latter category, 12 percent of exports of electronic computers went to Japan. For the Japanese, however, the goods listed in Table 5-5 were in many cases very important indeed. Of aircraft imports 99 percent came from the United States, power generating equipment 81 percent, electrical machinery 70 percent. Of all Japan's imports of machinery and transport equipment, 60 percent came from the United States. American manufacturers and American industrial workers, however, simply do not have such a big stake in the Japanese market as American farmers and some other primary producers do.

Consumer manufactured goods are difficult to find among United States exports to Japan. By contrast, such manufactures stand out prominently among United States imports from Japan, as we shall see below. Imports have remained a very serious business for Japan, as they have been for over a century, involving very little beyond those primary and manufactured products essential for operating and developing the Japanese economy. To be sure, there is snob appeal in Japan for certain foreign products, including skis and golf clubs made in the U.S.A., but such imports, or any consumer manufactures made abroad, have not heretofore been easily visible in Japanese import statistics. Only now, especially since the trade policy changes of 1971, is Japan opening its market to consumer goods. Indeed, in May 1972 a Japanese businessman's mission came to the United States for the specific purpose of promoting sales of American products in Japan.[1]

The United States as a Less Developed Country in Trade with Japan? Because primary products make up over half of what American exporters sell in Japan,

Table 5-5
United States Exports of Manufactures to Japan, 1971

Product Code and Name	Value ($ million)	Share of U.S. Exports to Japan (%)	Japan's Share of U.S. Exports to All Countries (%)	U.S. Share of Japan's Imports from All Countries (%)
5 Chemicals	324	8.1	8.4	37.8
6 Manufactured goods by Chief Material	191	4.8	4.3	16.3
68 Nonferrous metals	44	1.1	6.9	7.7
7 Machinery and Transport Equipment	1,130	28.2	5.8	59.9
71 Machinery, nonelectric	533	13.3	6.3	47.6
711 Power generating equipment	95	2.4	6.1	81.1
714 Office machinery and parts	167	4.2	11.0	58.8
714.2 Electronic computers	55	1.4	12.0	53.0
715 Metalworking machinery	58	1.4	14.3	35.2
72 Electrical machinery	227	5.7	7.4	69.6
73 Transport equipment	369	9.2	4.7	73.5
734 Aircraft and parts	322	8.0	9.5	98.8
8 Miscellaneous manufactures	260	6.5	9.5	39.9
861 Scientific, optical, etc.	69	1.7	7.8	59.2
9 Items not classified by kind	18	0.4	1.2	22.1
Total codes 5-9 ("Manufactured")	1,923	47.9	6.0	40.5
Total codes 0-4 ("Primary")	2,068	51.5	18.0	19.2
Special category exports	22	0.5	1.5	n.a.
Total Exports	4,012	100.0	9.2	25.3

Note: Minor inconsistencies result from rounding.

Sources: Columns 1-3: U.S. Department of Commerce, Bureau of the Census, *Exports, Commodity by Country*, December 1971, FT 410-71-12, pp. 1-1 to 1-13; and U.S. Department of Commerce, National Technical Information Service, *U.S. Exports, Schedule B Commodity Groupings, World Area, Country, and Method of Transportation*, EM 450/455, pp. 540-51; Column 4: Calculated from Japan Tariff Association, *Japan Exports and Imports '71.12*.

the suggestion crops up from time to time that the United States is playing the role of the less developed country. Traditional and colonial patterns of trade called for the less developed countries, or colonies, to supply crude materials, and the industrial countries, or metropolitan powers, to provide the manufactured products.

In trans-Pacific trade, most Japanese exports to the United States are manufactured goods, while the flow to Japan from the United States is what we have just seen—slightly more primary products than manufactures.

But one need not take very seriously the less-developed country idea. Colonial days are largely past, and less developed countries like Hong Kong, Taiwan, and Korea are exporting manufactured products, especially to high-income countries. The United States has very rich agricultural and mineral resources, unlike poorly endowed Japan, and in addition, American methods of production are highly advanced. Consequently, American production of the primary products sold to Japan is very efficient, both technically and economically. To an economist, export of such products makes excellent sense.

At the same time the United States sells large and rapidly growing quantities of manufactured goods to Japan, especially machinery. Japan still depends heavily on the United States for new technology and the best of new machinery that embodies such technology. The share of manufactured goods in American exports to Japan is rising, and has doubled since 1954, as these figures show:

Share of Total U.S. Exports to Japan (%)[2]

	Primary Products	Manufactures
1954	77	23
1960	67	33
1971	52	48

There is one way in which the United States does indeed share the disadvantage of any primary exporting country. This drop in the share of primary exports to Japan reflects partly Japanese shifts to purchasing in other countries, but also in part Japan's declining general dependence on primary imports, in that such imports rise less rapidly than production and income in Japan. The reasons include technical advances in Japanese agriculture, artificial supports to Japanese agriculture, technical improvements in manufacturing that economize on raw materials, and production of synthetic substitutes for imported primary products. Thus, while United States sales of manufactures to Japan in 1971 were almost ten times those of 1954, sales of primary products were only a little over three times their earlier figure. To make a might-have-been calculation, if primary product sales to Japan had risen as much as sales of manufactured goods, then in 1971 United States sales to Japan would have been: primary $6,323 million, manufactured $1,923 million, total $8,246 million, or more than double actual total exports and $985 million more than actual imports.[3]

Japan has traditionally felt disadvantaged by the need to import large quantities of primary products. Is it now Japan, or the United States, that suffers?

Commodities Moving to the United States

Composition of the Trade. The United States has been the largest outlet for Japanese exports during nearly all the period since Japan commenced trading abroad in the nineteenth century. But what Japan has to sell, and what the United States wants—or is willing—to buy, are radically different now from what they used to be. In the 1920s and earlier, Japan's principal export was raw silk, and the United States was by a wide margin the largest market for this product. In 1934 for the first time, raw silk was displaced, and cotton textiles took the number-one position among Japanese exports. Toys and "sundry goods" also became more significant export items. Many of these new products came to the United States. Such light manufactures, unlike silk, competed with American production, a serious matter in the economically deprived 1930s. Protectionism joined with political opposition to Japan's aggressive ventures in Asia to arouse strong American opposition to Japanese goods and to trading with Japan. The low quality of many Japanese manufactures received frequent comment, but it did not prevent a rapid increase in Japanese exports, either to the United States or to other markets. In the early years after World War II, as Japanese exports slowly recovered, it was these same light manufactures that first began to flow abroad. The same problems of quality existed, combined with other problems, such as design and cost, as well as the familiar opposition in the United States and elsewhere to competition from Japanese products.

As the 1950s wore on, new products appeared in the export list one after another. During the 1960s new products came to dominate both Japan's total exports and the growing share of these exports that was coming to the United States. In 1960, 53 percent of Japan's exports to the United States consisted of textiles, clothing, and miscellaneous products such as toys, footwear, plywood and pearls. Radios and all other electric machinery accounted for just under 10 percent of the total, and transportation machinery of all kinds less than 1 percent.[4] In 1970 textiles and all the other light manufactures together made up only 23.7 percent of total exports to the United States, while "heavy and chemical products" made up 72.4 percent.[5]

Table 5-6 lists the principal commodity groups and subgroups of imports into the United States from Japan in 1971. The predominance of manufactures is so nearly complete that the first five commodity groups (codes 0-4), covering primary products, account for only 3.1 percent of total 1971 imports. More than half of this small total is in one subgroup—fish.

The manufactured goods include a very wide array of both traditional light manufactures and of the now more important heavy manufactures.

Table 5-6
United States Imports from Japan by Commodity Group, with Principal Subgroups, 1971

Commodity Code and Name	Value ($ million)	Share of U.S. Imports from Japan (%)	Japan's Share of U.S. Imports from All Countries (%)	U.S. Share of Japan's Exports to All Countries (%)
0 Food and Live Animals	167	2.3	3.0	20.6
03 Fish and preparations	128	1.8	14.6	27.7
1 Beverages and Tobacco	3	0.04	0.3	16.1
2 Crude Materials, inedible	43	0.6	1.3	9.1
3 Mineral Fuels, Lubricants, etc.	4	0.06	0.1	7.4
4 Oils and Fats, Animal and Vegetable	7	0.1	4.1	25.8
Total codes 0-4 ("Primary")	224	3.1	1.6	16.1
5 Chemicals	196	2.7	12.2	12.9
6 Manufactures, by Material	2,158	29.7	22.6	27.9
62 Rubber manufactures	56	0.8	21.3	25.1
631 Plywood, veneer, etc.	55	0.8	15.7	64.6
632 Other wood manufactures	25	0.3	17.6	59.7
64 Paper and products	27	0.4	2.3	13.2
65 Textiles	376	5.2	27.0	19.1
66 Nonmetallic mineral manufactures	142	2.0	14.1	37.6
67 Iron and Steel	1,080	14.9	39.6	28.3
68 Nonferrous metal	56	0.8	3.6	25.7
69 Metal manufactures, other	334	4.6	39.9	42.3
7 Machinery and Transport Equipment	3,214	44.3	23.1	33.5
71 Machinery, other than electric	513	7.1	15.0	20.0
714 Office machine and parts	171	2.4	30.2	41.1

717	Textile and leather machinery & parts	82	1.1	16.4	20.5
72	Electrical machinery	1,132	15.6	44.3	44.9
722	Electric power machinery	68	0.9	25.9	19.9
723	Equipment for distributing electricity	29	0.4	27.4	26.0
724	Telecommunications apparatus	821	11.3	62.2	55.7
724.1	Television receivers	323	4.4	77.8	67.4
724.2	Radio receivers	327	4.5	65.7	56.9
725	Electric household appliances	58	0.8	36.7	44.3
73	Transport equipment	1,569	21.6	19.8	33.5
732.1	Motor vehicles	1,025	13.8	18.8	57.1
732.9	Motor cycles	432	5.9	82.4	70.6
8	Miscellaneous Manufactured Articles	1,377	19.0	25.6	47.1
84	Clothing and accessories	275	3.8	18.1	62.0
85	Footwear	95	1.3	12.5	67.5
86	Professional photographic, etc., goods, clocks	244	3.4	35.0	30.9
861	Scientific and optical apparatus	187	2.6	49.1	29.0
861.4 &.5	Cameras and projectors	88	1.2	72.7	33.9
891.1	Phonographs, tape recorders, etc.	369	5.1	81.1	54.8
891.4 &.8	Pianos and other musical instruments	40	0.6	60.6	50.5
894.2	Children's toys, Christmas decorations	73	1.0	28.9	54.8
894.4	Fishing, hunting, sports equipment	45	0.6	29.4	55.3
9	Items not classified by kind	92	1.3	6.2	42.7
	Total codes 5-9 ("Manufactured")	7,037	96.9	22.0	32.0
	Total Imports	7,261	100.00	15.9	31.2

Note: Minor inconsistencies result from rounding.

Sources: Columns 1-3: U.S. Department of Commerce, Bureau of the Census, *General Imports, World Area by Commodity Groupings*, annual 1971, pp. 1-18, 391-99; Column 4: Japan Tariff Association, *Japan Exports and Imports '71.12*, Commodity by Country, pp. 1-21, and Country by Commodity, pp. 547-566.

Importance in Japanese Exports. The United States market is a very large factor in Japan's exports; in 1971 the overall share was 31.2 percent. To achieve such a high overall figure, the United States has to take a far larger proportion of some individual products. The highest share shown in the last column of Table 5-6 is 71 percent for motorcycles. But altogether $3,225 million of 1971 imports from Japan, or 45 percent of the total, consisted of categories for which the United States took half or more of total Japanese exports. The categories were:

Category	Share of Japanese Exports Going to the United States, 1971
	(%)
Motorcycles	71
Footwear	68
Plywood	65
Clothing	62
Other wood manufactures	60
Motor vehicles	57
Telecommunications apparatus (includes television receivers (67), radio receivers (57) and other items)	56
Sporting goods	55
Phonographs, tape recorders, etc.	55
Children's toys and Christmas decorations	55
Pianos and other musical instruments	51

Japanese exporters generally, and especially producers of these particular products, rely on the American market to an extent that far exceeds the dependence of most American producers on the Japanese market. No wonder that Japanese are so apprehensive at potential, as well as actual, threats to their sales in the United States.

Importance in United States Imports. Imports from Japan are generally a less important factor for American importers than for Japanese exporters. As the last figure in the third column of Table 5-6 shows in comparison with the last figure in the fourth column, Japanese sales in the United States make up only 16 percent of U.S. imports but 31 percent of Japanese exports.[a] For manufactured goods alone, Japan is somewhat more important to the United States and the figures are 22 and 32 percent, respectively, in the last two columns of Table 5-6.

Still, Japanese sources provide the bulk of some imports, and in a few cases dominate even more than the United States market stands out in sales of

---

[a]Because total U.S. imports in 1971 were almost twice the total of Japanese exports. The figures were $45,602 million and $24,019 million, respectively.

Japanese exports. The following categories show 60 percent or more of total 1971 imports as coming from Japan:

Category	Share of Total U.S. Imports That Came from Japan, 1971 (%)
Motorcycles	82
Phonographs, tape recorders, etc.	81
Cameras and projectors	73
Telecommunications apparatus (includes television receivers (78), radio receivers (66) and other items)	62
Pianos and other musical instruments	61

Balances of Trade in Primary Products and Manufactures

Combining the total figures for the primary products and manufactures groups in Tables 5-4, 5-5, and 5-6, we get the following pattern for 1971:

(millions of dollars)	U.S. Exports to Japan	U.S. Imports from Japan	Balance
Primary products	2068	224	+1844
Manufactures	1923	7037	−5114
Total (excluding special category)	3991	7261	−3270

Thus primary products moved overwhelmingly toward Japan, the return flow from Japan to the United States being little over one-tenth as large. Manufactures moved in both directions, but the flow from Japan to the United States was well over three times as large as the flow from here to Japan, and the net import into the United States exceeded $5 billion. This contrast of primary products moving outward from the United States and manufactured products moving mostly inward is sharper than in American trade with any other country. And the import surplus of over $5 billion in manufactured goods is unique in American foreign trade experience.

The American Market as a Key Factor in a
Basically Successful International Economy

The reasons why Japan is so highly efficient in producing these various export products are analyzed in much of the literature on the Japanese economy and its growth. The world has been surprised by the phenomenal success of the Japanese in making modern products so well and so cheaply. Most attention is going to this production and growth "miracle." The other side of the export story lies in foreign markets. Here there has been a turnaround as unexpected as it is successful for Japan. Indeed, if one had looked carefully at Japan's economic experience up to 1945, it should perhaps have been foreseen that the capable and energetic Japanese would succeed in modern technology, economic organization, management and production. Few, perhaps, might have expected the phenomenal degree of success the Japanese have shown in recent years, but general success was predictable.

It is the availability of export and import markets that was less predictable. Commercial policy has been a difficult area for Japan from the beginning of foreign trade after the forced opening in 1854. Colonial empires and trade patterns, as well as the tariffs and quotas encountered in Japan's export drive in the 1930s, were substantial elements in the origins of the Japanese policy of seeking a Greater East Asia Co-Prosperity Sphere. Japan did not expect to be able to export enough to pay for necessary imports without Japanese control over a large area.

Only during the latter half of the 1960s did the balance-of-payments constraint relax to the point where Japanese and others could agree that exports were not deficient and that Japan could count on paying its way in the world. Now confidence in export markets, although far from complete, is high enough so that most discussions of Japanese economic growth concentrate mainly on domestic factors.

The United States and the American market have been crucial in this phenomenal change. The American market has been open to Japanese products to a degree that was not predictable. Much of the literature about trade barriers and United States commercial policy throughout the postwar period seems to suggest that U.S. import barriers might make impossible a rise of imports from Japan of the magnitude that has occurred. But the United States government has resisted with notable, although far from complete, success various protectionist pressures against Japanese goods. And the United States led in the establishment of international economic and financial policies that have fostered world trade and let Japan prosper. All the advanced industrial countries have avoided severe economic depression, and most, including the United States in the 1960s, have expanded their economies (and import markets) at moderate to brisk rates. Perhaps in all the world Japan is the country most benefited by the new international economic circumstances that included convertibility of currencies, tariff reductions, opposition to quantitative import restrictions, and the appearance of both institutions and policies aimed at liberalizing trade, freeing payments and promoting economic growth in rich and poor countries alike.

One result has been that the United States has absorbed a rising share of Japan's phenomenally expanding exports, most of which are—or were at first—competitive with American products. Thus the record to date does great credit, not only to Japanese producers and exporters and to American importers, who have in many cases taken the initiative, but also to American policy, as well as to the principles and policies espoused by liberal economists everywhere.

One important implication of Japan's experience seldom receives attention. Ever since beginning with cotton textiles and other light manufactures before World War II, Japan has been a pioneer in the export of factory products to countries more industrialized than itself, countries with higher per-capita production than Japan. This movement is the opposite of colonial trade, in which the metropolitan center did the manufacturing for the empire, and factory goods flowed "downhill" to the less developed colonies, in return for primary products. What Japan has done in selling very large quantities of factory manufactures to the United States and other leading industrial countries is new in economic history. Following Japan, now Hong Kong, Taiwan, Korea and a growing number of other developing countries have begun to export manufactures "uphill." There is a substantial body of opinion to the effect that such export from low-income countries is hopeless because of the import barriers imposed by the high-income countries. But the vast amount of manufactures of a great many kinds flowing from Japan, and now from other countries, to the high-income countries gives evidence that the market is there and import barriers do not, at least not yet, prevent the flow from continuing and rapidly increasing.

The implications for the developing countries are very hopeful indeed. The textile quotas of 1971 imposed on Hong Kong, Taiwan, and Korea, as well as Japan, remind the world that the United States market is not completely free. But the United States has accepted very large and very rapidly growing amounts of a wide range of imports that compete with domestic production. The textile and steel quotas, although serious in very important product areas, still leave possible a wide range and large volume of sales.

This profound new fact of large and rapidly increasing flows into the United States of manufactured goods that compete with American products has changed Japan's foreign trade as fundamentally as modernization and growth have changed Japan's domestic economy. Other high-income markets in Europe, Australia, New Zealand, and Canada are also buying increasing amounts of Japanese goods, although none compares with the United States in size and importance, nor in tolerance for competitive imports from Japan. Together the high-income countries account for over half of Japanese exports, and the share is still rising.

Trade Problems and Issues

New Problems Along with Old

The recent upsurge of trade between Japan and the United States has exacerbated some old problems and also created new ones. Both kinds are made more difficult by the lopsidedness of recent growth and the very different economic and political significance of the bilateral trade relationship between the two countries.

The familiar problems made more serious by recent events relate mainly to the openness or protectedness of the American and Japanese markets for imports. Japanese regard the American market as vital and react strongly to anything that appears to limit or endanger the market. In the United States, Japanese competition has become a problem for more industries and workers than ever before, and Japan is a significant element of the background to a series of strong protectionist moves in Washington. The American market thus threatens to become less open to imports from Japan than in recent years. The Japanese market, on the other hand, has been tightly controlled and imports have been restricted. By now import liberalization in Japan has gone a long way, but American businessmen are still not satisfied; they want a much more open market in Japan.

The newer problems concern the United States balance of payments, the international monetary system, and the international trading system. Trade with Japan had by the end of 1971 accumulated $8 billion of deficits since 1964, and these are a significant element in the balance of payments of each of the countries—in Japan's mounting surplus and the growing American deficit. This latter became so large in 1971, after two decades of persistence, that the United States took drastic action, upsetting the international monetary system, centered around the International Monetary Fund. At the same time, the United States has initiated a series of trade restrictions, affecting textiles and steel formally and a number of other products less formally, with various results that include questions about the liberal trade principles embodied in the General Agreement on Tariffs and Trade. In the international discussions since President Nixon's dramatic actions of August 1971, the United States has sought to link monetary and trade matters. As matters stood in mid-1972, there was serious doubt about the future of both the world monetary system and the world trading system.

The old and new problems are converging to push the United States toward more protectionist trade policies. At the same time much else is changing in the domestic and foreign affairs of the United States and of Japan, in the arrangements, institutions, and understandings that govern international relations, and in international economic relationships. Trade issues between Japan and the United States are by no means wholly susceptible to bilateral solutions.

Balance-of-Payments Disequilibria

Although commodity trade is a major element in the balances of payments of both Japan and the United States, there is both doubt and debate about the extent to which trade measures could or should serve to eliminate the present large disequilibria in their balances of payments. The foreign exchange rate changes made in the December 1971 Smithsonian Agreement and later will surely in time do much to reduce Japan's surplus disequilibrium and the American deficit disequilibrium. But we do not yet know whether the rate changes are enough, or even how long we need to wait for results. In both Japan and the United States, but especially here, there is heavy pressure to take other actions, meanwhile, to supplement the exchange rate changes, or for other reasons.

Standard economic theory says that there is some exchange rate that will tend to bring about equilibrium in a balance of payments under most circumstances. But not every one seems to accept this theory as feasible for the United States or for Japan. And in any case there remains doubt that the Smithsonian rates will prove to be equilibrium rates, especially since the pound sterling has already been floated from its Smithsonian rate. Meanwhile, the massive momentum of Japan's commodity trade surplus seems undiminished six months after the Smithsonian Agreement. There were, however, reports that contracts for future Japanese exports were beginning to show a lower rate of increase than before.[6] Despite these qualifications, the exchange rate is, in my view, the proper main reliance for basic change in the trade and payments balances.

An economic slowdown in Japan (to *only* 5.7 percent increase in real g.n.p. in Japan's fiscal year, April 1971-March 1972!)[7] has reduced the Japanese demand for imports of both raw materials and machinery, leading to a reduction in United States exports to Japan in 1971. Demand will pick up with expected recovery. If at the same time the effects of the Smithsonian Agreement are beginning to show, there could be a sharp change in the bilateral trade balance.

A major reason why the balance-of-payments disequilibria interfere with settlement of bilateral trade questions is that international circumstances cannot be predicted. It is frequently suggested that another yen revaluation may soon be necessary; so the exchange rate between the yen and the dollar is uncertain. The details of a new monetary system to succeed the Bretton Woods system cannot be anticipated. Nor is it possible to predict what major new trade circumstances or rules may result from international trade negotiations during the next year or two. In all three of these matters, persistence of recent large disequilibria in balances of payments would very likely lead to results substantially different from those to be expected if disequilibria decline substantially by, say, the middle of 1973.

Balance-of-payments disequilibria are being used as the basis for various action proposals in both Japan and the United States, including further import liberalization by Japan and more vigorous export efforts by American firms, which were proposed in the June 1972 Joint Communique of the joint businessmen's committees.[b] Some suggestions are for severely restrictive United States import policies, for instance the comprehensive quotas called for in the Burke-Hartke bill.[8] Whatever happens to this particular bill, the balance-of-payments deficit is a convenient excuse for almost any proposal to limit imports. As long as the American deficit is a serious problem, we can expect it to be used as a basis for such proposals.

We come to the question of what policy is appropriate concerning the bilateral trade balance. Because trade is only part, although a large part, of the balance of payments, and for other reasons including the possible results to be expected from the Smithsonian Agreement, it is hazardous to base policy on the trade balance, especially if the policy might possibly stay in effect longer than the trade deficit lasts. What is preferable is to push even harder, because of the deficit, for policies that seem desirable in any case, deficit or no. Action directed to affecting the trade balance by the United States should avoid directly restricting imports and focus instead on stimulating exports.

Such proposals as those in the Joint Communique of June 17, 1972, cited above, seem eminently desirable. On the Japanese side, further import liberalization is a basic economic measure, which can be expected to yield returns to the Japanese economy in wider choice to buyers and lower prices. Both economic and political relations with the United States would be improved by such measures, which will probably help to reduce the imbalance of trade between the two countries.

Measures to strengthen the export efforts and competitiveness of American producers are desirable for various reasons, including the impact on the deficits in our trade and payments. But such measures take time to have effect, and once they reach that stage, it would be neither practicable nor wise to try to stop their momentum quickly at some future time. Japan's export momentum today reflects competitiveness that has become institutionalized.

I do not see justification for restrictions on imports into the United States on balance-of-payments grounds, as long as there are reasonable means to finance the balance-of-payments deficits. But I do see many reasons to seek to approach equilibrium in the balance of payments. Among these reasons are the dangers of protectionist arguments based on the present deficit. Such arguments, even though weak economically, remain a potential threat that is increased as long as the deficit persists. A somewhat parallel point might be made with respect to

---

[b]Issued on June 17, 1972 at the conclusion of the annual meeting of the Japan-U.S. Economic Council and the Advisory Council on Japan-U.S. Economic Relations. The businessmen urged several such immediate actions and added, "In the U.S. view, such measures should in aggregate dollar terms be large enough to reduce the trade deficit substantially below last year's $3.2 billion." p. 4.

Japan's balance-of-payments surplus. As long as a large surplus persists, Japan will be under international pressure of one sort or another, and possibly also domestic pressure, to take action Japan's leaders may not want, or which may be economically foolish.

One measure that Japan might well adopt is to establish national reserves of essential imported materials, against such hazards as war, or other possible interference to shipping. Japan's main vulnerability is interruption of petroleum imports. Assuming that storage facilities can be prepared with adequate protection against earthquake, Japan might well choose to keep several months' supply in reserve. Details of such a policy have not been announced, but there are fairly large swings in Japanese imports of primary products as Japanese business accelerates and decelerates. As we have seen, this is the main reason for slack U.S. exports to Japan recently, including a 13 percent decline from 1970 to 1971. The change here contemplated might well be combined with public funding to even out import flows. Once Japan undertook such policies, it would encounter the usual problems of the stockpiler, especially difficulties in knowing when to intervene in commodity markets. But Japan is becoming such an enormous consumer and importer of primary products that the world must expect Japanese actions to have progressively more influence on commodity markets. From Japan's point of view, a large balance-of-payments surplus is one factor that might accelerate buying for stockpile. Others would include mainly price, but increasingly also considerations related to capacity operation of Japanese-owned mines and other facilities abroad and to honoring long-term purchase contracts.

Such measures as these fall far short of setting quantitative goals for the bilateral balance of trade. What is needed is something approaching equilibrium in the balance of *payments*. Just now, both trade and payments show large American deficits and large Japanese surpluses. Measures to reduce these are appropriate. The principal measure is to seek an equilibrium rate of exchange. But these, and any other appropriate measure, will take time to be effective. And when equilibrium arrives, Japan-United States trade should not be saddled with restrictions or rigidities that have outlived an original purpose related to the balance of trade.

Market Access—Japanese and American

The most basic of the familiar problems of Japan-United States trade is market access. Commodore Perry was the first to tackle it successfully. Nowadays both Japanese and American businessmen are seeking fuller and freer access to the import market in the other country. Japan is becoming more and more liberal toward foreign goods, while the United States is becoming less liberal. Some observers say the Japanese is now the more open of the two markets, but the matter is still debatable.

The Japanese Market. In Japan, import liberalization consists of dismantling a complex array of laws, regulations, practices, and habits built up over the years as a means of assuring that scarce foreign exchange would be used only for the most necessary and useful purposes. Present import restrictions are the residue of controls introduced during the occupation, and these in turn had a background of wartime controls. For well over a decade now, restrictions have been relaxed progressively until there are only a few categories of goods still subject to formal quantitative import control.

Not surprisingly, Japanese habits of control have held on longer than most observers, especially American exporters, have considered appropriate, while Japan's balance of payments has been growing stronger, especially during the 1960s. Bureaucratic lag and business habits resisted acknowledging in full the degree to which defenses were becoming unnecessary against former threats to the balance of payments. But as the balance-of-payments basis for import restrictions has receded, Japanese protectionist policy has become more evident. As matters now stand, the main American complaint relates less to the few residual formal controls (although some still rankle among Americans[c]). The main target is the less visible and formal controls that are part of Japanese practice, notably "administrative guidance," and government-business consensus.[9] Some Americans regard the import resistances originating here as both severe and particularly difficult to change. Japanese, on the other hand, often deny that these processes restrict imports unduly, and urge American exporters to get closer to the inner workings of the Japanese economy by learning the Japanese language and finding out about administrative practice and individual Japanese industrial activities. Indeed, Japanese are beginning to provide assistance to American exporters, as noted earlier.

The problem of market access in Japan now seems to me to be less one of specific restrictions than of trade flows and psychology. As long as the trade and payments balances are far from satisfactory, people will complain, and Japanese practices will be an object of the complaint. Once the balances stop being a problem, complaints may continue but shift to Japanese distribution and marketing policy internally. Japanese practice is different from that in the United States. It will take a higher degree of sophistication in things Japanese before most Americans attempting to do business in Japan can evaluate accurately the openness of the Japanese import market and take full advantage of it.

The American Market. Japanese have long been apprehensive about foreign import barriers, especially in the United States market. The large proportion of Japanese exports going to the United States, the large shares Japan now provides of United States imports of some particular products, and Japan's likely need for

---

[c]The Joint Communique cited above mentions integrated circuits, computers and "other high-technology intensive goods." p. 3.

further rapid increases in exports, reinforce such apprehensions, in view of the strong protectionist sentiments now influencing U.S. policy. Until now, or at least until recently, these Japanese apprehensions have proved far too pessimistic, as reality has proved far more favorable than even the most optimistic projections.

On the American side, firms that compete with imports from Japan share with workers and their unions a fear of losses from imports. Here too, such apprehensions in the past have proved far too pessimistic, and unexpectedly large imports from Japan have caused unexpectedly little difficulty in the American economy. Now, with a substantial worldwide import surplus, the United States is very likely importing goods that represent more employment than goes into American exports.[d] If the purpose of foreign trade were to create work, then American trade would now be failing, as protectionists contend. But economists view foreign trade, along with technology, principally as a means to maximize output per unit of input, and by this criterion American foreign trade is a most useful economic sector. Still, since many American individuals and interest groups think in terms of jobs, the present position makes liberal trade policy vulnerable.

For a generation since World War II, the United States has followed a liberal trade policy and led the world in erecting institutions that have fostered such policies, especially among the major trading nations. There was a strong spirit behind United States leadership in creating GATT and in making the Bretton Woods system work. The failure of Congress to approve ITO was a reverse, raising many doubts about Japan's commercial future after the occupation. But United States leadership continued, and the new institutions and policies worked. The circumstances of world trade grew generally better until the mid-1960s.

An important related point for Japan was American concern for Japan's economic success. Special American consideration for Japan began during the occupation, grew rapidly as cold war considerations made sharply clear the advantages for the United States of a strong and friendly Japan, and received a further boost in the Korean War when the United States depended heavily on Japan as a military base. This American concern for Japan led the United States to sponsor Japan in GATT, the UN, OECD and other organizations, and strengthened the resolve of successive administrations in Washington in their efforts to resist protectionist moves that would hurt Japanese trade.

Now this special relationship between the United States and Japan has ended. President Nixon seemed to intend to shock Japan in the way he announced in

---

[d]The Trade Relations Council, Washington, D.C., prepares figures in great detail showing the "net job equivalent" of imports and exports. For 1969, even before the 1971 trade deficit, the effect of foreign trade in manufactures (leaving out agriculture, forestry, mining and other fields) was calculated to reduce employment by a net figure of 151,650 jobs. Trade Relations Council of the United States, Inc., *Employment, Output, and Foreign Trade of U.S. Manufacturing Industries, 1958-69/70* (Washington, D.C., 1972), pp. ix-x.

July 1971 that he planned to visit Peking. Clearly the economic policy changes announced in August 1971 sought to change the yen's value more than that of any other currency (since the mark and other strong currencies had already appreciated to some extent). And the threat of unilateral textile import quotas under the authority of the Trading-with-the-Enemy Act was aimed primarily at Japan. It was evident that the Nixon Administration regarded Japan as too strong to need special American consideration any longer, and strong enough to accede to American demands (although not strong enough to resist them).

If Japan can no longer count on special consideration from Washington, what is the prospect that general United States commercial policy will be sufficiently successful to meet Japan's needs? Today's circumstances and today's mood in the United States are very different from those following World War II. Far from feeling strong and confident and being determined to lead toward freer world trade, American leadership today seems defensive about Vietnam and many unsolved domestic problems, and tends to show resentment that past American support is not more appreciated and present American policies more supported.

Other reasons for doubt about American policy arise from the wave of protectionist sentiment that has arisen since the end of the Kennedy Round negotiations in mid-1967. The AFL-CIO is no longer a supporter of liberal United States trade policies, but instead now advocates quota restrictions on imports, in particular supporting the rigid Burke-Hartke bill, as mentioned above. The unemployment caused by President Nixon's antiinflationary policy has strengthened the protectionist position of organized labor. Never since World War II have protectionist forces seemed so strong.

Recent American restrictions on imports include not only the new textile quotas but also quotas on steel, as well as a number of less formal restrictions. In deference to American concern, Japanese automobile producers are now reportedly holding back on sales in the United States.[10] In the name of "orderly marketing," a number of other Japanese commodities are reportedly being similarly restrained without public acknowledgment.

In addition, the Nixon administration has tightened up the administration of two old laws, and this action looks like import restriction, despite official denials. They relate to dumping, and to countervailing duties to offset foreign export subsidies.[11] Tightening of the antidumping law has reached a point where Japanese domestic prices are watched closely and compared with prices of the same Japanese goods in the United States. During the first half of 1972, this scrutiny extended to checking price changes after the Smithsonian Agreement. The Treasury Department contended that sales prices in the United States should rise by the full 16.88 percent that the yen had risen in dollar terms, unless prices in Japan were reduced.

Cases affecting Japan include antidumping charges on television receivers and a charge of Japanese subsidy to "certain electronic products." The effect of such cases, and of the policies behind them, is to increase substantially the risk a

Japanese exporter undertakes in selling in the United States. Throughout an investigation all sales made involve the possibility of later additional import duty. The time involved has been shortened, but substantial hazard remains.[e]

Japanese goods in the American market are sometimes called "excessive," especially in the share of total Japanese exports that come to the United States. This share, recently above 30 percent overall and much higher for certain products, is certainly large, more than twice that of any other country to which Japan exports. But how would one judge whether the American share is "excessive"? Not by any consumer resistance in the United States. Not by any universal or abstract rule about what is too much in a market economy. Possibly by a finding that the effects on the American economy are in some ways more painful than the gains from trade are worth, but such a finding would relate to the *volume* of Japanese goods coming in, not their proportion as compared with those going to other countries.

There are two ways that one might possibly say the American share of Japanese exports was too high. One would relate to the problems caused by imports from Japan and would apply if these problems would be notably eased simply by larger Japanese sales in other markets, without any change in Japanese sales here. Such a case seems most unlikely, since Americans who protest against imports usually are thinking of little beyond their own particular interests.

The other way to say that the United States is taking an excessive share of Japanese exports would be simply to say that other markets are taking too little, however one might define too much or too little. It certainly seems true that Europe, with its high per capita incomes, large foreign trade, and high demand for products such as Japan exports, could gain economically by taking more advantage of Japanese goods and Japanese prices. Here lies a task for Japanese exporters, made more difficult by what appears to be strong and possibly rising European resistance to Japanese products, based mainly on protectionist grounds, but also on psychological grounds.

I do not regard as excessive either the amount or the share of Japanese exports that come into the American market. But I do hope Japan can succeed better in other markets. This hope is based on concern for Japan's economic health and for economic development in the whole world, as well as on dissatisfaction with protection anywhere and with the other motives that appear to lie behind European resistance to Japanese goods. My hope is related also to a preference for freer international trade generally.

---

[e]On a worldwide basis, "antidumping investigations which previously took two to three years are generally being completed now by the Treasury in nine to twelve months. Complaints filed during the past three years have been 50 percent greater than during 1966-1968. And the number of final decisions published by the Treasury over the same time period has increased by 80 percent." Rossides, cited, p. 6.: "one of the consequences of the new approach was to make it more difficult for them [foreign exporters] to sell their merchandise in the United States." Ibid., p. 7.

Orderly Marketing and Economic Readjustment

Throughout nearly all the two decades since the end of the occupation, Japan has experienced rapid export growth. One element in this growth has been the introduction of one product after another that has rapidly gained large sales in foreign markets. The first recorded case was women's blouses in the 1950s, whose export to the United States rose as follows:

Year	000 Dozen Blouses[1][2]
1953	5
1954	171
1955	3,996

The figure for 1955, 47,952,000 blouses, was enough for almost every American woman of blouse-wearing age in a total population that was then 166 million. This influx in two years from the first arrival of any Japanese blouses could only have been disruptive to American blousemakers, even though the low price of the Japanese "dollar blouses" attracted a new and far larger market than had existed for the higher priced American blouses.

The result was more violent than usual for new Japanese products, just as the explosive increase in shipments of blouses exceeded growth in most other cases. Before the end of 1955, the secretary of state "personally advised representatives of the Japanese government that they should exercise restraint in their exports and not attempt to capture so much of the American market that an American industry will be injured."[13] This statement referred not only to blouses but also to other cotton manufactures that were flowing into the United States in rapidly rising volume. Quotas appeared almost immediately, informal for the year 1956, and quite formal thereafter. These quotas followed discussions between American and Japanese representatives, amidst a background of publicity in the United States, escape-clause proceedings in the Tariff Commission, and several state laws requiring the retail stores concerned to display large signs saying "Japanese Textiles Sold Here."[14] Quotas have restrained Japanese cotton textile shipments to the United States ever since.*

Only a few other Japanese products, mostly cotton textile items, have involved so much public discussion as blouses. Not until the discussions over quotas on man-made and woolen textiles, 1969-71, did another quota discussion become a matter of major high-level governmental tension between Japan and the United States. Quotas have been applied to steel much less noisily, and to various other products even more quietly, although now they reportedly apply to such Japanese exports as automobiles.

What has happened is that the Japanese have found ways to gauge American

---

*See Chapter 7.

political tolerance as well as customer preferences. By avoiding undue "market disruption," through "orderly marketing," Japanese exporters have been able to make rapidly increasing sales, usually without a public uproar. Only when imports pass some critical tolerance limit does the public hear about an issue. It is impossible to tell when Japanese exporters may have misjudged on the other side and stopped short of making all possible sales within the political tolerance of the Americans.

Such "voluntary restraint" by the Japanese is sometimes wholly voluntary on their part. Often, however, official discussions are involved, before or after the initiation of Japanese restraint action. Sometimes the degree of pressure applied by the United States government is very great, most of all in the 1971 textile quotas, when the president himself was involved, and the United States threatened to impose import quotas under the Trading-with-the-Enemy Act.

The Japanese have thus found a way to succeed in the American market and at the same time minimize the specific cases of uproar and resistance over particular products. In doing so, Japanese exporters have acted like oligopolists, who must take account of the market effects of their own actions, by contrast with individual sellers in a purely competitive market, where no seller can detect the effects on the market of his own action. This whole development reflects a high and rising degree of sophistication on the part of the Japanese in relation to the American market.

Now we are hearing the suggestion that such "economic diplomacy" be applied not only to individual products but also to the totality of Japanese exports to the United States, as well as to sensitive import products in cases of shortage. There is nothing in the Japanese background to suggest opposition to such "diplomacy" except that, of course, the Japanese concerned in any case must be convinced of the need for restraint or other action; that is they must see the alternatives as less satisfactory to them and to Japan.

Japan's "shock" at President Nixon's radical economic policy reversals in August 1971 represents failure of "economic diplomacy" at the highest level. But the failure was not one of principle. There was no opposition to taking such action as would pragmatically advance Japanese interest. The failure in August 1971 resulted from misjudgments about the situation, about American concern for its own balance of payments, and about President Nixon's readiness to be stern with Japan.

My conclusion is that the pragmatic Japanese are psychologically ready for whatever may appear to be necessary or advantageous to Japan under any of the terms here placed in quotation marks: "Orderly marketing" through "voluntary restraint" to avoid "market disruption," or even "economic diplomacy." This last term is often used in Japan in another sense to relate to foreign aid and other policies toward less developed countries, but my use of the term here is consistent with that other Japanese usage.

What then are the issues? I see two. First, the Japanese need to understand the rules under which they are carrying on their foreign trade. They have not always understood them adequately. Within the rules, the Japanese, like any other players, need to operate effectively, and even on this score the 1971 shock showed lagging Japanese performance. But in general I expect from the Japanese very skillful activities within accepted rules.

Second, I see a very serious problem indeed for American trade policy. "Orderly marketing" and the rest are ways of controlling trade, not of making it free. As indicated above, "voluntary restraint" admits the imperfection of competition and calls for conduct becoming an oligopolist. American trade policy has not formally made such admission. Formally, American trade policy seeks the freest possible trade and much American trade policy actively continues to seek to reduce trade barriers.

Japanese may justifiably complain when American policy professes to seek freer trade but also presses Japan repeatedly to impose restrictions on trade. It has not been the Japanese who professed free trade as a doctrine. But it has been against Japanese exports that the majority of American initiatives have sought "voluntary restraint" and "orderly marketing."

To make "orderly marketing" consistent with the liberal trade principles professed by the United States since World War II, some principles or rules are necessary. To be really valuable such principles should be multilateral and apply to all trading nations, especially the major industrial countries. Space is not available here for detailed explanation of a set of proposed rules on "orderly marketing." But if the United States still seeks freer trade, here are some conditions to keep "orderly marketing" from becoming a new form of the old-fashioned cartel:

1. Every market restraint should have a time limit, with strict limitations on renewals. It should hardly ever, if at all, be necessary to continue restraints for as long as the sixteen years during which Japan has already restrained exports of cotton textiles.
2. With a terminal date compulsory, every market restraint must relax progressively, at a pace that removes all restraint in the time provided.
3. Along with such progressively less stringent restraints must go measures to assist the affected industry, workers, communities, etc. In some cases the assistance can make the industry competitive by the end of the restraints. Other cases will call for the relocation of displaced labor and other factors. Failure of readjustment assistance thus far in the United States puts more burden than is necessary or justified on the individuals, communities, etc., affected by imports.
4. GATT or some other international organization should police the arrangements, to make sure they aid in transition from restrained, controlled trade to free competition. This last requirement may prove even more difficult than the others.

This brief list of requirements for "civilizing" the quotas, voluntary or otherwise, suggests how far present "orderly marketing" is from the basic principles of liberal trade. Japan is now strong enough to have a large stake in such principles. If the United States wishes to have Japan move further toward free trade, something like these requirements will have to come into effect. If they do, and if Japan adopts generally liberal trading principles, Japan can continue to prosper. So will other countries that trade with Japan, including the United States, which would be limiting its commitment to support noncompetitive industries and simultaneously signaling such industries that limitations on imports will no longer be an endless process.

Notes

1. "Basically the aim of the mission is to inform Americans of the growing potentials of the Japanese consumer market." Japan-U.S. Economic Council, "U.S.-Export-to-Japan Promotion Mission, May 15-26, 1972" (Tokyo: Author, 1972), p. 1.

2. Figures for 1971 from Tables 5-4 and 5-5. Earlier figures from Warren S. Hunsberger, JAPAN AND THE UNITED STATES IN WORLD TRADE (New York: Harper and Row for Council on Foreign Relations, 1964), pp. 198-99.

3. Calculated from ibid. and Table 5-1 above.

4. Japan External Trade Organization (JETRO), FOREIGN TRADE OF JAPAN, 1961, p. 184.

5. Ibid., 1971, pp. 162-3.

6. U.S.-Japan Trade Council, Washington, D.C., 6 July 1972.

7. Bank of Tokyo, WEEKLY REVIEW, June 19, 1972, p. 1.

8. Nat Goldfinger (Research Director, AFL-CIO), "Imports Undermine American Industry," WASHINGTON POST June 25, 1972, p. F 1. The Burke-Hartke bill, which is strongly supported by the AFL-CIO, provides (among other things including controls over foreign investment) for a commission with power to establish quantitative controls over any imports. "The Foreign Trade and Investment Act of 1972," Title III Quantitative Restraints on Imports. The Senate form of this bill, S. 2592, was introduced on September 28, 1971 by Senator Hartke of Indiana. The bill had not passed either House by June 30, 1972, but there appeared a possibility that parts of it may be enacted, perhaps as riders on other legislation.

9. Described, for instance, in Eugene J. Kaplan, JAPAN, THE GOVERN-MENT-BUSINESS RELATIONSHIP (U.S. Department of Commerce, Bureau of International Commerce, Washington, D.C.: GPO, February 1972), Chapter 4 and elsewhere.

10. U.S.-Japan Trade Council, 6 July 1972.

11. See, for instance, Eugene T. Rossides, Assistant Secretary of the Treasury for Enforcement, Tariff and Trade Affairs, and Operations, "Antidumping and Countervailing Duty Laws: Instruments for Freer Trade; Three and One-Half Years of Rejuvenation," address before the U.S. Council, International Chamber of Commerce, New York, N.Y., June 28, 1972 (Washington, D.C.: Department of the Treasury NEWS, June 28, 1972, p. 11).

12. Warren S. Hunsberger, JAPAN AND THE UNITED STATES IN WORLD TRADE (New York: Harper and Row for Council on Foreign Relations, 1964), p. 293, from Japan Textile Products Exporters' Association.

13. Hunsberger, cited, p. 317.

14. Ibid., pp. 310-24.

6

Evolution of Foreign Direct Investment: The United States and Japan

Lawrence B. Krause

The economies of both Japan and the United States are directed by a mixture of market forces and government activity with the former predominating. This basic similarity is often overlooked or underweighted in the comparison of the two economies. There are, of course, numerous and important differences in public and private institutions that rightfully deserve attention, but the basic forces underlying the economies are similar. Thus understanding the experience of one economy helps in the appraisal of the future of the other, and the analysis can be conducted in both directions. Crucial to the analysis is the role of long-run profit maximization as the motivating force for private business decisions and the central position of the private sectors in both economies.

A particularly interesting application of a comparative examination relates to the role of foreign direct investment by Japan and the United States. Direct investment is the most advanced form of foreign involvement that can be undertaken by a business firm. While not the first major country to send abroad large amounts of direct investment, the United States is now the world's largest direct foreign investor and its experience should be relevant to the understanding of Japanese foreign investment. Japan may now be following an investment pattern similar to that of the United States in an earlier period. The following analysis begins by viewing foreign investment from the point of view of the business firm and then focuses on the aggregative consequences of this activity for the economy as a whole.

Foreign Involvement of Business Firms

Business firms prefer to conduct all their business at home, especially in the early stages of their development. This results from the fact that firms are at a tremendous disadvantage when they operate abroad in competition with local business. Among the numerous reasons for this disadvantage, the most important one is the firms' own ignorance. Lack of knowledge of the language, legal system, governmental machinery, commercial and financial channels, labor markets, business traditions, and consumers' tastes in foreign countries are

---

The views expressed are those of the author and should not be attributed to the Staff, Officers or Trustees of the Brookings Institution.

among the factors, and they all combine to make commerce difficult if not impossible for the foreigner. As is well known, the cost of obtaining knowledge is great and its value is always rather uncertain.

Another handicap to foreign firms is loyalty to local producers—or looked at from the other side of the same coin—natural prejudice against foreigners as expressed by consumers, local producers, or by extra-legal actions of government. In addition, legal discriminations against foreigners in the form of taxes or regulations are universally enforced by governments. These legal discriminations may be motivated by purely political consideration, may represent an effort by the government to improve the economic well-being of domestic residents at the expense of foreigners, or may reflect mercantilist ideas that result in the redistribution of income within the economy toward privileged producers.

Taken together, these various factors provide ample justification for firms to remain at home to avoid difficulties and to benefit from discrimination against foreigners. The substantial internationalization of the horizons of businessmen that has in recent years taken place everywhere and particularly in the United States and Japan is thus quite remarkable.

If firms are going to do business abroad, then the motivation must be substantial, especially in the initial venture. Firms are likely to want to minimize their foreign involvement so as not to become overexposed to risk. Four stages of foreign involvement can be identified by type of activity, and they can be ordered by depth of commitment. The most common form of activity involves only export and import transactions and requires the least commitment by the firm. In the extreme, a firm may be completely passive in the sense that it might conduct foreign sales only by filling orders which it does not solicit and by making foreign purchases only when actively solicited by others. Foreign involvement of this type requires little commitment and by its nature is likely to remain a very small portion of a firm's business.

In order to conduct a sizeable amount of foreign trade, firms must make a much greater effort; this involves committing more resources and taking greater risks. At some point, as foreign trade becomes a larger share of the firm's activity, it usually becomes necessary to establish a permanent agent near its principal markets. While in form, the setting up of a sales or purchasing agent is an act of direct foreign investment, it grows directly out of export-import transactions and is the next step in foreign involvement. This type of foreign investment has been undertaken intensively by the major Japanese trading firms. It permits better servicing of customers and broader scope for purchasing. On the other hand, the firm also runs a greater risk of having its foreign business interrupted or otherwise undermined.

Selling a very large volume of goods by exporting to a particular market involves such a high degree of risk for firms that many find it intolerable. The risk arises from the prospect of rival local production, which may capture the market because of its many advantages. An exception, of course, exists for natural resource-based exports when the resource or its substitute is not available locally in sufficient supply. One way to reduce the risk is to disperse the sales effort of the firm to avoid becoming overly dependent on any single market. This strategy has been suggested to Japanese firms in view of their heavy dependence on the U.S. market. But sales dispersion itself contains many inefficiencies, including higher transport costs, heavy promotional expenses and the like, and is unlikely to provide a lasting solution.

A more basic solution is to produce locally the product previously exported. In some instances, the easiest and least demanding way to provide local production is through licensing an already existing local firm to produce the product. Licensing permits a firm to have its product made locally without a commitment of its own capital and with a minimum use of its own management talent. Licensing is thus the third stage in foreign involvement. Foreigners have participated heavily in the Japanese economy through this route. Because it is limited in time, lacks enforceability, and a number of other reasons, however, licensing may not be an adequate solution for the firm.

As noted at the outset, the most demanding form of foreign involvement is direct investment. To make a foreign direct investment, a parent firm must provide equity capital that is embodied in physical assets located abroad and under the legal jurisdiction of the host country. A foreign subsidiary is a legal person of the country in which it is incorporated with all the benefits and risks of such a position.[a] Direct investment normally requires substantial amounts of executive talent along with financial resources so the decision to go abroad will not be taken lightly.

Direct Investment and Long-Run
Profit Maximization

Given the economic and political risks and the disadvantages facing the foreigner when making a direct investment, there generally have to be good prospects for making profit within some reasonable time frame to induce the decision. Furthermore, the profit prospects must be unique to foreign production or else the market will likely be served through exporting. Four types of advantages can be identified; cost reductions, sales expansion, suppression of competition, and portfolio diversification.

Costs might be reduced through local production in a number of ways. First and possibly most important, local production avoids the payment of tariffs and

---

[a]It is possible to operate abroad as a branch of a parent firm, but this subjects the earnings of the foreign operations to taxation of both the host country and the parent country and also risks the entire assets of the firm in the foreign venture. Thus the branch form of investment is used only under special circumstances such as crude petroleum production where depletion allowances offset all parent-country tax liabilities.

is not subject to quota restrictions or other harrassment of imports.[1] Also transportation costs are usually reduced by a significant amount with production closer to the market. Furthermore, local factors of production may be cheaper; these include lower wage rates or less expensive land and construction costs. In addition, local regulations concerning pollution may be less demanding and thus the costly process of restoring water and air may be avoided. It also may be possible to reduce raw material costs and make their supply more secure for the total operations of the firm if foreign direct investment stimulates the discovery and development of natural resources. Both avoidance of pollution cost and natural resource development are of particular importance to prospective Japanese investors. These cost-reductions depend, however, on the market being large enough to allow the investing firm to capture plant economies of scale.

If a firm decides not to export a product to an area, but instead to produce the product locally, sales can usually be increased in the host country and in other countries having special trading relations with the host country (for instance within the same customs union). The products made locally will avoid most of the antiforeign prejudice noted earlier. Also the better and faster service that can be provided to local customers may stimulate purchases from the firm, even of those products not made locally. Indeed, foreign subsidiaries become major customers of parent firms for raw materials and capital goods, and intermediate products as well as finished products. Some existing Japanese foreign investment in production facilities abroad was undertaken originally to increase exports from the Japanese parent firm. Furthermore, it is much easier to meet local consumer tastes through adaptation when producing on the spot, since special taste preferences are more easily identified and the skills required to make the adaptations are more readily available. This is a particularly important reason for American firms wanting to produce in Japan.

Another advantage of direct foreign investment can be appreciated by viewing the firm within the context of the world market of the industry in which it operates. Expansion of production into another country can represent a horizontal extension of the firm (producing the same good), a vertical extension (adding an earlier or later stage in the production process), or even possibly a conglomerate diversification, although the last is very rare.[2] A horizontal extension may be undertaken to forestall or discipline actual or potential competitors.[3] Direct investment does seem to be concentrated in those industries characterized by few sellers and in which product diversification is a major factor, adding credence to this view, although a full "conspiracy" against competition cannot be proven. Unwillingness to strengthen a foreign competitor, however, may be an important reason for a firm's reluctance to license advanced technology to a local producer.

A vertical extension may be undertaken to reduce the uncertainty involved in obtaining raw materials, to reduce a firm's reliance on other firms, or to raise barriers to entry of new firms into the industry. Thus by directly investing, the firm may strengthen its competitive position within the industry by maintaining or increasing its share of the world market. Undertaken either as an offensive or defensive measure, direct investment is designed to increase profits and to guarantee the perpetuation of the firm.

Another important attribute of direct investment involves the ownership of assets denominated in different currencies. Like other types of foreign assets, direct investment allows the attainment of diversification to offset the risks of currency fluctuations and also provides a mechanism for making speculative gains. Thus diversification may be an important objective sought by some risk-averse investors, as is the opportunity for speculating by other investors.[4] Since direct investment involves an operative venture comprising various financial dealings, it may permit an investor greater scope for accumulating both assets and liabilities in foreign currencies than other types of foreign investment. Thus direct investment may be a very effective method of attaining international portfolio balance for a firm, but this also explains why some governments—and particularly Japan—have been reluctant to permit such activity since it tends to undermine the effectiveness of domestic monetary policy.

The Firm and the Economy

Conventional economic theory suggests that when firms make foreign investment for their own benefit, they also improve the aggregative economic welfare of both the parent and host countries. If firms do earn higher profits by investing abroad than they could obtain by investing at home, then there is a presumption that resources are being transferred from lower to higher productive uses, and that, on balance, the firm contributes to a better allocation of world resources. This theory is fundamentally the same as that which supports the international trade of merchandise and thus is dependent on the assumption of equilibrium exchange rates. That a firm can contribute to a better distribution of world resources seems quite likely. A direct investment involves more than just the transfer of equity capital; it also includes entrepreneurship, technology, and other productive knowledge in a so-called industry-specific package. It hardly seems possible to obtain this package transfer through other means, particularly not through government-to-government transfers.

When business firms reach decisions, however, they are generally made without direct reference to the overall needs of the economy at that moment. This may bring the actions of individual firms into conflict with the stabilization desires or structural plans that the government may have for the economy. Since direct investment also affects a country's balance of payments, external needs of the country may also be perceived to be in conflict in the short run with a firm's desire to invest abroad. Thus governments of both parent and host countries may formulate policies which hinder or promote the inward or outward flow of direct investment.

There are a number of different instruments governments may utilize to bring foreign investment into line with aggregative economic policy goals. If governments want to stimulate inflows or outflows, they can supply loans to the direct investor, they can guarantee the investment against political and commercial risks, and they can provide tax incentives and other subsidies or exemptions. These incentives can be designed to provide general stimulation or to direct the investment into particular countries or regions or to particular types of business ventures. Likewise governments can retard either the inflow or outflow of direct investment. In the extreme, they can prohibit the activity, or they can impede it through licensing or taxation restraints. Again, the licensing or taxation measures can be used in a general way or be directed to particular investments in certain areas or activities. Both the United States and Japan have instituted various policies in this area. Clearly, other motivations beside economic ones may be involved in these government activities. Indeed, domestic political interests or foreign policy interests may be the most important considerations in policy formation.

The Case of the United States and Japan

It will be primarily as parent countries to direct investment that the United States and Japan will be examined; however, some mention need be made of their experience as hosts to direct investment of others. The United States from its inception has officially welcomed foreign direct investment. The first secretary of the treasury, Alexander Hamilton, by emphasizing the desirable aspects of this investment, set the tone which has not changed appreciably in 200 years. Nevertheless, there were periods when American nationalists resented foreign control of American enterprises. As a result of the government's welcome, good business prospects and close ties with Europe, foreign investment was attracted into the United States in substantial amounts. Until the Civil War most foreigners invested in U.S. debt or equity securities, but did not actively manage U.S. enterprises. Indeed in 1803, 45 percent of the nation's capitalized worth (through securities) was owned by foreigners, including over half of the national debt outstanding.[5] However, some direct investment had taken place even before the Civil War in trading firms, land companies, insurance companies, and iron works.[6] Subsequent to the war, foreign direct investment expanded in land development companies—some resulting via conversions from defaulted local and state government bonds—and some were vertically expanded to include cattle raising and meat processing. Investments were also made in mortgage companies, banks and other financial institutions, petroleum and mineral development, breweries, textile plants, soap production, steel-production facilities, scientific instruments and many others. Some smaller U.S. railroads were also directly controlled from abroad, although most U.S. railroads were controlled by Americans with foreign debt and equity participation.

Toward the latter part of the ninteenth century, income in the United States attained rapid growth, and American levels of technology approached those of the older industrial countries who were the investing countries; these factors combined to reduce the relative importance of foreign direct investment to domestic ownership in the resource-rich U.S. economy. Much foreign investment was actually liquidated during World War I or shortly thereafter, although some firms maintained their position. New foreign direct investment still is being made in the United States, but in modest amounts relative to outflows.

Starting in the 1870s, the United States became a parent to direct investment. Firms such as Colt Arms, Singer Sewing Machine, Westinghouse, and International Paper that developed technological leads over their international rivals recognized the advantage of direct investment and acted accordingly.[7] Expansion of this investment continued until World War I. The two world wars and the intervening period witnessed a stagnation or retrogression of direct investment everywhere and for obvious reasons. Subsequent to 1950, however, there has been new and prolonged growth in U.S. direct investment making the United States the largest investor in the world.

The experience of Japan as a host country for direct investment has differed greatly from that of the United States. Because of the long period of history in which Japan was isolated from the rest of the world, Japanese culture developed a distrust of foreigners, and official Japanese policy did not permit foreigners to forge business ties in Japan. Other than a few trading posts, foreign-owned business did not take root in Japan even when it was becoming common elsewhere. Japanese industrial development first reached a stage when it should have aroused great interest to foreigners between the world wars and some foreign firms were established, but the general climate for foreign investment was inopportune. In the 1930s, Ford and General Motors were forced to liquidate their early ventures, although Nestles', Air Liquide, and Otis Elevator did survive. Thus it was not until after World War II that direct investors made great efforts to establish themselves in Japan.

Most foreign participation in the Japanese economy was through licensing arrangements which were controlled but welcomed by the government. Between 1950 and 1969, over 13,000 separate licensing agreements were made, of which 1629 were in 1965 alone. It has been estimated that about 10 percent of all manufacturing activity in Japan is conducted with foreign technology; this figure is raised to between 25 and 30 percent for the modern sectors of industry.[8] The cost of foreign technology as seen in balance-of-payments accounts has risen from less than $100 million per year in 1960 to over $350 million in 1969. The relative importance of licensing arrangements, however, is likely to decline. Foreign firms, particularly those American-owned, are becoming more reluctant to share their technology in this way because of the rather meager returns they obtain and lest they help a potentially formidable competitor. Furthermore, Japan is now less in need of foreign technology than it was and is developing its own technology through rapidly increasing research and development expenditures. Indeed Japanese firms are increasingly providing technology to firms in other countries and earning returns therefrom. Earnings from this activity were only 2.4 percent of the corresponding (outgoing) payments in 1960, but had risen to 12.5 percent in 1969 ($46 million).

The present position of Japan as a parent of direct investment is a post-World War II phenomenon. Previous Japanese direct investment in the empire was liquidated as a result of the war itself. Japanese business firms had neither the desire nor the resources to make foreign investment immediately after the war. As economic advancement proceeded in the 1950s and early 1960s, Japanese firms began to rediscover the benefits of foreign investment, but official concern over balance-of-payments deficits kept capital resources from being used for this purpose. Thus substantial foreign direct investment by Japanese firms is a quite recent development.

To the present, therefore, the experience of the United States and Japan has been quite dissimilar with respect to direct investment. However, there is reason to believe they will become more alike in the future; indeed, the previous experience of the United States might well indicate trends for subsequent Japanese developments. Japanese society has already made the decision not to be content to earn only that standard of living that would be possible for a self-contained island country. Thus Japan is committed to the world market. As long as private business remains the principal form of economic activity and the world economy evolves as in the past, then Japanese firms may inevitably become as involved in foreign direct investment as their American counterparts.

Direct Investment: The U.S. Model

The characteristic that is common to all developed countries in the postwar period is their growing involvement in international commerce. For most countries, international trade in merchandise was the main form of this involvement; both imports and exports rose as a percentage of gross national products. This is also true of the United States, but to a lesser degree. In 1950, U.S. exports of goods amounted to 3.6 percent of GNP in that year. By 1960, U.S. exports had risen to 3.9 percent of GNP; and by 1970, exports reached 4.3 percent of GNP. Thus, as in other countries, U.S. merchandise exports became relatively more important to the economy, but this growth was outdistanced by direct investment.[b] U.S. direct investment was valued at $11.8 billion in 1950,

---

[b]For present purposes, direct investment is measured by the book value of assets, which is a "stock" concept rather than a "flow" concept like exports and GNP. The comparison is not misleading if the output-capital ratio remains relatively constant which it apparently has done over the last decade at around 2.4, and as it is assumed to do in the future. A value-added measure of direct investment enterprises would obviously be a superior measure, but the data are not available.

equal to 4.1 percent of GNP or approximately the same dollar amount as U.S. exports. This investment, however, almost tripled by 1960 and reached a value of $32.8 billion, amounting to 6.5 percent of GNP and substantially more than exports. By 1970, U.S. direct investment was valued at $78.1 billion, or equal to 8.0 percent of GNP and almost twice the value of exports. Thus the U.S. economy was increasingly tied to foreign markets through direct investment, with exports playing a lesser role.

The growth of U.S. direct investment has shown some interesting geographical and industrial patterns. One would expect that firms would try to minimize the risks and uncertainties of direct investment by investing in countries that are particularly well known and which have developed close relations with the investing country. Thus neighboring countries and ones having special historical or cultural ties are often the first countries in which firms will risk their equity. As is seen in Table 6-1, U.S. direct investment followed this pattern. In 1950, 34 percent of all U.S. direct investment was in Canada and Mexico. Another 35 percent was located in Latin America (less Mexico), possibly reflecting the "Monroe Doctrine" approach in U.S. relations with that area. Of the remaining, an inordinate share—7 percent of all investment—was located in the United Kingdom which reflects the factors noted above. By contrast, less than 3 percent was located in the Far East, despite the history of U.S. ties to the Philippines. There was only a trace of U.S. investment in Japan.

With the passage of time and the continuation of political stability and

Table 6-1
Book Value and Percentage Distribution of U.S. Direct Investments Abroad (by Area, Selected Years), 1950-1970

| | Millions of Dollars | | | | | % Distribution | | |
	1950	1957	1960	1966	1970[a]	1950	1960	1970
Total	$11,788	$25,394	$32,765	$54,711	$78,090	100.0	100.0	100.0
Canada, Mexico	3,994	9,508	11,993	18,247	24,575	33.9	36.6	31.5
Latin America (-Mexico)	4,161	7,313	8,476	10,200	12,909	35.3	25.9	16.5
United Kingdom	847	1,974	3,194	5,657	8,015	7.2	9.7	10.3
Other Europe	886	2,177	3,451	10,552	16,465	7.5	10.5	21.1
Japan	19	185	254	756	1,491	.2	.8	1.9
Africa – Non-Oil	163	390	518	930	1,388	1.4	1.6	1.8
Africa – Oil	124	274	407	1,104	2,088	1.1	1.2	2.8
Middle East	692	1,138	1,163	1,669	1,645	5.9	3.5	2.1
Far East (-Japan)	291	696	898	1,471	2,477	2.5	2.7	3.2
Other	612	1,739	2,412	4.085	7,048	5.0	7.5	8.8

[a]Preliminary

Source: *Survey of Current Business* and Department of Commerce, Office of Business Economics, *Balance of Payments: Statistical Supplement* (1963).

economic growth, American direct investment became more venturesome and spread to other areas. In particular, Europe became much more attractive to American investors. Not only the United Kingdom, but also Continental Europe gained many new U.S. ventures. The formation of the European Economic Community and the European Free Trade Association no doubt had important stimulative effects.[9] While U.S. investment did increase in Japan, the amounts were quite modest given the attractions of Japanese growth. This can be explained by the severity of Japanese government restrictions limiting investment inflows.

The industry distribution of U.S. investment over time also exhibits some interesting factors as seen in Table 6-2. Again firms are to be expected to maximize profits while minimizing risks. This can be accomplished through vertical expansion, particularly by investing in the production of a raw material like petroleum, although political risks may be great. Likewise vertical expansion into trade in other countries is attractive. Firms also expand horizontally, particularly in industries marked by oligopoly. Thus manufacturing investment as a whole has expanded, and within it, chemicals, machinery, and transport equipment have grown extremely fast. Industries not particularly promising from a profit standpoint or unusually risky from a political point of view have not attracted new investments. Thus agriculture, public utilities, and certain types of mining and smelting have either stagnated or declined. The concentration of new investment in manufacturing also explains the European focus noted above, as manufacturing is conducted near or in expanding markets, and Europe has grown very rapidly.

The profit implications of foreign direct investment for the U.S. economy can be seen in Table 6-3 and 6-4. Corporate profits are an especially important magnitude because of their impact on business investment both at home and abroad and on financial markets of all sorts. Because direct investment is a package operation, it permits a parent firm not only to earn interest, dividends, and branch earnings, but also to collect management fees and royalties from its foreign affiliate. These fees and royalties are approximately one-third the size of earnings and add to the profits of the parent firm. A much smaller amount of fees and royalties are also earned from unaffiliated foreign firms and constitute a type of foreign involvement, although not dependent on direct investment. The magnitude of these inflows into the United States as an aggregate can be appreciated by comparing them to corporate profits after taxes.[c] One is struck immediately by their large relative size. It strongly suggests that the American economy has greater foreign dependence than is generally believed.

---

[c]This comparison somewhat exaggerates the importance of foreign flows because the U.S. tax liability has not been subtracted from them. The data on these liabilities are not available, but it is well known that they represent a very small portion of the aggregate because of the combined operation of the foreign income tax credit, depletion rules, tax treaties, and provisions for the Western Hemisphere Trade Corporation. See Nathan N. Gordon, "Tax Aspects of U.S. Foreign Direct Investment," vol. 1 in *United States International Economic Policy in an Interdependent World*, pp. 953-64.

Table 6-2
Book Value and Percentage Distribution of U.S. Direct Investment Abroad (by Industry, Selected Years), 1950-1970

	Book Value (Millions of Dollars)					% Distribution				
	1950	1957	1960a	1966	1970	1950	1957	1960	1966	1970
Total	$11,788	$25,394	$32,765	$54,711	$78,090	100.0	100.0	100.0	100.0	100.0
Manufacturing	3,831	8,009	11,152	22,058	32,231	32.5	31.5	34.0	40.3	41.3
Food	483	723	943	n.a.	n.a.	4.1	2.8	2.9	n.a.	n.a.
Paper, allied products	378	722	861	n.a.	n.a.	3.2	2.8	2.6	n.a.	n.a.
Chemicals	512	1,378	1,902	n.a.	n.a.	4.3	5.4	5.8	n.a.	n.a.
Rubber products	182	401	520	n.a.	n.a.	1.5	1.6	1.6	n.a.	n.a.
Primary, fabricated metals	385	941	1,256	n.a.	n.a.	3.3	3.7	3.8	n.a.	n.a.
Machinery	420	927	1,333	n.a.	n.a.	3.6	3.6	4.1	n.a.	n.a.
Electrical machinery	387	731	918	n.a.	n.a.	3.3	2.9	2.8	n.a.	n.a.
Transportation	485	1,204	2,118	n.a.	n.a.	4.1	4.7	6.5	n.a.	n.a.
Other	599	983	1,301	n.a.	n.a.	5.1	3.9	4.0	n.a.	n.a.
Agriculture	589	680	687	n.a.	n.a.	5.0	2.7	2.1	n.a.	n.a.
Mining, smelting	1,129	2,361	3,011	4,315	6,137	9.6	9.3	9.2	7.9	7.9
Petroleum	3,390	9,055	10,948	16,205	21,790	28.8	35.7	33.4	29.6	27.9
Public utilities	1,425	2,145	2,548	2,284	n.a.	12.1	8.4	7.8	4.2	n.a.
Trade	762	1,668	2,397	4,716	n.a.	6.5	6.6	7.3	8.6	n.a.
Miscellaneous	662	1,476	2,022	5,133	17,932	5.5	5.8	6.2	9.4	22.9

aRevised figures for 1960 direct investment value are available but do not include an industry breakdown for manufacturing. Similar breakdowns for 1966 and 1970 will be available upon publication of the 1966 Census. Figures may not add to totals because of rounding.

Source: Survey of Current Business and Balance of Payments: Statistical Supplement (1963).

Table 6-3
U.S. Income from Abroad (Millions of Dollars), 1950-1970

Item Inflow	1950	1960	1961	1962	1963	1964	1965	1966	1967	1968	1969	1970
Direct investment interest, dividends, branch earnings	$1,294	$2,355	$2,768	$3,044	$3,129	$3,674	$3,963	$4,045	$4,518	$4,973	$5,658	$6,026
Fees, royalties from unaffiliated foreigners	n.a.	247	244	256	273	301	335	353	407	461	523	600
Direct investment fees and royalties	126	590	662	800	890	1,013	1,199	1,329	1,438	1,546	1,682	1,880
Gross earnings of corporate sector.	1,420	3,192	3,674	4,100	4,292	4,988	5,497	5,727	6,363	6,980	7,863	8,506
Income from other private assets	190	646	793	904	1,022	1,256	1,421	1,614	1,717	1,949	2,267	2,597
Gross earnings	1,610	3,838	4,467	5,004	5,314	6,244	6,918	7,341	8,080	8,929	10,130	11,103
Outflow												
Direct investment fees and royalties	n.a.	−35	−43	−57	−61	−67	−68	−64	−62	−80	−101	−111
Direct investment interest, dividends, branch earnings	n.a.	−220	−194	−185	−223	−202	−299	−372	−381	−388	−417	−441
Income paid on other private liabilities	n.a.	−511	−535	−586	−701	−802	−942	−1,221	−1,382	−1,843	−3,269	−3,591
Gross outflow	−338	−766	−772	−828	−985	−1,071	−1,309	−1,657	−1,825	−2,311	−3,787	−4,143
Net private foreign earnings of U.S.	1,272	3,072	3,695	4,176	4,329	5,173	5,609	5,684	6,255	6,618	6,343	6,960
Corporate profits after tax	24,864	26,680	27,245	31,229	33,077	38,444	46,461	49,943	46,638	47,778	44,490	41,242

Source: *Survey of Current Business.*

Table 6-4
U.S. Income from Abroad as a Percentage of Corporate Profits after Tax, 1950-1970

	Gross Corporate Earnings from Abroad (%)	Net Private Foreign Earnings of U.S. (%)	Corporate Profits after Tax (Millions of Dollars)
1950	5.71	5.12	$24,864
1960	11.96	11.51	26,680
1961	13.48	13.56	27,245
1962	13.13	13.37	31,229
1963	12.98	13.09	33.077
1964	12.97	13.46	38,444
1965	11.83	12.07	46,461
1966	11.47	11.38	49,943
1967	13.64	13.41	46,638
1968	14.61	13.85	47,778
1969	17.67	14.26	44,490
1970	20.62	16.88	41,242

Source: Table 6-3.

There are several ways of analyzing the income effect of foreign investment. Looking first at the top row of Table 6-3, the size of what one might call the pure foreign earnings flows can be seen. Pure earnings between 1950 and 1970 rose by $4.7 billion or nearly fivefold. Total after-tax corporate profits during this same period rose only $16.4 billion, less than a doubling. Thus the pure foreign profit contribution to American corporations increased considerably and by 1970 represented 15 percent of after-tax profits. The associated earnings flows from fees and royalties are listed in the next two rows. These flows between 1950 and 1970 increased by $2.4 billion. When these flows are added to pure foreign earnings, they indicate that 5.7 percent of corporate profits in 1950 could be attributed to foreign operations, 12.0 percent in 1960 and as high as 20.6 percent in 1970. It should be noted that income of foreign subsidiaries not distributed as dividends to U.S. parents is not included in these figures. Undistributed profits in 1970 amounted to $2.0 billion. If these earnings were added to both foreign earnings and total corporate profits, the contribution of foreign operations to American corporations would now appear to be about 26 percent.

The net contribution of foreign operations to the U.S. economy as a whole differs from these magnitudes because earnings on foreign-owned assets in the United States represent a drain on American incomes. Much foreign investment in the United States which yields earnings to foreigners is in forms other than direct investment. To arrive at a comprehensive concept for the net current contribution of foreign operations to American incomes, returns to foreigners on all their private assets in the United States have been subtracted from the total of U.S. private returns from abroad (excluding reinvested subsidiary earnings).[d] This net flow was $1.3 billion in 1950, rose to 3.1 billion in 1960, and was $7.0 billion in 1970. These net inflows clearly have exceeded the growth rate of corporate profits and GNP as a whole. What all of these magnitudes indicate is that the U.S. economy has a large and growing interest in world markets and this interest arises primarily through the operations of direct investment.

One notable attribute of this relationship is the countercyclical tie between foreign earnings and domestic earnings. Foreign earnings obviously respond to foreign business conditions. Unless there is perfect correspondence between foreign and American cyclical conditions, foreign earnings will cushion the impact of temporary weakness in the U.S. domestic economy. Thus the $3.3 billion decline of U.S. corporate profits between 1966 and 1967 would have been over $4 billion without the growth of foreign corporate earnings. Likewise the $3.3 billion decline of corporate profits between 1968 and 1969 and the further $3.2 billion decline in 1970 would have been $4.2 billion and $3.7 billion respectively without the moderating effect of foreign corporate earnings. Foreign earnings are, therefore, a type of safety-valve for the U.S. economy in a recession somewhat similar at times to exports of merchandise for the Japanese economy.

U.S. Direct Investment in Japan

American firms have made direct investments in Japan, but as noted earlier, these ventures have been rather small and many have been undertaken only recently. The amounts and major distribution by industry of U.S. direct investment in Japan are shown in Table 6-5. In 1950 this represented a mere 0.2 percent of total U.S. direct investment, only 0.8 percent in 1960, and still only 1.9 percent in 1970, even though it had by then reached $1.5 billion. However, the U.S. share of total foreign direct investment in Japan amounts to about 70 percent of the total.[10] Thus while Japan received a relatively small part of U.S. investment, U.S. investment was large from a Japanese perspective, even though the totality of foreign investment in Japan is modest.

Japan can be described as, at best, a reluctant host to foreign direct investment. This follows directly from the long tradition of Japan's suspicion of foreigners and wish to be independent of foreign control.[11] While other concerns

---

[d]Return to the U.S. government on its foreign assets and its payments on foreign liabilities are not included. These flows approximately offset one another. Inflows generally were greater than outflows until 1970, but the net balance was reversed in 1971. The net amounts are small.

Table 6-5
Book Value of U.S. Direct Investment in Japan, Selected Years (Millions of Dollars), 1950-1970

	1950	1955	1960	1961	1962	1963	1964	1965	1966	1967	1968	1969	1970
Total	19	129	254	310	369	472	598	675	756	870	1,050	1,244	1,491
Manufacturing	5	28	91	110	119	145	207	275	334	425	522	646	753
Petroleum	a	a	a	a	a	260	315	321	331	347	405	447	540
Trade	0	5	27	b	b	b	b	b	b	b	b	b	b
Other	14	96	136	200	250	67	77	79	91	98	123	150	198

Note: Figures may not add to total because of rounding.
aUntil 1963, petroleum investments were included in "Other".
bSince 1961, trade investments have been included in "Other".
Source: *Survey of Current Business* and *Balance of Payments: Statistical Supplement* (1963).

and desires have influenced Japanese policy from time to time, the underlying temper of reluctance has remained. In the early postwar period, there was intense concern over the weakness in the balance of payments; this led to the enactment in 1949 of the Foreign Exchange Control Law and its extension in 1950 with the Law Concerning Foreign Investment. Under this law a licensing procedure was established whereby the Foreign Investment Council could validate foreign investment in Japan. Investment was permitted only when it contributed to the attainment of Japanese self-sufficiency and to the improvement of the balance of payments, and then only up to 49 percent ownership of the enterprise. In 1956 an important exception to the procedure was introduced. Foreign firms were permitted to invest in Japan and with full ownership if they would forgo the explicit right to repatriate profits and principal. Such enterprises were known as "yen-based companies" and included such well known firms as Coca Cola and Johnson & Johnson.

As balance-of-payments fears receded by the early 1960s, more foreign investments were licensed, but new criteria were also instituted. Investment was allowed only if it did not unduly challenge small-sized enterprises, seriously disturb industrial order, or severely impede the advancement of Japanese technology. Further liberalizations were announced in 1963 when Japan accepted Article 8 status in the International Monetary Fund and began participating in the Organization for Economic Cooperation and Development. Still other liberalizations were implemented in July 1967, March 1969, September 1970, and in August 1971.[12] Liberalizations have taken the form of more automatic screening, reductions in the number of restricted industries, and increases in the permitted share of foreign ownership. Distinctions are still drawn between new ventures and take-overs of existing companies, with the former activity being treated more liberally than the latter. In particular, the permitted percentage of foreign ownership is considerably lower in already existing enterprises.

United States investors responded to these liberalizations with a burst of new investment in 1963 and 1964 and with a large and growing flow of investment since 1967. American investment has been particularly heavy in the petroleum industry and petroleum is the only industry in Japan in which foreigners predominate, owning approximately 60 percent of the total. Foreign firms have been more severely restrained in the distribution of petroleum products than in the provision of crude petroleum or refined products.[e] Most foreign investment and half of all U.S. investment is in manufacturing and accounted for 3.3 percent of total sales of Japanese manufacturing firms in 1966. Foreign firms are spread rather widely throughout manufacturing, but many are concentrated in machinery and chemicals and are responsible for about 5 percent of sales in these two areas. Foreign firms are important in rubber products and account for about 19 percent of sales.

---

[e]U.S. investment in Okinawa has not been included in the figures for Japan in the past, but will be so incorporated after May 1972. The only major U.S. investment in Okinawa is in petroleum.

The operations of American and other foreign enterprises in Japan are notable because their relationship to domestic enterprises is so similar to that relationship in other developed countries. One might have expected that due to the elaborate screening procedure and the great reluctance of the Japanese authorities, they would have somehow been quite different, but that is not the case. Other than demonstrating the attribute of a lower foreign ownership share, foreign enterprises in Japan exhibit standard basic characteristics even though they have a real handicap in competing with Japanese-owned firms.

The primary motive for foreign firms to invest in Japan (as a developed economy) is the attraction of the growing market, just as elsewhere. Japanese firms, like firms in other countries, desire foreign partners primarily to obtain new productive technology. As noted previously, since Japanese firms have become formidable international competitors, they have found greater difficulty in obtaining foreign technology through licensing and have thus entered into joint ventures. Acceptance of foreign direct investment has also been spurred by the recognition that Japanese exports and Japanese foreign investment will not be accepted in other countries without reciprocal treatment. Furthermore, there was some concern that foreign investment might settle elsewhere in Asia and export goods competitive with Japan, and the Japanese prefer investment in Japan to that alternative. There was also some realization that consumers and the economy in general would benefit from the presence of some foreign investment.

After foreign enterprises became established, they attempted to conform to the business practices of Japan and thus tried to blend into Japanese society. This was accomplished by having Japanese partners take the predominate role in areas like labor relations and intrabusiness negotiating, or by using Japanese employees in sensitive management positions. This is exactly what profit maximizing behavior would dictate and is standard practice among multinational firms. In their business experience, foreign-owned enterprises have grown faster than wholly Japanese-owned firms in the same industry; they have earned higher profits than their Japanese counterparts; and they have exported a larger share of their output than their Japanese competitors. This mirrors the experience of American direct investment in many countries.[13]

The picture that emerges of foreign enterprise in Japan is that of successful businesses that have learned how to adapt to local conditions. Of course, while this generalization refers to those that have survived, some have not. Foreign-owned firms, however, are not identical to Japanese-owned firms and in some respects, they may be leaders in the economy. For instance, laborers in foreign-owned enterprise are likely to work fewer hours and are likely to work a five-day week rather than the five-and-a-half day standard Japanese workweek. Some Japanese firms are also moving toward the shorter workweek. Foreign enterprises also attempted at times to circumvent the overly-structured Japanese distribution system. Indeed the great success of Coca Cola in Japan is in part due to its innovation of selling directly to retailers. A foreign-owned enterprise is also likely to be doing somewhat less research in Japan than its Japanese counterparts, but this may be only a temporary phenomenon growing out of the selection bias. Foreign enterprises were permitted into Japan because of superior technology of the parent firms and are thus likely to rely on it in the early years. But the advantage of indigenous research is likely to weigh heavily in the future. Lower costs of doing research in Japan relative to the United States on the one hand, and the great expansion of R and D efforts by competitive Japanese firms on the other, will force foreign enterprises to emulate domestic firms in their research efforts.[14] From all this, one is tempted to conclude that the fear of many Japanese that foreign firms would change their society is unjustified from the experience to date.

Japan as Parent to Direct Investment

Japanese direct investment in other countries began again in 1951, but it was strictly controlled under the 1949 and 1950 legislation noted above. Firms were permitted to invest abroad if the investment would promote exports from Japan or develop natural resources unavailable or scarce in Japan. Proposals would be rejected if they involved too great a drain on the balance of payments. Direct investment was also curtailed lest it undermine the effectiveness of domestic monetary policy—a very major stabilization instrument in Japan. Finally, investment was controlled to prevent "excessive" competition, a euphemism for hurting other Japanese firms at home. The analysis could be improved by examining rejected proposals, but unfortunately several factors combine to make this impossible. Records of such proposals are not made public by the Foreign Investment Council. Some projects were headed off by the Bank of Japan and so were never even submitted to the council. Furthermore, direct investment could be limited by the Export-Import Bank of Japan not providing financial support. Desirable projects, on the other hand, received great support in particular from the Japan Petroleum Development Corporation, the Metalic Minerals Exploration Agency of Japan, as well as from the Export-Import Bank.

The nature of the direct investments undertaken by Japanese firms conforms to what one would expect from a country in the early stages of foreign investment and does not seem to be particularly distorted by the control procedure. No doubt the amount of investment was held down, but with the easing of Japan's balance-of-payments constraint, direct investments have been rising. The value of Japanese direct investments is recorded in Tables 6-6 and 6-7.[f] As with most things Japanese, the most striking characteristic is its rapid

---

[f]Japanese data are of two sorts: approval data as reported by the Ministry of Finance and Ministry of International Trade and Industry, and balance-of-payments data as reported by the Bank of Japan. They differ rather considerably with approval data being much larger and reported in greater detail. They differ because approvals precede expenditures leading to

rate of growth. Almost 60 (59.5) percent of total investment has occurred in the last three years, reaching a value of $3.6 billion by March 1971. In fiscal 1970 alone, over $900 million was authorized, a one-third increase in a single year.

The motivations of Japanese firms investing abroad have been investigated by the Export-Import Bank of Japan.[15] The answers indicate that more than half of all ventures have been undertaken to maintain or increase exports from Japanese parent firms. A large number of investments to develop raw material sources were also reported. Both motives reflect the early stages of Japanese foreign involvement through direct investment and the limiting effect of government policy. The one unique feature of Japanese investment is the large number of ventures in cotton textile production that were begun in the early years. This may well reflect the "voluntary" and subsequent mandatory cotton textile program of the United States and other countries which limited exports from Japan, but did permit Japanese firms to set up production in other countries to export to these markets. The wage differential between Japan and Hong Kong, Taiwan, and Korea would not alone have justified such ventures at the time they were started, but very large differentials have subsequently developed. Thus the cotton textile investments were just ahead of their time and are now among the most profitable of Japanese foreign investments.

Japanese firms, like those of other countries, generally prefer where possible to have 100 percent ownership of their foreign ventures rather than share the equity. Of 40 ventures selected because of the large values involved (but excluding those investing in natural resources), fully 21 were 100 percent Japanese-owned, and all but 7 were 50 percent or more owned by the Japanese parents.[16] The two notable exceptions are the steel ventures in Brazil and Malaysia reflecting the large commercial and political risks involved. However, Japanese firms do seek out joint venture partners for natural resource investments among both host-country firms and those of third countries for the purpose of reducing the economic and especially the political risks involved in such investments. Also it is the large Japanese firms that do the foreign investing. About one out of every four foreign ventures is undertaken by the ten leading general trading firms, with Mitsui and Mitsubishi the leaders. These ten firms together had fifty ventures in the United States alone.

The distributions of Japanese direct investment by industry and area are shown in Table 6-8 and 6-9. The characteristics that one would expect to find are in fact present. Natural resource investment accounts for over 40 percent of

a timing difference. Approvals are more broadly defined to include all management ties while the data for payments have a minimum cut off of 25 percent ownership; approval data also recognize currency adjustments and the like and thus come close to the U.S. concept of book value. Approval data indicate different forms of direct investment, all of which would appear as direct investment under U.S. definitions. All Japanese data include investment in Okinawa. Most of the subsequent analysis will be based on approval data.*

*See Saburo Okita, "The Experience and Problems of Japan's Private Foreign Investment in Latin America" in *IA-ECOSOC Sixth Annual Meeting of Experts*, Port-of-Spain, June 1969.

Table 6-6
Japanese Direct Investments Abroad, by Type, 1951-70

Fiscal Year	Value						Number of Cases	
	Securities	Loans	Direct investment	Branch investment	All types of investment	% distribution	All types of investment	% distribution
	(Millions of Dollars)							
1951-58	70	56	12	5	143	4.0	445	11.3
1959	22	20	9	2	53	1.5	123	3.1
1960	33	21	37	2	93	2.6	151	3.8
1961	47	39	78	1	165	4.6	133	3.4
1962	40	31	25	4	99	2.8	179	4.5
1963	63	23	37	3	126	3.5	223	5.7
1964	69	39	12	1	120	3.3	193	4.9
1965	75	69	12	1	157	4.4	209	5.3
1966	74	122	31	1	227	6.3	253	6.4
1967	118	132	20	5	275	7.6	306	7.8
1968	201	326	29	1	557	15.5	384	9.8
1969	224	404	37	2	668	18.6	568	14.4
1970	299	572	36	6	913	25.4	768	19.5
Total 1951-70	1,334	1,854	375	33	3,596	100.0	3,935	100.0
% distribution	37.1	51.6	10.4	0.9	100.0			

Note: Figures are rounded and will not necessarily add to totals.

Source: MITI, Trade Promotion Bureau, *Keizai Kyōryōku no Genjō to Mondaiten*, [Present Situation of International Economic Cooperation and Its Programs], 1972, in Japanese.

Table 6-7
Capital and Income Flows of Japanese Direct Investment Abroad,
1961-70 (Millions of Dollars)

Fiscal Year	Capital outflow	Income
1961	104	9
1962	62	11
1963	125	12
1964	44	12
1965	105	15
1966	101	21
1967	137	27
1968	228	37
1969	230	48
1970	397	90

Source: Foreign Department, Bank of Japan, *Balance of Payments Monthly*, August 1971.

the total and three of the four largest ventures: oil in Saudi Arabia and Kuwait, oil in North Sumatra, and wood pulp in Alaska (steel production in Brazil is the fourth). Japanese investment in addition has ventured into iron ore, copper, uranium, bauxite, nickel, natural gas, industrial salt and other resources in small amounts. The location of the natural resource obviously determines where these investments need to be made, but where choice exists, the Japanese have opted for sites close to the home islands.

The Japanese have been particularly innovative with respect to their natural resource investment in Australia. In addition to forming joint ventures, they have instituted long-term purchase contracts with the new ventures and thus have almost guaranteed the success of the investment along with obtaining a needed raw material. While Japanese investment in Australia is now rather small, worth only about $240 million, it may expand rapidly in the future.[17]

The pattern of Japan's export markets has been very important in determining where Japanese firms make direct investment. Thus the large percentage of Japanese investment in North America, over 25 percent (or one quarter) of the total, reflects the fact that close to one-third of the total Japanese exports are sent to this area. As noted at the outset, exports lead to direct investment to defend and expand markets. Almost 22 percent of Japanese investment has gone into Southeast Asia. This results both from export markets and from neighboring-country incentives. Much of Japanese manufacturing investment has been directed to South Korea, Taiwan, and Hong Kong for the same reasons that Americans invest in Canada and Great Britain. On the other hand, there has been a conscious effort by the Japanese to become less Asia oriented. Japanese firms have risked some capital in Latin America, but very little in Africa. In the

170

Table 6-8

Japanese Foreign Investment, by Industry, Total 1951-70 (Approval Basis Cumulative to the End of March 1970)

	Number of cases	Amount (millions of dollars)	% Distribution Number of cases	Amount
Manufacturing	1,391	963	35.3	26.8
Food	135	61	3.4	1.7
Textiles	259	190	6.6	5.3
Timber and pulp	44	212	1.1	5.9
Chemicals	175	60	4.4	1.7
Iron, other metals	99	138	2.5	3.8
Machinery	138	67	3.5	1.9
Electrical machinery	206	71	5.2	2.0
Transportation	43	103	1.1	2.9
Other	292	61	7.4	1.7
Agriculture	94	58	2.4	1.6
Fishing	96	27	2.4	0.8
Mining	195	1,127	5.0	31.3
Construction	32	38	0.8	1.1
Commercial	1,112	370	28.3	10.3
Banking, insurance	115	322	2.9	9.0
Other	520	659	13.2	18.3
Subtotal	3,555	3,563	90.3	99.1
Branch investment	380	33	9.7	0.9
Total	3,935	3,596	100.0	100.0

Note: Figures are rounded and will not necessarily add to totals.

Source: MITI, Trade Promotion Bureau, *Present Situation of Economic Cooperation and Its Programs* (1972, in Japanese).

aggregate, about 60 percent of Japanese direct investment is in less developed countries and forms an important part of Japanese cooperation with them.

It has been suggested that direct investment will be the Achilles heel of the Japanese economic miracle, that Japanese firms cannot make a success of direct investment in other countries. It is argued that the insular nature of the Japanese and their great suspicion of foreigners that has protected the home islands from foreign business incursions will also keep Japanese firms from properly managing enterprises in other countries. This attitude becomes manifest in a number of business practices. Japanese firms tend to centralize too many of their business

Table 6-9
Japanese Foreign Investment, by Area (End of Fiscal Year 1970)

		Millions of Dollars	% Distribution
North America –	1968	185	33.2
	1969	129	19.4
	1970	192	21.0
	1951-70	912	25.4
Latin America –	1968	40	7.2
	1969	101	15.1
	1970	46	5.0
	1951-70	559	15.5
Southeast Asia –	1968	80	14.3
	1969	199	29.8
	1970	176	19.2
	1951-70	779	21.7
Europe –	1968	151	27.1
	1969	94	14.0
	1970	336	36.7
	1951-70	638	17.8
Middle and Near East –	1968	28	5.0
	1969	38	5.7
	1970	28	3.0
	1951-70	334	9.3
Africa –	1968	43	7.7
	1969	18	2.8
	1970	14	1.5
	1951-70	92	2.6
Oceana –	1968	31	5.5
	1969	89	13.3
	1970	123	13.4
	1951-70	281	7.8
All Areas –	1968	557	100.0
	1969	668	100.0
	1970	913	100.0
	1951-70	3,596	100.0

Note: Figures are rounded and will not necessarily add to totals.

Source: MITI, Trade Promotion Bureau, *Present Situation of Economic Cooperation and Its Programs* (1971 and 1972, in Japanese).

decisions in Tokyo rather than in the foreign subsidiaries themselves. They insist on using Japanese nationals rather than local people in too many management positions. They continue to use Japanese ways of doing business rather than adapting to local practices. These factors combine to engender labor problems and to stir resentment in general.[18] Poor business practices result in poor profits performance. Indeed up to now only about half of Japanese foreign investment has proven profitable at all, much less profitable enough to offset the risk.

However, it is really too early to evaluate the profit experience of Japanese direct investment with any degree of certainty. According to surveys made in 1968 and 1969, 60 percent of overseas ventures were currently profitable, another 5 percent or 6 percent were breaking even, and the remaining 34 or 35 percent were incurring losses. Since new ventures take some time to turn a profit and new ventures weigh heavily in Japan's total, the high percentage of losses does not seem unusual. Indeed there has been a noticeable improvement in the profit picture since the 1965 survey. Only half of the ventures earning profits are currently paying dividends to their Japanese parents.

Again Japanese direct investors behave similarly to those of other countries by reinvesting much of their profits in foreign ventures. This also reinforces the theory that foreign ventures are the children of large corporations, which in the interest of long-run profits are willing and able to absorb losses for a few years. The absolute amount of returned profits has been rising and reached the considerable figure of $90 million in 1970 (113 in calendar year 1971). Furthermore, the large Japanese trading companies may be an institution particularly well suited to direct investment. Trading companies are probably superior to multinational corporations in their ability to organize the talents of various business enterprises that are needed in foreign ventures.

One can characterize Japanese direct investment by 1970 as only having begun to develop. The problems that Japanese firms now face are not much different from those American firms encountered when first investing in Europe.[19] There is no evidence to support the conclusion that Japanese firms will be any less adaptable and will not in time earn large profits. In 1961 pure earnings from abroad represented only 0.2 percent of Japanese corporate profits after taxes. By 1969 this percentage had more than tripled to 0.7 percent and certainly exceeded 1 percent of corporate profits in 1970. But these figures are still very small. If the United States is an appropriate model to judge by, these figures will not remain small for very much longer. The Japanese investment base is growing abroad and should be a major contributor to Japanese incomes and economic stability sometime in the future.

Future of Japanese Direct Investment

One need not depend on either a naive historical model or simple extrapolation to predict future growth of Japanese direct investment. There are many sound economic reasons why increased direct investment should be forthcoming. First of all there will be growing need for raw materials that cannot be supplied domestically in Japan. Japanese firms (like those in other countries) have shown they prefer to extend their investments abroad to complete the vertical integration of the enterprise to the alternative of depending on vital imports for continued existence of their enterprise. Second, the growing shortage of Japanese labor, which will not be relieved by inflows of foreign workers, will force up Japanese wages so that foreign workers will have a decided competitive advantage in some fields despite higher levels of productivity in Japan. Japanese firms operating in these labor-intensive industries will increasingly be forced to move production abroad to lower wage areas to survive. Third, the shortage of land in Japan is raising the cost of new plant sites. New industrial areas are only a partial answer since labor relocation may be involved. Thus some land-intensive industries may go abroad in search of cheaper locations.

A fourth factor closely related to the third concerns the cost of pollution. Japan is so densely developed—highest GNP per useable acre in the world—that pollution is a very serious problem. Industrial wastes that are easily dissipated elsewhere reinforce each other in Japan. Thus what comes free in other countries may become increasingly expensive in Japan as the government begins to enforce more stringent antipollution regulations. Some Japanese industries that are heavy polluters may find it more profitable to produce abroad in countries where nature can still handle more wastes without cost, or where the government is less concerned over the consequences of pollution. (Of course, many countries will not welcome industrial polluters and will bar them.) Already some Japanese mineral producers are smelting ores in other countries for this reason.

Two other general reasons for investing abroad may also become more important in the future. With the rise of incomes and the improvement and extension of higher education in Japan, a surplus of management talent relative to workers may develop. This means that the real opportunity costs to foreign investment may go down for Japanese firms. Thus, like the United States, Japan will "export" its management skills and techniques through direct investment. Also as capital investment continues to deepen in Japan, the real cost of capital should begin to decline. While this may be further down the road than the other factors mentioned previously, in time it should be quite significant and permit much more capital to be invested abroad.

Problems of Japanese Direct Investment

As more Japanese firms invest abroad, it is likely that they will face more of the problems already noted, as well as additional difficulties encountered by firms of other countries. Foreign investment always stirs certain resentments as some local firms suffer under the added competition. The more able the Japanese firms abroad, the more likely it is that they will be resented. Furthermore, nationalistic feeling is particularly agitated by foreign investment in natural resources, especially nonreplaceable resources like petroleum and minerals. Since these industries are of great interest to Japanese investors, some difficulties are certain to arise.

These problems will create a major challenge to Japanese firms. They will have to learn how to survive in a somewhat hostile environment. Local participation in equity may well be a partial answer to some of these problems. But as the recent experience of American copper companies in Chile indicate, local participation even by the government is no guarantee against expropriation. The danger of expropriation is always present to some degree, and firms must learn how to evaluate the probability of such actions if they are to be successful.

There is little opposition to outward direct investment today in Japan, but this might well change in the future. Some groups in society can be hurt by foreign direct investment, like labor groups that have skills specific to certain industries. As in the United States, a time may come when these groups will make a public issue of their opposition. One might think that this might occur only in the distant future, given the state of Japanese labor unions, but the future has a way of arriving very quickly in Japan.

Because of Japan's geographical and economic position, Japanese firms may face one set of unique challenges, namely, how to set up workable direct investments in the Soviet Union. The Asian regions of the USSR contain some undeveloped but valuable natural resources. Japanese technology, capital, and markets could add immeasurably to the value of these resources. The Russians have shown some interest in working out an arrangement somewhat similar to that which permits Japanese participation in the development of Australia's resources. The challenge to Japanese firms will be to determine on the one hand whether they can gain sufficient protection of their investment to justify the risks, and on the other, whether they can steer clear of the Sino-Soviet dispute, which is centered near the areas of some of the most promising developments.

Conclusion

Japanese foreign direct investment may never exactly mirror that of the United States, but not because of something unique to Japanese culture. Rather the economic factors facing Japanese firms are somewhat different—like greater concern over sources of raw material—and these factors will determine a different pattern of investment. But the behavior of Japanese firms can be understood within the same motivational framework as their American counterparts. In terms of general interest, it seems certain that Japanese direct investment will make a much more prominent place in the future than it has in the past.

Notes

1. See U.S. Department of Commerce, U.S. MULTINATIONAL ENTER-PRISES AND THE U.S. ECONOMY, January 1972 (Stobaugh study) for supporting evidence from U.S. case studies.

2. Richard E. Caves, "International Corporations: The Industrial Economics of Foreign Investment" ECONOMICA, February 1971.

3. Stephen H. Hymer, "The Efficiency (Contradictions) of Multinational Corporations," AMERICAN ECONOMIC REVIEW, 60, no. 2, May 1970.

4. Robert Z. Aliber, "A Theory of Direct Foreign Investment," in Charles P. Kindleberger (ed.) THE INTERNATIONAL CORPORATION (MIT Press, 1971).

5. Louis M. Hacker, FOREIGN INVESTMENTS IN AMERICA'S GROWTH, U.S. Information Service, dated 11/1/67 (processed).

6. Cleona Lewis, AMERICA'S STAKE IN INTERNATIONAL INVEST-MENT, Brookings Institution, 1938, Chapter 5.

7. Raymond Vernon, "The Economic Consequences of U.S. Direct Invest-ment," in UNITED STATES INTERNATIONAL ECONOMIC POLICY IN AN INTERDEPENDENT WORLD, Williams Commission, (Washington, D.C.: U.S. Government Printing Office, 1971), vol. 1, p. 929-52.

8. The Boston Consulting Group, James C. Abegglen, Editor, BUSINESS STRATEGIES FOR JAPAN, Sophia University, Tokyo, 1970, p. 118.

9. Lawrence B. Krause, EUROPEAN ECONOMIC INTEGRATION AND THE UNITED STATES, The Brookings Institution, 1968, Chapter 5.

10. MITI, "Special Report on Foreign Owned Firms in Japan," Processed, Dated September 25, 1968.

11. M.Y. Yoshino, "Japan as Host to the International Corporation," in Charles P. Kindleberger (ed.) Chap. 14, THE INTERNATIONAL CORPORA-TION (MIT Press, 1971).

12. Ministry of Finance and Bank of Japan, MANUAL OF FOREIGN INVESTMENT IN JAPAN, November 1971.

13. D.T. Brash, AMERICAN INVESTMENT IN AUSTRALIAN INDUSTRY, Canberra, 1966, J.H. Dunning, THE ROLE OF AMERICAN INVESTMENT IN THE BRITISH ECONOMY, PEP Broadsheet no. 507, 1969, A.E. Safarian, THE PERFORMANCE OF FOREIGN-OWNED FIRMS IN CANADA, Montreal, 1969, and MITI, "SPECIAL STUDY ON FOREIGN ENTERPRISES IN JAPAN," 1971 processed.

14. Boston Consulting Group, BUSINESS STRATEGIES FOR JAPAN, Chapter 7.

15. The 1968 special survey was reported by Koichi Hamada, "Japanese Investment Abroad," at the Third Pacific Trade and Development Conference, Sydney, 22 August 1970, and the 1969 special survey in THE ORIENTAL

ECONOMIST, June 1971 in an article entitled "Are Japanese Foreign Ventures Profiting?" p. 14-17.

16. THE ORIENTAL ECONOMIST, "Are Japanese Foreign Ventures Profiting?"

17. Robert Trumbull, "Japanese Study Australian Sites," special to the NEW YORK TIMES, February 12, 1972.

18. Ian Stewart, "Japanese Stir Asian Resentment," special to the NEW YORK TIMES, January 10, 1972.

19. A.W. Johnstone, UNITED STATES DIRECT INVESTMENT IN FRANCE: AN INVESTIGATION OF THE FRENCH CHARGES, Cambridge, Mass.: MIT Press, 1965.

7 The Textile Confrontation

Gary Saxonhouse

On October 15, 1971, brandishing the legal power endowed by the 1917 Trading with the Enemy Act, buttressed by the inherent asymmetry in the economic power relations between the two countries and following hard upon the earlier Nixon shocks, the United States forced the Japanese (as well as other Asian countries) to agree to "voluntary" textile export restraints. The agreement's key features include a 5 percent limit on the growth of man-made textile exports to the United States. The growth limit will be administered on an item by item basis. In most respects the agreement is not unlike the voluntary restraint agreements on cotton textile imports into the United States which had been negotiated during the late 1950s and early 1960s under GATT auspices, save that the category by category controls seem to be stricter.

The acceptance by the Japanese government of American demands for this latest restraint measure ended two and one-half years of acrimonious negotiations. American government leaders hailed the decision as a turning point in the battle against increasing popular sentiment for isolationist foreign economic policies. Presumably protectionism's appetite was to be sated by the special characteristics of the bone of textile quotas. The American textile and apparel industry, while acknowledging the Nixon administration's efforts on their behalf, felt the agreement could do little more than save the rump of an already battered sector of the economy. Southern politicians and industry spokesmen claimed that while the negotiations had been going on, well over 100,000 jobs had been lost.

In Japan, where these two and one-half years of negotiations had been given voluminous coverage by the news media, there was widespread condemnation of the nakedly coercive tactics employed by the American negotiators. Major newspapers suggested that serious damage was being capriciously inflicted on the Japanese economy. The South Carolina campaign promise of presidential nominee Nixon notwithstanding, there seemed to be no economic or social bases on which the demands for restriction could be justified. Moreover, Japanese textile industry leaders predicted 300,000 jobs would be lost as a consequence of this particular Sato Capitulation.

Interference with Free Trade

The Textile Confrontation is over. While not eternally resolved, difficulties in this product line are not expected in the immediate future. Nonetheless, further study of this issue is certainly worthwhile. Bound up in this controversy are larger economic issues which transcend the narrow considerations so often emphasized in the Japanese and American press.

Japan is a very large, very rapidly growing export-oriented economy. Unlike other developed countries, which both import and export relatively large amounts of manufactures often within the same industrial line, Japan has a decidedly nineteenth-century pattern of trade, exporting manufactures primarily and importing, as a percentage of gross national product, disproportionate amounts of raw materials. As a follower country, Japan's exports tend to be in industrial lines that have been developed and remain substantial elsewhere. The impact of the large, rapidly growing, newly efficient Japanese industries has since, at least as early as the 1930s, created serious international tensions. In spite of everything that has happened recently, one suspects that the international difficulties resulting from Japan's growth process are increasing rather than receding. In examining the textile issue, one must try to be mindful of how the general problem can best be handled.

As a long-term proposition, most economists in Japan and the United States, and to a lesser extent policy-makers in these countries, agree that resources should flow into and out of national industries in accordance with comparative advantage. Such a policy with its free-trade corollary, in a world of equilibrium exchange rates, will maximize world welfare. Free trade like all free-market policies requires adjustment on the part of the inefficient. This adjustment can be painful for some.

Inefficient industries have their workers and managers with accumulated specialized training, their stockholders with claims over plant and equipment, their localities whose special characteristics have been capitalized, all of whom lose to the extent that they cannot transfer themselves readily to industries for which a national comparative advantage exists. In the event that very large, very rapid adjustments are required, the possibility exists that a socially intolerable situation may develop. The history of economic policy in the twentieth century in the United States, and perhaps more so elsewhere, is the history of attempts to mitigate the unfettered ravages of the market economy. While macroeconomic policies have been designed to curb the vagaries of the business cycle, and responsible balance of payment behavior has been defined, if not always practiced, internationally acceptable policies which can ease the burden of structural adjustment due to import competition remain to be developed. It is widely recognized, however, that to the extent that a serious adjustment problem does exist, some kind of interference with free trade is legitimate.

A benign social policy need not be the only justification for interference with free trade. It is possible a national industry's potential comparative advantage is not being actualized. That is to say, it is not modernizing when this ought to be its policy. The absence of modernizing behavior need not be attributed necessarily to the incompetence of management. Modernization may not be occurring simply because the gestation costs of such activity are high and the individual firm management may feel that it will be impossible to recoup fully such outlays. For example, why train a labor force to do radically different things when your workers when trained may join your competitors? Again, why be a guinea pig for a machinery manufacturer's new design? It may be that only some intervention with free trade will encourage this nationally-useful industrial modernization.

It is possible that an industry which ought to be internationally competitive is found not to be, not because of the modernizing problems mentioned above, but rather because the industry is not operating in a competitively healthy economy. For example, capital markets may not be operating in a manner as to insure that the most efficient firms and industries are getting their share of resources. Again labor market institutions may distort what should be an intimate connection between wages and productivity. In such instances explicit or implicit government intervention may be necessary. Finally, it is possible that an industry for which a national comparative advantage may exist may not be competitive with imports because of the interference with free trade on the part of foreign governments. Given a cosmopolitan perspective, subsidies by foreign governments to industries exporting to the United States may well have to be balanced by subsidies of some kind to American industries.

What kinds of departures from free trade might be appropriate? In the abstract, this is a very difficult question. In the case where the social consequences of import competition with a declining industry are paramount, policies must be designed to move resources gently into more productive areas. Otherwise it is a matter of getting a faltering or an infant industry on a competitive footing. Government help may be proffered in a wide variety of forms. Direct grants to the firms involved are possible. Special tax provisions can encourage investment in capital goods and/or training and retraining of labor. Tariffs and quotas are implicit subsidies, less obvious to the taxpayer, more noticeable by the foreign competitor. Suffice it to say here, a priori, one cannot rule out completely any of the above policy instruments. Depending on the technological imperatives of industrial modernization, depending on the political decision-making process, depending on the economic distortions at home and abroad, any of the policy instruments may be a useful aid to attaining national objectives.

The American Textile and Apparel Industries—
The Position of Capital and Labor in the Industry

Can it be argued in consequence of increased import competition in recent years that an adjustment of a socially intolerable magnitude has been required of the American textile and apparel industry? Below there is presented a set of tables which attempt to characterize the aggregate well-being of this industry. In these tables cottons and woolens have been aggregated together with man-made textiles. To talk about declining cotton employment and production when cotton capital and labor are simply shifting into man-made fabrics is to manufacture a problem where none may exist. Similarly, to discuss rapidly increasing man-made imports while ignoring controlled and stagnating cotton imports and declining woolen imports is to indulge in a curious exaggeration.

Clearly, while imports do not dominate the American textile and apparel market, they nonetheless control a not insubstantial share. While this is true of textile and apparel imports as a whole, this cannot be said of imports from Japan taken individually. This control of a substantial and growing share of the American market by foreign manufacturers does not appear to have had an impact of socially intolerable proportions on domestic manufacturers. While the textile mill rate of return to stockholder equity figures seem somewhat low and the industry unemployment rate seems somewhat higher than average, there is nothing at this level of aggregation which suggests that a special suspension of a liberal trade outlook is required (see Tables 7-1, 7-2, 7-3, 7-4, and 7-5).

It should be pointed out that both indicators of industrial well-being used here are fraught with very real limitations. Some have argued that because of the age structure of the textile and apparel industry capital stock, calculation of industry net worth has been biased downward and calculation of profits biased upward, thus making the published and relatively low rate of return figures upward-biased estimates of the true rate of return figures. Insofar as the

Table 7-1
Profits after Federal Income Taxes as a Percentage of Stockholder Equity, 1960-1971

	U.S. Manufacturing	U.S. Textiles	U.S.Apparel
1960	9.2%	5.8%	7.7%
1961	8.9	5.0	7.2
1962	9.8	6.2	9.3
1963	10.3	6.1	7.7
1964	11.6	8.5	11.7
1965	13.0	10.9	12.7
1966	13.4	10.1	13.3
1967	11.7	7.6	12.0
1968	12.1	8.8	13.0
1969	11.5	7.9	11.9
1970	9.3	5.1	9.3
1971[a]	9.6	6.1	9.6

[a]First three quarters only.

Source: *Federal Reserve Bulletin*.

Table 7-2
U.S. Employment Rates: 1950-71

	Total U.S. Private Nonagricultural	U.S. Manufacturing (Including Textiles and Apparel)	U.S. Textile and Apparel
1950	39196	15241	2458
1955	43761	16882	2269
1960	45881	16796	2158
1965	50741	18062	2280
1966	53163	19214	2365
1967	54459	19447	2355
1968	56070	19781	2399
1969	58083	20167	2410
1970	58081	19367	2350
1971	57835	18608	2325

Source: United States Department of Labor, Bureau of Labor Statistics, *Employment and Earnings.*

Table 7-3
U.S. Unemployment Rates: 1965-71

	U.S. Manufacturing	U.S. Textile and Apparel
1965	4.0%	6.5%
1966	3.2	5.9
1967	3.7	4.5
1968	3.3	4.9
1969	3.3	5.2
1970	5.6	7.3
1971	6.8	8.1

Source: United States Department of Labor, Bureau of Labor Statistics, *Employment and Earnings.*

unemployment figures are concerned, it should be understood that industrial unemployment rates are tabulated by asking individuals unemployed and looking for work what was the industry in which they held their last job. To the extent that displaced textile and apparel workers stop looking for jobs, to the extent that textile and apparel workers in finding jobs displace workers in other industries or new entrants to the labor force, to the extent that workers in finding new jobs sustain substantial cuts in pay and incur substantial relocation costs, the unemployment rate might not adequately reflect the impact of imports on the industry labor force. In reviewing the above observations, these qualifications should be kept in mind.

Table 7-4
Textile Imports and Textile Production, 1965-1971 (in Millions of Current Dollars)

	U.S. Textile Imports from Japan	Total U.S. Textile Imports	Total U.S. Textile Production
1965	189	716	19611
1966	206	774	19550
1967	172	704	19401
1968	221	847	21785
1969	238	888	23208
1970	264	1008	22040
1971	346	1268	22818

Source: U.S. Department of Commerce, Bureau of the Census, *Highlights of U.S. Exports and Imports*; U.S. Department of Commerce, Office of Business Economics, *Survey of Current Business.*

Table 7-5
U.S. Apparel Imports (Millions of Current Dollars), 1965-1971

	U.S. Apparel Imports from Japan	Total U.S. Apparel Imports	U.S. Apparel Production
1965	159	593	21588
1966	183	654	21671
1967	176	699	21688
1968	211	884	22977
1969	268	1100	23289
1970	284	1249	23529
1971	294.2	1507	23726

Source: U.S. Department of Commerce, Bureau of the Census, *Highlights of U.S. Exports and Imports*; U.S. Department of Commerce, Office of Business Economics, *Survey of Current Business.*

In considering the impact of imports one must be struck by the absence of new employment opportunities in the postwar period in the American textile and apparel industries. Given the relatively small proportion of the textile and apparel market occupied by imports, it is difficult to lay this phenomenon entirely at import competition's doorstep. Nonetheless, in understanding the structural evolution of industries, it is instructive to analyze the determinants of employment in textiles and apparel.

Decisions regarding employment are made by individual firm managers. In an effort to explain and project employment levels, economists often caricature this decision-making process algebraically. Thus, if it is assumed that managers maximize profits subject to the constraints of technology and consumer demand, and if these constraints are represented algebraically in ways which are widely, if not universally acceptable, then the textile and apparel industry labor force can be shown to be a function of textile and apparel technology, wage rates, the cost of capital, price of materials, real disposable personal income, and population.

Concretely, firm managers maximize

Revenue − Costs, say profits $= po - wl - sr - qk$

where $p \equiv$ price of output

$o \equiv$ quantity of output

$w \equiv$ hourly costs of workers

$l \equiv$ worked man-hours

$s \equiv$ price of materials

$r \equiv$ raw materials

$q \equiv$ cost of capital

$k \equiv$ capital services

subject to the two constraints of technology and demand. The techonology constraint means output is constrained by the amount of capital, labor, and raw materials used. That is to say, the production of additional output requires the use of additional inputs. It is assumed that this relationship between inputs and outputs can be expressed algebraically in the following manner.

$$o = a^e t_l^b k^c r^d ,$$

where a, b, c, d and e are constants or parameters and $t \equiv$ sometime index which increases regularly with the passing years. The numerical values which the parameters take on indicate the responsiveness of output to changes in the various inputs. Thus, if b takes on the value 0.3, this means that a 10 percent increase in man-hours will lead to a 3 percent increase in output. The above algebraic formulation of the relation between inputs and outputs is widely used by economists. At the very least, it may be viewed as a good, if simple, approximation of the more complex relations between inputs and outputs.

The demand constraint means that the price of textile output is functionally related to the quantity of output produced, personal disposable income, population, and the price of textile imports. That such a relationship exists should be intuitively clear. Price may have to decline in order for a market to absorb additional output. With a given output, an increase in personal disposable income should force up prices. Again, decrease in the prices of imported goods should force down domestic prices. The demand constraint is assumed to take on the following form.

$$p = v_0 \left(\frac{o}{n}\right)^{v_1} \left(\frac{y}{n}\right)^{v_2} (xp_j)^{v_3} ,$$

where v_0, v_1, v_2, and v_3 are the parameters and

$y \equiv$ disposable personal income

$p_J \equiv$ price of textile and apparel imports in foreign currency

$x \equiv$ exchange rate of foreign currency into dollars

$n \equiv$ population.

The algebraic form of the demand constraint is analogous with that of the technological constraint. The parameters of this relationship can again be easily interpreted. For example, if $v_3 = 1$, a 1 percent decline in textile import prices will lead to a 7 percent decline in domestic textile prices. The values which the parameters take on give a quantitative specification of the qualitative relations discussed above in connection with the demand constraint.

Taking the technology and demand constraints and simulating the maximization of profits by using the optimizing calculus, one arrives, after considerable manipulation, at the following equation which purports to explain textile industry employment.

$$\bar{L} = a^* - b^* \bar{W} + c^* \bar{Q} + d^* \bar{S} + e^* t + f^* \bar{Y} + g^* (\bar{XP_J}) + h^* \bar{N} \qquad (8.1)$$

where

$\bar{L} \equiv$ logarithm l
$$a^* \equiv \frac{1 \text{ logarithm} \left\{ cv_0 \left[\left(\frac{b}{c}\right)^b \left(\frac{d}{c}\right)^d \right]^{v_1 + 1} \right\}}{[1 - (v_1 + 1)(b + c + d)]}$$

$\bar{W} \equiv$ logarithm w
$$b^* \equiv - \frac{(v_1 + 1)(c + d) - 1}{[1 - (v_1 + 1)(b + c + d)]}$$

$\bar{Q} \equiv$ logarithm q
$$c^* \equiv - \frac{(v_1 + 1)c}{[1 - (v_1 + 1)(b + c + d)]}$$

$\bar{S} \equiv$ logarithm s
$$d^* \equiv - \frac{(v_1 + 1)d}{[1 - (v_1 + 1)(b + c + d)]}$$

$$\overline{Y} \equiv \text{logarithm } y \qquad f^* \equiv \frac{v_2}{[1 - (v_1 + 1)(b + c + d)]}$$

$$\overline{XP_J} \equiv \text{logarithm } xp_J \qquad g^* \equiv \frac{v_3}{[1 - (v_1 + 1)(b + c + d)]}$$

$$\overline{N} \equiv \text{logarithm } n \qquad h^* \equiv - \frac{(v_1 + v_2)}{[1 - (v_1 + 1)(b + c + d)]}$$

$$\overline{A} \equiv \text{logarithm } a \qquad e^* \equiv \frac{(v_1 + 1)e\hat{A}}{1 - (v_1 + 1)(b + c + d)}$$

The complexity of the above equation is more apparent than real. The coefficients of import price, personal disposable income, population and the input prices are functions of the parameters of the constraint relations. Considering what has already been said, it is not surprising to find that there has been considerable speculation and research among economists as to what values these parameters may take on. Taking advantage of this shelf of research on these questions at the industry and product level one can arrive at a set of plausible figures for these parameters which at the same time explain employment trends in the textile and apparel industry. Table 7-6 presents the results of this exercise.

The explanation proposed in Table 7-6 should not be viewed as definitive. It does rest on a very reasonable set of parameter values and a decision-making model, most elements of which have been found to be highly useful for prediction and heuristic purposes. In any case, it would seem that only a very small part of the lack of secular growth in employment opportunities in the textile and apparel industry can be attributed to import competition. By itself import competition has been responsible for a 1.4 percent decline in textile and apparel industry labor force in the twenty-one years since 1950. This effect is really quite minor when compared with the impact on employment of a rising wage rate, improved production processes, and a relatively low rate of increase in demand for textiles. In the absence of countervailing forces, rising wages would have been responsible between 1950 and 1971 for something like an 70 percent decline in textile and apparel labor!

What is seen at work here is the natural evolution of the American economy being responsible for the lack of employment growth. As the American economy develops, its growth outstrips the natural increase in the labor force. This leads to an increase in the wages which the textile industry must pay its workers. This, in turn, leads to an increasingly capital-intensive structure of production. This

Table 7-6

Explanation of Change in Total Man-Hours Worked in Textile and Apparel Industry: 1950-71

Change in total man-hours	−5.6%
Attributable to	
improved processes and inputs	−31.2
change in the wage rate	−69.8
change in capital cost	+17.9
change in raw material prices	+0.8
change in personal disposable income	+58.5
change in population	+16.1
import competition	− 1.4

$v_1 = -2; v_2 = 1.34; v_3 = 1; b = 0.3; c = 0.25; d = 0.45; e = 0.015$

$a = 2.718$ are the assumed values for the parameters

Source: Data used in the construction of this table has been taken from Bureau of Labor Statistics, *Employment and Earnings*; Office of Business Economics, *Survey of Current Business*; Federal Reserve Board, *Federal Reserve Bulletin*; Nihon Ginko, *Yushutsunyū bukka shisū nempō*. See appendix for a discussion of the plausibility of parameter values.

trend may have been accelerated in the early and mid-1960s when special depreciation guidelines were adopted for the textile industry by the U.S. Treasury Department as part of a program to modernize the industry. At the same time that this structural adjustment in the industry has been occurring, the demand for the product of this industry has been growing relatively slowly. When compared with most other consumer goods, textiles are a necessity. As per capita income grows in the United States, it is expected that the proportion of income spent on textiles declines. Thus, as part and parcel of the evolution of the American economy, the textile industry diminishes in relative importance, while, at the same time, it attempts to remain efficient through the substitution of capital equipment embodying the latest technological advances for increasingly expensive labor.

This last point requires emphasis. The American textile industry is highly efficient. Taken as a whole, the management of this industry have not missed many opportunities to reduce costs. Also, when compared with other textile industries in other countries, best-practice techniques seem very widely diffused in the American industry. Too often the extremely low research and development expenditures as a percentage of textile industry sales are taken as indicative of some technological lag. These statistics ignore the extensive research and development work undertaken by the textile machinery industry. Interestingly, most of this research work has been carried out in recent years by the European machinery industries.

It should be understood, however, that technological progress can only do so much. An efficient American textile industry has lost its export markets. Notwithstanding the widespread opportunities available for substituting capital equipment for labor, this industry remains relative to other industries, quite labor-intensive. Technological sophistication cannot completely offset American labor scarcity and the continued decline of the industry can be expected. To the extent that such a continued decline is not socially disruptive, nor attributable to market distortions or failures, the analysis presented earlier suggests it should be viewed with equanimity.

Local Problems

Even though the aggregate data do not reveal a major crisis in an efficient American textile industry, and even though the destiny of the industry seems largely determined by the evolution of the American economy, it is still possible that the aggregate data and the general trends mask local problems of considerable importance. Determining the extent to which this is true is an extremely difficult problem. There are only six American states whose economies depend mainly upon the textile and apparel industries. These states include North Carolina, South Carolina, Georgia, Alabama, Mississippi, and Tennessee. Interestingly enough, the unemployment rates for these six states have in recent years been below the national average. While the usefulness of state unemployment rates as welfare indicators are impaired by the possibility of interstate migration, the above observation, nonetheless, retains its significance. That the trend of unemployment has been up in some of these states does not negate this observation at all. The mild loosening of a tight regional labor market cannot be thought of as a serious social problem.

One can pursue the problem at yet a further level of disaggregation. With the aid of the Census of Manufactures, it is possible to identify those metropolitan regions (SMSA) for which the textile and apparel industries are an important component of the local economy. Of the more than forty-five textile-dependent districts in the United States, only five have had higher than average unemployment rates in recent years. These five cities—Lowell and New Bedford in Massachusetts; Johnstown, Scranton, and Wilkes-Barre in Pennsylvania all lie outside the South. Indeed, Greenville, South Carolina, the city where President Nixon made his famous campaign promise, and probably the most textile-dominated metropolitan area in the country, has had unemployment rates significantly lower than the national average for quite some time.

It would seem that on the basis of what local evidence exists, it is difficult to find local crises. Five cities in Pennsylvania and Massachusetts seem to be in some trouble, but even here it is not clear that this unemployment has any connection with the textile industry, much less that import competition has been responsible for the loss of jobs that has occurred. Textile industries in the

Northeast have sustained serious and measurable damage for years from Southern competition.

Still it must be remembered that 61 percent of all textile and apparel jobs are located in nonmetropolitan areas. It is possible that it is some of these mills that have been affected by foreign competition. Such mills would have to be sufficiently dispersed by state to explain why their difficulties do not appear in the state statistics. At the same time the number of mills so affected could not be sufficiently large as to be reflected in the national industrial statistics. So defined, a local problem may yet exist, but it is hardly reasonable to proceed on the presumption that this in fact is the case.

Other Justifications for Interference with Free Trade

American textile quotas have been justified largely as an ameliorative social policy. It has been shown that the basis for such justification is dubious at best. Is it possible to justify intervention on any of the other grounds discussed above? As noted above, the notion that the American textile and apparel industry has not been willing or able to modernize is categorically rejected. Unprecedently heavy capital expenditures have been made in the last seven years. Nor can it be argued that there are special, unusual distortions operating in the labor market which the textile and apparel industry faces, making it difficult for the industry to meet international competition. Only 25 percent of the workers in this sector of the economy are covered by collective bargaining agreements. Wages in textiles and apparel, since 1960, have been rising at about the same rate as wages in manufacturing as a whole. Over the longer period since World War II, textile and apparel wages have lagged well behind wages in other manufacturing industries.

Finally, there remains the problem of distortions in foreign economies which give special advantages to foreign textile and apparel producers in competition with American manufacturers. The visible issue here concerns direct subsidies given by the Japanese government to its textile industry. In the absence of other distortions in the Japanese and American economies, these grants, running into the hundreds of millions of dollars, given to encourage the industry to scrap old machinery, consolidate small firms, and invest in new plant and equipment, could certainly be thought of as giving the Japanese industry an edge inconsistent with the principle of world allocation of resources in accordance with comparative advantage. Putting aside any special implicit subsidies which may be given the American textile and apparel industry by its government, the vast departures from the competitive allocation of capital resources in the Japanese economy deserve recognition here. It may well be that the grants given the Japanese textile industry have corrected to some extent for the biases against allocation of resources to an industry not seen by Japanese economic planners as part of the wave of the future. To the degree that this is true, an American policy which singles out textile imports from Japan for special retribution would be an economic mistake.

The American Market, the Japanese Textile Industry and the Japanese Economy

If voluntary export quotas cannot be justified either on social or economic grounds, it is fair to ask at this juncture what effect American restrictions will have on the Japanese textile industry. Japanese textile exports to the United States are less than 4 percent of Japanese textile production (see Table 7-7). From the viewpoint of the aggregate economic health of this industry, the American market would not seem to be of crucial importance. Nor is this market crucial from the balance-of-payments perspective.

Lest the Japanese textile industry's importance be viewed through glasses of the 1930s, it should be pointed out that the industry is hardly more important for the Japanese economy than it is for the American economy. In both countries, as Tables 7-8 and 7-9 show, textiles' relative importance has been declining for years.

What of the claim that a serious crisis will develop in Japan as a result of the American restrictions? In the same way that American producer decisions were caricatured, Japanese textile and apparel manufacturers can be thought of as maximizing their profits subject to the constraints of technology and demand. In this instance, there can be many demand constraints—a demand constraint for the home market and demand constraints for foreign markets. Again, as a consequence of this maximization process, Japanese textile and apparel prices, production, exports to foreign markets, employment and the employment levels of other industry inputs can be determined. The following equation which

Table 7-7
Japanese Textile and Apparel Production and the American Market (Millions of Current Dollars), 1965-1969

	Total Japanese Textile and Apparel Production	Japanese Textile and Apparel Exports to U.S.	Total Japanese Exports
1965	8428	348	8451
1966	9464	389	9776
1967	10546	348	10442
1968	11552	432	12972
1969	13058	506	15990

Source: Tsūsanshō, Kōgyō Tōkei Nempō; Nihon Ginko, Keizai Tokei Nempo.

Table 7-8

Value Added in Textiles and Wearing Apparel as a Proportion of Total Value Added in Manufacturing in Japan and the United States, 1965-1969

	Japan	U.S.
1955	12.9%	8.1%
1960	9.5	7.8
1965	8.2	7.2
1966	7.6	7.2
1967	7.3	7.1
1968	6.8	7.3
1969	6.3	–

Source: Keizai Kikakuchō, *Kokumin Shotoku Tōkei Nempō*; Office of Business Economics, *Survey of Current Business*.

Table 7-9

Textile and Apparel Employment and Manufacturing Employment in Japan and the United States (Thousands of Workers), 1965-1969

	Japan		United States	
	Textile and Apparel Employment	Manufacturing Employment	Textile and Apparel Employment	Manufacturing Employment
1961	1,493	8,751	2108	16,326
1965	1,638	9,920	2280	18,062
1966	1,668	10,291	2365	19,214
1967	1,666	10,554	2355	19,447
1968	1,647	10,863	2399	19,781
1969	1,663	11,412	2410	20,167

Source: Tsūsansho, *Kōgyo Tōkei Nempō*; Bureau of Labor Statistics *Employment and Earnings*.

explains Japanese textile exports to the American market is an implication of this process.

Table 7-10

The Explanation of Japanese Textile and Apparel Exports to the American Market

$$\overline{E} \equiv a^{**} - b_J{}^{**}\overline{W}_J - c_J{}^{**}\overline{Q}_J - d_J{}^{**}\overline{S}_J + e_J{}^{**}t_J + f^{**}\overline{Y} - g^{**}\overline{X}$$

$$+ h^{**}\overline{N} + b_A{}^{**}\overline{W}_A + c_A{}^{**}\overline{Q}_A + d_A{}^{**}\overline{S}_A - e_A{}^{**}t_A \qquad (8.2)$$

where

$$\frac{p_J}{x} = v_0 {}^{**}E^{v_1}{}^{**}y^{v_2}{}^{**}p_A{}^{v_3}{}^{**}n^{-v_1}{}^{**}{}^{-v_2}{}^{**}$$

is the demand constraint for Japanese origin textile and apparel exports to the American market,

p_J $\equiv$ unit price (in yen) of these exports

x $\equiv$ yen-dollar exchange rate

E $\equiv$ Japanese textile and apparel exports to the American market

y $\equiv$ American personal disposal income

p_A $\equiv$ unit price (in dollars) of American made textile and apparel

n $\equiv$ American population,

where

$$o_J = a_J e^{f^t} l_J{}^{b_J} k_J{}^{c_J} r_J{}^{d_J}$$

and

$$o_A = a_A e^{A^t} l_A{}^{b_A} k_A{}^{c_A} r_A{}^{d_A}$$

are the Japanese and American technology constraints and it is assumed $b_J + c_J + d_J = 1$ and $b_A + c_A + d_A = 1$

l_J $\equiv$ labor employed in the Japanese textile and apparel industry

k_J $\equiv$ capital employed in the Japanese textile and apparel industry

r_J $\equiv$ raw materials used in the Japanese textile and apparel industry

o_J $\equiv$ output produced in the Japanese textile and apparel industry

l_A $\equiv$ labor employed in the American textile and apparel industry

k_A $\equiv$ capital employed in the American textile and apparel industry

r_A $\equiv$ raw materials used in the American textile and apparel industry

o_A $\equiv$ output produced in the American textile and apparel industry

and where

$\overline{E}$ $\equiv$ logarithm E $\overline{Y} \equiv$ logarithm y

$$\overline{X} \equiv \text{logarithm } x \qquad\qquad \overline{N} \equiv \text{logarithm } n$$

$$\overline{W}_A \equiv \text{logarithm of American wage rate} \qquad \overline{W}_J \equiv \text{logarithm of Japanese wage rate}$$

$$\overline{Q}_A \equiv \text{logarithm of American capital cost} \qquad \overline{Q}_J \equiv \text{logarithm of Japanese capital cost}$$

$$\overline{S}_A \equiv \text{logarithm of American raw material cost} \qquad \overline{S}_J \equiv \text{logarithm of Japanese raw material cost}$$

$$t_A \equiv \text{American time index} \qquad t_A \equiv \text{Japanese time index}$$

$$a^{**} \equiv -\frac{1}{v_1^{**}} \text{logarithm} \left[b_J^{\,b_J} c_J^{\,c_J} d_J^{\,d_J} v_o^{**}(v_1^{**}+1) \right]$$

$$+ \frac{v_3^{**}}{v_1^{**}} \text{logarithm} \left(b_A^{\,b_A} c_A^{\,c_A} d_A^{\,d_A} \right)$$

$$b_J^{**} \equiv \frac{b_J}{v_1^{**}} \qquad\qquad b_A^{**} \equiv -\frac{v_3^{**} b_A}{v_1^{**}}$$

$$c_J^{**} \equiv \frac{c_J}{v_1^{**}} \qquad\qquad c_A^{**} \equiv -\frac{v_3^{**} c_A}{v_1^{**}}$$

$$d_J^{**} \equiv \frac{d_J}{v_1^{**}} \qquad\qquad d_A^{**} \equiv -\frac{v_3^{**}}{v_1^{**}} d_A$$

$$e_J^{**} \equiv -\frac{e_J}{v_1^{**}} \text{logarithm } a_J \qquad e_A^{**} \equiv +\frac{v_3^{**}}{v_1^{**}} e_A \text{logarithm } a_A$$

$$f^{**} \equiv -\frac{v_2^{**}}{v_1^{**}} \qquad\qquad g^{**} \equiv \frac{1}{v_1^{**}}$$

$$h^{**} \equiv \frac{v_1^{**} + v_2^{**}}{v_1^{**}}$$

Equation (2) in Table 7-10 sees Japanese textile and apparel exports to the United States as a function of industry input prices in the two countries, technological change in the two countries, the yen-dollar exchange rate, American disposable income and American population. Note that the explanation of international trade flows is not seen simply as a matter of looking at relative wage increases. Given the possibility of offsetting changes in a wide variety of other variables, rapid increases in relative wages are potentially consistent with zero import growth, decline in import dependence or indeed export growth.

In attempting to understand the consequences for Japan of the American restrictions, the above equation can be used to predict what would have happened in 1972 and 1973 in the absence of restrictions on man-made and woolen textiles. The results of this prediction are presented in Table 7-11. Given the projected 9.2 percent decline of Japanese textile and apparel exports to this country during 1972 and the rather modest increase predicted for 1973, it does not appear that the October 15 Agreement negotiated in the midst of so much heat and ill-will was really necessary. Even if one accepts the premise that limiting Japanese textile and apparel exports is desirable, the American devaluation, the Japanese appreciation, and the antiinflation elements of Nixon's New Economic Program might have been enough to accomplish this end. Since the negotiated restrictions are likely to be largely inoperative, it is unnecessary to talk of their impact. In any event, the American market absorbs such a small proportion of Japanese textile and apparel production that almost any develop-

Table 7-11

Japanese Textile and Apparel Exports to the United States in 1972 and 1973 in the Absence of Restrictions on Man-Made and Woolen Exports[a]

	1972	1973
Change in exports	− 9.2%	5.7%
Attributable to		
change in Japanese wage rate	− 6.3	−6.4
change in Japanese capital cost	0.3	1.5
change in Japanese raw material prices	12.6	−
improved Japanese processes and inputs	3.4	3.4
change in American wage rate	2.7	2.7
change in American capital cost	2.6	3.4
change in American raw material prices	−−	−
improved American processes and inputs	− 2.6	−2.6
change in yen-dollar exchange rate	−25.2	−
change in American real disposable income	3.1	3.1
change in American population	0.2	0.2

[a]$v_1{}^{**} = -0.66; v_2{}^{**} = 0.5; v_3{}^{**} = 1; b_A = 0.3; c_A = 0.25; d_A = 0.45; e_A = 0.0175; a_A = 2.718; b_J = 0.3; c_J = 0.2; d_J = 0.5; e_J = 0.0275; a_J = 2.718$ are assumed values for the constraint parameters. See the appendix for a discussion of the plausibility of these values. The predictions on Japanese input prices, American input prices and American disposable income have been constructed with the aid of forecasts made available by the Japan Economic Research Center and the University of Michigan Research Seminar on Quantitative Economics.

ment in that market is unlikely to have a large impact on the Japanese industry. The projected 9.2 percent decline in Japanese exports to the United States will force down industry employment by no more than 0.3 percent.

This again does not mean that certain small subsectors and certain localities of this industry will not be hurt as a result. In general, however, structural adjustment should not be as serious a problem in the rapidly growing Japanese economy as it might be in the more slowly growing American economy. It is important to understand in this connection the rather special nature of the Japanese industry labor force. While the American textile industry work force is about 65 percent female and middle-aged, the Japanese textile industry work force is about 75 percent female and young. The modal entrant to the textile industry in Japan is a recent junior high school graduate who will work for a few years in a mill prior to marriage. The average age of female spinners is not more than twenty-one years, and the average duration of employment is three years. For women in the apparel industry, the average duration of employment is the same and the average age is twenty-five years. To the extent that the textile-industry labor force is made up of transients who have not made a heavy investment in the acquisition of skills and who do not anticipate long-term employment, the problem of structural adjustment is eased.

Why the Political Flap?

Given that the Japan-American textile trade has little consequence for either the Japanese or American textile industries, one may well ask what was responsible for the confrontation and the bitter recriminations. Policy formation is a very subtle process. Given unequal distribution of access to this process, strange things can happen. All it takes is one aggrieved party with perfect access to develop a general policy catering to a special interest. While the American textile industry in general was in good shape, and while no geographic regions were in serious trouble, one does not lack for aggrieved parties in the product line. For example, more than 50 percent of knit blouses, sweaters, women's knit slacks, women's coats, knit sport shirts, and knit and woven dress shirts are foreign imports. In spite of geographic dispersion, the industrial proximity of these manufacturers is presumably sufficient to allow for the manufacturers and unions in these lines to organize as an effective interest group in favor of the limitation of foreign imports.

It is not only desperation which leads groups to attempt to influence government policy. If gain can be achieved relatively inexpensively, one imagines any route is fair game. When President Nixon evolved a southern strategy, the influential textile interests in that area of the country may well have seen an opportunity to get a measure of protection rather inexpensively. While foreign imports had yet to make a serious impact on domestic markets, the threat of international competition was always present. Moreover, the rather large investments in labor-saving equipment made during the 1960s by the industry had often been legitimatized by the need to stay ahead of foreign manufacturers. Certainly both President Nixon and the southern textile interest did not anticipate the Japanese reaction to their proposal for quantitative restrictions on man-made fibers and woolen goods. Presumably they imagined that their proposal would be viewed as a natural extension of the 1962 agreement on cotton textiles. This agreement, which had originally applied only to Japan, had during the course of the 1960s been successively applied to a large number of countries which, taking advantage of the restraints on Japan exports, had expanded their exports to the United States. While the existence of restraints on cotton goods imports is not sufficient to explain the increase in the imports of man-made fiber products to this country, they certainly are part of the explanation. It might be argued that the extension of the agreement to man-made fibers was necessary to accomplish the aims of the original agreement.

Even if there was the expectation that quotas could be had without too much reaction from foreign producers, one must wonder why the Nixon administration persisted in its efforts for very strict controls when it became apparent that a major international controversy was in the making. During the first year of negotiations it was not entirely obvious that there would be unusual difficulties. From all information available, it seems that President Nixon felt the problem had been favorably disposed of in the course of his Okinawa discussions with Prime Minister Sato in November 1969. While this may have been President Nixon's understanding, and a secret agreement may well have been concluded, nothing in either Japanese or English versions of the communique alludes directly or indirectly to the Voluntary Textile Quota issue. In any event, when negotiations did not proceed as smoothly as expected, the Nixon administration unofficially justified its intransigence on the grounds that the Japanese were reneging on an understanding which was inextricably if informally tied to the all important Okinawa Reversion Understanding.

United States annoyance was exacerbated by an acceleration in textile imports while negotiations were underway. This acceleration, ironically, was the consequence of the expectation that a quota agreement would be successfully negotiated and that shares of the quota would be allocated on the basis of shares of the American market held shortly before the time of the agreement. As such an acceleration makes quotas, indeed very strict quotas, almost inevitable, one might expect some voluntary restraint during the course of negotiation.

Unfortunately, textile and apparel technology is sufficiently diffused so that the industry in Japan is only one of many industries exporting textiles to the United States. Concerted action across national boundaries is difficult, particularly when such action is seen by other countries as designed to preserve Japan's historically large share of the American textile import market. Restraint is difficult even within the Japanese industry and for much the same reasons.

The industry has a relatively large number of firms and newer entrants into the American market are unwilling to concede large market shares to older firms. It is this outlook which accounted for an increase in exporting capacity at just the time when the threat of quotas might have been enough to deter investment.

While evidence of bad faith at least fueled the Nixon administration's interest in continuing its advocacy of very strict quotas, what accounts for continued Japanese opposition? The locus of the Japanese opposition was not so much the government as it was the industry and the textile unions. Why the violent industry opposition if the economic impact was not likely to be very large? As in the case of the American government, it need not be true that the representative organs of labor and capital in the Japanese textile industry are so organized as to represent accurately the views of the industry in general.

Beyond this possibility, it is clear that industry leaders were preoccupied with long-term considerations. In the wake of loosening trade restrictions, imports of cheaper grades of textiles had been increasing rather substantially in the Japanese home markets. The 16 percent of domestic production going to export markets was being threatened by the newer textile industries in other Asian countries.

Textile industry management, largely in its sixties and seventies, has been conditioned by experience to expect structural changes of fundamental magnitude. Within the adult recollection of these leaders is the growth of Japanese textiles from a domestically oriented small-scale industry before World War I, to a major export role during World War I, to world dominance in the 1930s, to utter destruction during World War II, to a rebirth in the postwar period as an important but not preeminent manufacturing industry in a much more rapidly growing Japanese economy.

Given the industry's structural adjustment program of the last few years, it is very clear that industry leadership hoped to maintain and even substantially develop the industry's position in export markets through dominating the most sophisticated end of the textile industry product line. As a long-term prospect, it was hoped that a Japanese combination of good technology and relatively cheap labor would lead to a rapid erosion of the market shares of American and European manufacturers.

If the current very strict three-year U.S. quotas on man-made fiber textile imports persist indefinitely, as seems likely, this hoped-for possibility is foreclosed. As the earlier projection makes clear, in the short run, one does not expect that the quotas will have much real influence. In the long run, however, given changes in tastes, the very strict category rules will work to inhibit real growth in Japanese exports to American markets. Given the American precedent of restricting growing textile imports, rapid expansion of Japanese textile exports into other markets may also be stymied.

It may well be that to look for serious damage to either textile industry or to look for some small group diverting public policy to its own ends is seriously to misunderstand historical process. Large wars are fought over small bits of land. As was pointed out earlier, the textile issue had and has tremendous symbolic importance. On what terms will the fruits of Japan's newly efficient manufacturing industries be allowed into the American market? Elements in the United States are increasingly seeing the 1962 GATT agreement on cotton as the paradigm, while Japan, in a rather remarkable change of attitude, is beginning to support worldwide free trade. Once it became apparent that any textile agreement hammered out might well be an important building block in a new world trading order, agreement by the governments involved became at least somewhat more difficult.

Even if this intervention in the international textile and apparel trade had been justified, and even if it was necessary, the instrument of intervention, economically speaking, was a very poor choice. Inflexible, seemingly permanent import quotas, allocated on the basis of historical shares and administered by the foreign exporting industries are no way to build a new world order. Unless one assumes that optimum efficiency stems from perfect security, this system seems to encourage sloth and does so at the same time that it implicitly pays a very large bribe to foreign manufacturers to weaken their opposition to a system which typically will rob American consumers of the benefits of international specialization.

Appendix To Chapter 7

The parameter values chosen for the production and demand relations (see p. 183) define a competitive industry producing a relatively income inelastic product. Given the extremely low concentration ratios in the American textile and apparel industries the competitive characterization seems entirely warranted. Otto Eckstein's recent study of industry pricing behavior tends to confirm this view. If the industry is competitive, under a given technology, constant unit costs can be expected. Within the context of the caricature being discussed here, this implies $b + c + d = 1$. (Under a competitive regime, profit maximization by the firm, existing and potential, does not lead inevitably to maximum aggregate profits for the industry. Instead of using the firm optimum condition, marginal revenue = marginal cost as was done implicitly in deriving Equation 1, the competitive industry socially optimum condition, average revenue equals average cost, might better be used. This change, while conceptually important, alters only the constant term in Equation 1. The constant term is irrelevant to the construction of Table 7-6.) The actual choice of values for b, c and d has been guided by technological information on the American industry available in the British Textile Council's study *Cotton and Allied Textiles*.

Given that clothing is a necessary consumption item, it is reasonable to expect that the demand for the output of the textile and apparel industries will be income inelastic. In this study an elasticity of 0.67 has been used. For each 1 percent increase in per capita income there will be a 0.67 percent increase in per capita demand for textile and apparel products. This assumed value is consistent with the findings presented by Houthakker and Taylor in their recent consumer demand study and with work done on this subject by Bela Balassa.

The same studies which confirm this income inelasticity of demand also suggest that the "textile price relative to the general price level" elasticity of demand is zero. On the other hand, casual reflection as well as the results of econometric studies by Moriguchi and Ueno suggest that the "domestic textile price relative to the imported textile price" elasticity is nonzero and negative. v_3 and v_1 have been chosen such that this elasticity is -0.5.

The parameter values chosen for system used in projecting Japanese textile and apparel exports to the United States in the absence of import restrictions can be rationalized on grounds much the same as those just presented. In the first place, the American technological constraint is the same in both the export determination and the labor determination systems. As for the Japanese technological constraint, low concentration ratios in this industry again argue for $b_J + c_J + d_J = 1$. The British study referred to earlier has again been used to determine the precise values for these coefficients. Finally the American import demand constraint parameter values have been chosen with the Moriguchi-Ueno Japanese export-demand functions in mind.

8 Competitive Development of the Japanese Steel Industry

James van B. Dresser, Jr., Thomas M. Hout, and
William V. Rapp

Introduction

The brilliant success of Japan's steel industry is frequently attributed to, in varying combinations, cheap labor, unfair price competition, and government assistance. In fact, these alleged factors have had little or no impact on the Japanese steel industry's recent performance. Japanese unit labor costs have dropped relative to the United States steadily since 1965, yet Japanese steelmakers' wages have increased three times faster. The unfair pricing hypothesis has never been satisfactorily documented, and under voluntary steel export quotas Japanese steel prices in the United States have become artificially high. The government did provide significant financial assistance and incentives during the industry's postwar redevelopment. As this report will suggest, however, government's cooperation with industry over the last decade has been neither economically decisive nor operationally mysterious. It is easy to overestimate the government's impact on Japan's competitive position.

A more accurate explanation of Japan's success would emphasize a modern physical steelmaking capacity resulting from the highest investment levels per ton in the developed world, application of highly effective raw material acquisition and logistics systems, and productivity gains which overcome rapidly rising labor wages and lowered actual unit labor costs over the 1960s. In a context of rapid growth in the domestic market and a supportive national government policy, Japan has become the low-cost broad line steel producer in the world. This paper describes the historical development and competitive economics of this remarkable performance.

Industry Evolution

Prewar Pattern

Steel is traditionally the *sine qua non* of industrial development and military adventure. Japan's sustained and rapid rate of industrialization and her periodic military episodes created large, often sudden demands on steel production. The

201

country, however, has little iron ore and only limited coal deposits; hence domestic production has required from the beginning the import of basic materials. The small production scale and the logistics of raw material acquisition made early Japanese steelmaking decidedly uncompetitive. Private capital was not attracted in significant amounts to steelmaking until the twentieth century. The Japanese government, in order to ensure an adequate steel supply, directly or indirectly controlled the industry for nearly the entire period from the Meiji Restoration through the Second World War.

At the turn of the century, the government established Japan's first large modern mill. The Yawata Mill dominated production, the remainder of which was shared among older state-owned and scattered private mills. The mill was built on the northern coast of Kyushu to eliminate the overland haul of ore and coal from mainland China. Finished steel imports exacerbated the chronic foreign exchange problem, so the government subsidized the Yawata mill for ten years until its operations were reasonably competitive with imports.

World War I launched the steel industry in Japan as requirements rose dramatically and imports of finished steel from Europe diminished. All of today's major private firms including Fuji (later merged with Yawata into Japan Steel), Sumitomo, Kobe, Kawasaki, and Nihon Kokan were established in the first fifteen years of the century. Production was stimulated by special wartime tax exemptions.

Overcapacity, which plagued the industry during the 1920s, became critical during the depression of the early 1930s. The government responded with the Important Industry Law of 1931, conferring on government the authority to organize production and allocate markets. In 1934, the Japan Steel Company was organized by consolidating Yawata with the six largest private steel companies. The state was directly responsible for its creation and, through Yawata, owned 70 percent of the consolidated firm. War with China in 1937 enlarged the role of the state's bureaucracy in the industry. The Ministry of Commerce and Industry, MITI's predecessor, both allocated production among steelmakers and rationed output to end-users during the military buildup of the late 1930s. In 1941 full operating control passed to the government and remained there throughout the war.

The prewar pattern, then, was not one of simply close cooperations but of frequent direct control. The management of steel producers were accustomed to reporting alternately to shareholders and government officials. The necessity which Japan faced of rapidly expanding wartime production and allocating imported raw materials among producers drew government into the industry's operations. The practice of placing former vice ministers of government on the boards of large manufacturing firms had its origins in the immediate prewar period, and the steel industry was the leading practitioner. Until its dissolution at the war's end, Japan Steel Company was effectively an extension of the Japanese government.

Postwar Recovery

Steel was identified early in the postwar period as an absolutely critical redevelopment priority. In August 1945 only three of Japan's thirty-five wartime blast furnaces were in operation. Significantly, the decline in production had resulted more from disruption of raw material supplies into Japan than from destruction of the plants. Japan's industry had been turned off at the port. Consequently, the problem was not to rebuild the nation's steel capacity but to restore them to production.

One of the first major postwar joint economic policies of the Japanese Cabinet and the General Headquarters of the Allied Powers was to designate steel, coal, electric power generation, and chemical fertilizer as the key recovery industries.

Funds for steel industry rehabilitation came from two broad sources: government subsidies and a mixture of government and private borrowings. The postwar production cost of steel exceeded both the prewar level and, more importantly, the economically desirable level for supplying the critical basic material in Japan's reconstruction. Consequently, subsidies were provided at both the steel resale price level and the imported raw material level. The critical subsidy was the former: from 1947 through 1950, cumulative price of steel to end-users was reduced by over one-quarter of a billion dollars from producer cost levels. This sum represented nearly 30 percent of all price subsidies awarded to strategic postwar industries including coal, fertilizer, power, and food. Coal price subsidies, which accrued indirectly to steel producers, accounted for an additional 15 percent.

Renovation of existing capacity was financed by a mixture of debt instruments. The Reconstruction Finance Bank, a government financial institution, responded to the Cabinet's designation of priorities and became the single major creditor of the industry during the immediate postwar period. The commercial banks themselves loaned roughly $14 million to the industry from 1947 to 1950. Private bank capital was scarce, and Tokyo's city banks responded to the administrative guidance of the Bank of Japan in directing funds to the economy's various sectors. A strong, almost tacit consensus existed on the necessity to completely restore production in the vital industries.

There was a distinction, however, between restoring capacity and expanding capacity, and it was this issue which occasioned the first visible policy disagreement over the recovery strategy for the steel industry. The postwar inflation caused the government in 1949 to cut back the economy's recovery program. As a result, the steel industry which by 1949 had roughly recovered its 1935 production level of 4.7 million crude metric tons experienced reduced price and import subsidies, causing the cost of steel to rise and the demand to fall. Yataro Nishiyama, president of Kawasaki Steel, which was and remains an aggressive firm, announced his intention to build a major new steel plant, the first substantial capacity increase since the war. The Bank of Japan, under the direction of Hisato Ichimada who was nicknamed "The Pope" in light of the bank's powerful influence at the time, had helped to initiate, and strongly supported, the deflationary economic policy. The Bank discouraged the expansion, pointing out its inflationary effect and the existing unutilized industry capacity. Kawasaki, seeking to gain market share, argued that domestic demand would rapidly increase after the temporary countercyclical policy expired and that adequate construction lead time recommended Kawasaki's plan. Kawasaki did build its plant. The Bank of Japan continued to advise against it but did not attempt to impose its position on Kawasaki's banks, and the plant was financed domestically. Kawasaki emerged prophetic when shortly after, in June 1950, the North Korean Army entered South Korea and steel demand rose sharply.

Subsequently, a First Rationalization Plan was announced by MITI. The plan's objectives were to increase the productivity of existing plants and stimulate the building of new ones over the period 1951-55. Assistance by government was in two categories: broad tax and duty exemptions and loans from government financial institutions. The tax and duty measures were enacted in 1952 and provided:

1. Import duty exemption on designated steelmaking equipment. (Sixty percent of such equipment was imported at that time.)
2. Fifty percent increase in depreciation base allowed on designated equipment.
3. Reserve for price changes in inventories and securities established as tax-free contingency measure.
4. Revaluation of assets permitted, effectively increasing the depreciation base.
5. Additional bad debt reserves permitted.

The effect of these measures was to increase the funds from operations available for reinvestment and, in particular, toward specific types of investments. Over the five-year period (1951-55) when steel output doubled from 4.8 to 9.6 million tons, internal funds generation accounted for one-quarter of the $145 million capital expenditures in the industry. Another 10 percent was financed through new equity issue while the remaining two-thirds was through debt instruments. It is evident that Japan's steel industry, now well-known outside Japan for its aggressive high-debt financial policies, was forced to accept high debt levels at an early postwar date in order to finance its growth.

The borrowings from government financial institutions during this period were characteristically large in amount and further leveragable with private commercial banks. The Japan Development Bank, the Industrial Bank of Japan, and the Long Term Credit Bank—all governmental or quasi-governmental banks—lent to the steel industry and accounted for roughly half of the $95 million in debt undertaken during this period. Commercial banks were encouraged to finance the steel expansion, and the Ministry of Finance permitted $11 million of foreign exchange loans to the industry.

The First Appearance of Overcapacity

Steel remained an industry of critical policy interest, and a Second Rationalization Plan for 1955-60 was developed by MITI and the industry. It was during this period that Japan's steel industry began to develop its modern, efficient steelmaking capability. Capacity more than doubled over the five years. Moreover, Japan's investment per ton produced was easily the highest in the world over the period and nearly twice that of the United States.

The late 1950s are also notable for the first postwar appearance of temporary overcapacity and the resulting creation of one of the oldest cooperative arrangements in the industry called the public sales system. The mild recession of 1957, when Japan's economic growth rate receded in the midst of the steel capacity boom, created a serious overcapacity situation. Because Japan's steelmakers operate with exceptionally high fixed financial and labor costs, and because rapid trend growth was encouraging larger regular increments to capacity, the cash-flow crisis resulting from substantial underutilization was severe. Prices became extremely flexible downward in an attempt to restore normal operating ratios. As the crisis deepened, severe price-cutting began to appear.

Self-motivated collusion among firms to restrict production and stabilize prices would have violated the Anti-Monopoly Act, the antitrust legacy of the occupation. MITI held informal consultations with industry management in search of a solution, and the public sales system emerged. Under this arrangement, steel producers reported their scheduled monthly production levels to MITI along with price schedules. Prices were made public, and the industry's entire monthly output was to be sold at the announced prices. Production limits and price levels were not made unilaterally by MITI; lengthy discussions usually preceded shifts in the announced levels. The system has survived in one form or another since 1958 and has dampened but not eliminated the spread between announced and actual prices. More serious overcapacity situations have led to MITI-sanctioned price cartels.

Artificial price agreements, however, do not at all accurately describe the competitive environment in steel. The essential fact about Japanese steel prices is not their cyclical instability but rather their long-run trend of sustained decline. The prices of both crude and specialty steels have decreased steadily (in both current and constant yen) since the middle 1950s as scale improvements, rapid productivity gains in excess of wage increases, integrated basic oxygen furnace installations, and progress in raw material logistics have significantly reduced the cost of making steel in Japan. Price competition has been intense. In Figure 8-1, the industry real price index is plotted (double logarithmically) against total industry accumulated production in tons. The evidence indicates a strong functional relationship between the two.

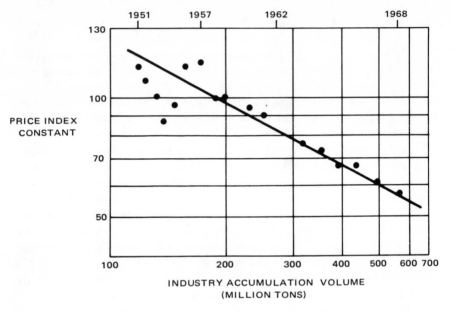

Figure 8-1. Crude Steel: Post-Reconstruction Japan.

The Politics of Capacity Additions

Since the postwar recovery period, it has been obvious to both ministries of government and management of steelmakers that a joint determination of the rate of capacity additions was in the interests of both. The macroeconomic impact of steel expansion's massive financial requirements and of any imbalance in demand and supply of steel dictated that the government influence the growth rate of capacity. On the other hand, the cash flow crises and price instability which follow overbuilding usually persuade the steelmakers to cooperate among themselves and with MITI. There remains a general, although not always unanimous, feeling among producers that consensus with government on capacity decisions is desirable and prudent.

The process, although it has shifted somewhat over time, generally begins with representatives of the privately-owned steel producers gathering within the Japan Iron and Steel Federation tentatively to present and discuss investment intentions for the coming year. Nothing is decided at this meeting or series of meetings, but the producers' plans are evaluated in view of the demand outlook for the industry and the existing pattern of market shares. Often these representatives, usually managing directors, are MITI alumni. Subsequent to these meetings and informal discussions among management and officials of the Iron and Steel Section of MITI's Heavy Industries Bureau, the presidents of the steel producers will seriously discuss and seek consensus on the rate and timing of individual producers' major investments. MITI will participate ex officio in these meetings, bringing its point of view to bear. The periodic frequency of consensus meetings at both levels varies with the complexity of the problem. After a consensus is reached a report is traditionally issued by MITI recommending a course of action to the industry.

This process should not be viewed in terms of the Western public-versus-private dichotomy. The government neither plans nor dictates the rate of capacity expansion. The officials and advisory councils within MITI do not unilaterally and formally accept or reject the industry's consensus, but rather evaluate it in view of Japan's wider economic objectives. Some observers of the industry suggest that no application for a capacity increment from a major firm has ever been flatly rejected, although some have been delayed. This, of course, is the mechanism of the consensus process; the expanding firm is either persuaded to delay his application or is persuaded to accept a delayed approval. When this persuasion doesn't materialize, consensus is frustrated.

The government's sources of authority in this process are both official and traditional. Among official instruments of policy, MITI's control of imported basic materials has been critical. Japan imports 98 percent of her iron ore and 84 percent of her coal needs. MITI directly controlled the importation and allocation of these materials through foreign exchange import quotas. Ore quotas were liberalized in 1965 and coal imports were essentially freed in 1971. Historically, this has been MITI's most immediate control. Foreign exchange control also permits the Bank of Japan to limit steel producers' borrowing from foreign banks. Foreign capital financed 8 percent of Japanese steelmakers' capital budgets during the 1950s and remains an important source. The Bank of Japan establishes queuing rules for access to these funds and limits the rate of lending by individual foreign banks.

The Bank of Japan and the Ministry of Finance bring a macroeconomic and international payments balance perspective to the discussions regarding financing of steel expansions. While MITI's international perspective focuses on the relative competitiveness and growth of Japanese steel, the financial authorities share broader concerns. Hence, in 1970 the bank denied requests for increased foreign borrowings in order to avoid undermining its domestic deflationary policy and depress the rate of increase in dollar reserves. This forced the delay of capacity additions, some of which will be further delayed through 1972 in view of continuing soft demand.

The influence of the steel industry's traditional relationship with the bureaucracy and with the broader economic policy-making community in and out of government should not be overlooked. Their mutual recognition of Japan's dependence on steel is well founded. Early in 1970, steelmakers' preliminary capital budgets for the next five years indicated that a full 10 percent of the Japanese economy's total capital investment for the period would be in steel capacity. The industry has been easily the most critical element in Japan's remarkable postwar economic phenomenon. Its impact on the international competitiveness of Japanese ships, autos, bearings, and machinery has been profound. It is at once one of Japan's biggest importers and exporters. It dominates the domestic capital markets. Recognition of its critical position has been strong. If the thesis that Japan's leaders of business and government share common perceptions of Japan's national interest has any validity, it must apply to Japan's traditional steelmakers.

Current Situation

The current situation among elements of government and the steel industry is a predictable extension of the historical relationship. MITI and the industry continue to confer on capacity, production, and export issues, and the consensus system retains its central position. The exercise of direct controls such as MITI's allocation of imported coal and the Ministry of Finance's strict control of foreign exchange lending to steel is either dormant or infrequent.

In June of 1971, the Bureau of Heavy Industries obtained approval from the Industrial Structure Council of a new program to rationalize and modernize existing steel capacity. The plan, which was formulated with the assistance of the steelmakers, would make it mandatory to idle smaller, obsolescent furnaces as larger modern furnaces became operational. This plan is partially a response to the projected waning of steel demand growth in the intermediate term and partially an effort to retain Japan's position as the most competitive producer overall of steel internationally.

The FTC immediately announced its opposition to this plan, claiming that it is a government-authorized "production adjustment cartel running counter to the Anti-Monopoly Law." A negotiation followed, and after limited concessions from MITI, the FTC accepted the plan.

The major question facing the industry in 1971-72 was steel demand, both long and short run. Earlier estimates of a 150 million ton business by 1975—roughly a 60 percent increase over current levels—have become highly improbable as Japan's recovery from the current recession has failed to materialize.

The short-run implication of the 1971 recession has been overproduction. The persistence of the downturn necessitated a 10 percent reduction in output through midyear which was established by the industry on the basis of self-restraint. The New Economic Policy of the United States in the fall of 1971 prompted the industry to ask MITI to organize a "depression cartel" which would monitor production levels of individual manufacturers. MITI responded by organizing the cartel and negotiating approval of its operation with the Fair Trade Commission.

There are precedents for temporary, MITI-enforced production cartels. In both 1962 and 1965, selected products were cartelized in periods of weak demand. The Anti-Monopoly Law permits such actions when the market price of any product has declined below production cost and rationalization actions by producers do not prove effective remedies. This provision reflects Japan's flexible attitude toward officially-sanctioned market organization and an awareness of the potentially destructive recession economics of high fixed cost operations and intense competition for market share.

Industry Economics

Underlying the institutional dynamics described above has been a systematic improvement of Japan's cost structure and market share relative to the rest of the world. The following section traces the economics of the Japanese steel industry, concentrating on the elements of cost improvement and continued international competitiveness.

The conclusions of the analyses which follow are clear. Japanese steel producers have an absolute advantage over their U.S. counterparts in all three major factor cost categories: labor, raw material, and capital costs.

Labor Costs

Since 1965 Japanese steel labor wages have increased 17.2 percent per year, 3.5 times the U.S. annual rate of increase of 4.9 percent (Table 8-1). Naive commentators have extrapolated from these trends that Japanese wage rates will equal U.S. rates by 1981, penalizing Japanese producers. This comparison is meaningless in that it fails to consider the other side of the coin—productivity.

The Japanese made astounding labor productivity gains in the 1960s. Table 8-2 shows that output more than doubled between 1965 and 1970, while the input of man hours rose almost imperceptibly. The result was that physical output per man hour increased 125 percent in Japan during the past five years. The comparable U.S. statistic rose only 4 percent in the same period.

Only unit labor costs (labor dollars per ton) are relevant in international trade. The trend in this index can be obtained by dividing the wage index (labor dollars per hour) by the productivity index (tons per hour). Table 8-3 shows that

Table 8-1
Steel Labor Costs, Inclusive ($/Hour), 1965-1970

	U.S.	Japan
1965	4.48	0.82
1966	4.63	0.97
1967	4.76	1.10
1968	5.03	1.26
1969	5.38	1.50
1970	5.68	1.80
Compound rate of annual increase	4.9%	17.2%

Source: American Iron and Steel Institute (AISI); Japan Iron and Steel Federation (JISF)

Table 8-2
Steel Labor Productivity (Index: 1965 = 100), 1965-1970

	Japanese		Labor Productivity Index	
	Output[a] Index (A)	Input[b] Index (B)	Japan (A/B)	U.S.
1965	100.0	100.0	100.0	100.0
1966	115.6	96.2	120.1	102.6
1967	149.6	101.3	147.7	101.3
1968	168.4	102.8	163.8	106.0
1969	202.9	102.6	197.6	106.3
1970	230.9	102.6	225.2	104.1

[a]Based on total output of steel products weighted by value added.
[b]Total man-days worked.
Source: Japan Productivity Center.

Table 8-3
Unit Labor Costs, 1965-1970

	Unit Labor Cost (1965 = 100) (Wage Index/Productivity Index)	
	U.S.	Japan
1965	100.0	100.0
1966	100.9	99.0
1967	104.9	91.5
1968	106.1	94.7
1969	113.1	92.6
1970	122.1	97.5

Japanese productivity gains have overshadowed wage increases with the result that unit labor costs actually declined from 1965-70, as compared to a 22 percent increase in the United States.

Comparing absolute labor productivity levels (tons per man hour) between countries is extremely difficult because of differing statistical definitions. However, recent Japanese and U.S. studies of the subject indicate that labor productivity levels in the two countries' steel industries are equivalent today. The American Iron and Steel Institute calculates that in 1970 U.S. crude tons per man hour was .086 and Japan was .083 on a comparable basis. Japan Iron and Steel Federation data indicates that in 1968 U.S. productivity levels were 130.5 percent of Japan's. Applying the differential percentage changes since (Table 8-2) implies a productivity parity reached in 1970.

The conclusions of this analysis are clear.

- The Japanese steelworker has achieved U.S. productivity levels.
- His wages remain at one-third of U.S. levels.
- The unit labor cost gap (in labor dollars per ton of steel) is widening rather than narrowing.

The implications are equally obvious.

- Even if Japanese steelworkers were paid U.S. wages while Japanese and U.S. productivity increases continued at their present rates, unit labor costs in Japan would never exceed U.S. levels.
- Alternatively, even if Japanese productivity increases fell to the U.S. rate while Japanese wages continued to rise at their current rate, Japanese unit labor costs would not exceed the U.S. level for ten years.

If the advantage of the Japanese steel industry is traceable to "cheap labor," it is not the result of illiterate surplus labor used intensively and paid subsistence wages. It stems instead from massive capital investment supporting a highly skilled work force whose large pay increases can be justified by the productivity gains made possible by the capital improvements.

Material Cost

Raw materials account for more than 60 percent of the factory sales price of a ton of Japanese steel, and over 90 percent of the raw materials value is imported. The economics of mining, loading, transporting, and offloading basic materials has been of critical importance to the Japanese. Over the 1960s, the landed cost of iron ore, coking coal, and principal ferroalloys actually decreased in current dollars. 1970 landed costs were lower than 1960s. This was a result largely of major Japanese commitments on long-term supply contracts which insulated Japan from the basic materials inflation of the late 1960s and the unprecedented developments in ocean logistics for bulk handling and conveying.

Table 8-4 indicates the savings resulting from the use of larger bulk carriers alone. Table 8-5 shows the extent to which the Japanese are striving to take advantage of these potential cost savings. The low average tonnage per ship indicates that many logistics cost savings are yet to be realized.

Table 8-4
Savings from Use of Bulk Carrier

	Costs Per Ton Cargo	
Bulk Carrier	5,000 Miles	10,000 Miles
30,000 DWT	$6.00	$10.00
100,000 DWT	$3.50	$ 5.50
200,000 DWT	$2.90	$ 4.50

Table 8-5
Japanese Ore Carrier Fleet

	Number of Ships	Total Tonnage	Average Size
Present Fleet	159	9,130,000	52,400
Under Construction	9	1,170,000	130,000

Source: *Oriental Economist*, August 1971.

The implications of the logistics revolution were extraordinary for Japan:

— Seaborne trade in iron ore increased from 101 to 215 million tons between 1960 and 1969. Japan purchased 60 percent of this increase and in 1969, purchased 39 percent of all iron ore in seaborne trade.
— Coking coal in seaborne trade increased from 46 to 80 million tons in this period. Japan purchased 97 percent of this increment. In 1969, it bought 50 percent of all coking coal in seaborne trade.

Japan's paucity of iron ore and coal deposits forced the steel industry at an early date to search out long-term overseas sources of supply. Assistance from the government has been limited. There is direct financing of imports from government banks, primarily from the Export-Import Bank and the Overseas Economic Cooperation Fund. These institutions provided the assurance of long-term financing necessary in order to enter into supply agreements with overseas mining operations, some of whose total output was for Japan. In addition to providing long-term source of funds, the government designates iron ore and coal as priority import categories and ensures that foreign exchange is allocated to them. Currently, with Japan's surplus of foreign exchange, this designation is irrelevant, but for 20 postwar years this was a highly important provision to steel industry management.

In addition to financing imports, the government has assisted steelmakers in undertaking direct overseas resource development investment. Special sources of funds are designated by the Ministry of Finance in its annual budget in accordance with a standing policy to favor overseas investment for this purpose. Once again this provision is less critical now that the Ministry has relaxed its control of capital exports. During the 1950s and 1960s when Japan's currently productive resource development projects were undertaken, however, capital exports of scarce foreign exchange were authorized first for ore, coal, and petroleum exploration and mining ventures. Resource development accounted for 30 percent of total cumulative Japanese foreign investment through 1970.

A third form of government financial assistance has been tax incentives and insurance against development losses. A contingency reserve for possible losses and thorough development-loss insurance facilities are available to overseas ventures. The impact of these is slight, particularly when compared to depletion allowances.

Capital Costs

Many pages could be devoted to this subject; however, Japan's steadfast emphasis on large-scale plant investments and swift adoption of new technologies has been thoroughly documented in technical journals and need not be reproduced here.

A few statistics will serve to highlight the Japanese steel industry's accomplishments in this regard.

- Of the ten largest blast furnaces in the world, as of end of 1971, nine are in Japan.
- The largest, the Fukuyama #4 of Nippon Kokan, has a daily production capacity of 10,000 tons.
- This furnace raises Fukuyama's annual capacity to 12 million tons, the largest in the world for a single mill.
- In 1960 the daily production of pig iron per blast furnace was almost equal in the United States and Japan at 970 tons. By 1969, the figures were 2,723 for Japan, 1,465 for the United States, 1,644 for the USSR, 1,039 for West Germany, 845 in the United Kingdom, and 672 in France.
- In August 1969, Japan had as many continuous casting units (33) as the United States. By the end of 1970 the Japanese total had increased to 40.

The adoption of Linz-Donawitz converters by the Japanese industry deserves special mention. The L-D converter is less expensive to construct and produces crude steel approximately six times faster under normal operating conditions than an open hearth furnace (thus reducing labor and fuel costs). Since its perfection in the mid-1950s, it has been recognized as superior. However, as shown in Table 8-6, its adoption has proceeded more rapidly per tonnage in Japan than the United States.

Because of the apparent slowness of the U.S. industry in moving to the L-D converter, it has been frequently criticized for failure to recognize and adopt a superior new technology. However, the statistics displayed in Table 8-6 belie this criticism. In fact, a recent study indicates that in the 1956-64 period, L-D additions in the United States comprised a higher percentage of total capacity additions than in any other country. The U.S. industry actually added almost 30 percent more L-D capacity than its total net capacity additions during this period because large increments of Bessemer and open hearth capacity were scrapped.

The problem is traceable not to slow adoption by the U.S. industry but to the effects of relatively slower growth. As Table 8-6 shows, Japanese steel capacity increased 258 percent from 1956-64 versus only 10 percent in the United States. Therefore, even Japan's lower adoption rate enabled it to achieve a higher share of its capacity in L-D converters than the slower growing U.S. industry over an equal time period.

Table 8-6
Steel Capacity by Type: United States and Japan, 1956-1969

| | Percentage of Capacity Stock | | | | Percentage of Additions by Type 1959-64 | |
| | Japan | | U.S. | | | |
	1956	1969	1956	1969	Japan	U.S.
L-D Converter	−%	73%	1%	43%	61%	116%
Open Hearth	84	13	89	43	16	−40
Electric	16	14	8	14	23	26
Bessemer	−	−	2		−	−2
Total % addition to capacity 1956-64:					258%	10%

Source: Boston Consulting Group; *The Economic Journal*, September 1967.

Increasing Strength in Specialty Steel

In response to a voluntary tonnage quota in the United States and increasing competition among the 70 nations which produce carbon steel, the Japanese industry has increasingly emphasized specialty steel production and export.

As with carbon steel, the development of Japan's specialty steel capability did not take place in a competitive vacuum. It corresponded to a serious deterioration in the U.S. position in world stainless steel production. Table 8-7 shows the differential growth rates which have more than halved the U.S. industry's world market share since 1955.

Figure 8-2 plots real domestic price per ton of American and Japanese comparable stainless sheet against the total accumulated industry production tonnage of each country. The plot is on double logarithm paper, showing the percentage change in price against the percentage change in accumulated production experience. (Prices are real prices, deflated by GNP indices. In both cases the deflator base is 1968.) The data indicates that Japanese domestic prices in constant yen consistently decreased on trend by 20 percent each time accumulated production experience doubled. The sparse data for prewar U.S. prices indicates a similar rate of real price decline. Since the late 1940s, however, real prices have failed to decline in the United States until 1958 when the "price umbrella" was broken by imports. It is not coincidental that Japanese stainless imports into the United States began at about this time. Falling Japanese prices reached U.S. levels in 1958.

The period since 1958 illustrates the chronic disadvantage of the U.S. specialty steel industry today. The Japanese price has continued down, preserving the industry's customary margins. On the other hand, the U.S. industry has reacted aggressively, but too late to be successful, in meeting the import threat. The rapid U.S. price decline since 1958 is obviously steeper than could have been justified by cost declines; however, even the margin reduction which accompanies this price deterioration could not suffice to bring U.S. prices down as fast as Japanese prices due to Japan's higher growth rate (25 percent versus 2-3 percent annually).

The dilemma is evident. Without achieving faster production growth than Japanese competitors, the U.S. industry cannot achieve equivalent cost declines. And the U.S. industry cannot achieve sufficient production increases because Japanese competitors enjoy the powerful combination of lower prices, at least comparable (to us) cash-flow margins, and a strong foothold in the world's fastest growing markets—Asia, Africa, and Latin America. It is thus doubtful whether at this late date U.S. producers in specialty, as well as in carbon steels, can recover competitive equilibrium.

Table 8-7
U.S. Share of World Stainless Production, 1955 & 1968

	1955	1968	Annual Growth
U.S. Production Index	100	125	2%
World Production Index	100	600	15%
U.S. Share of World Production	65%	28%	

Source: International Nickel.

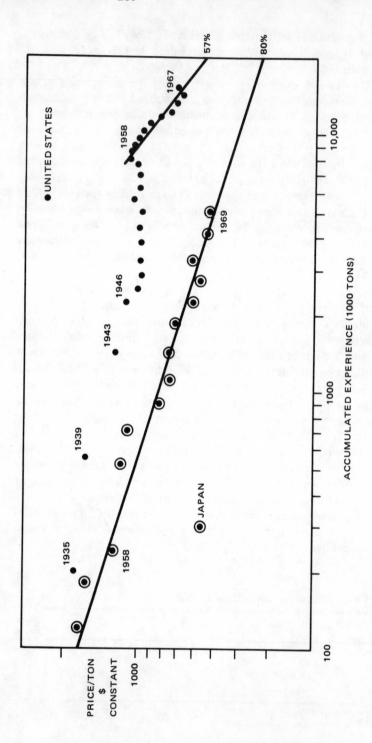

Figure 8-2. Comparative Experience Curve for Stainless Steel Sheets.

Conclusion: Future Japanese Competitive Strategy

The current competitive situation raises serious policy questions for the United States since quotas or other protection for the U.S. steel producers make large steel users less competitive relative to their foreign competition, as is already apparent in appliances and automobiles. On the other hand, one might argue that the Japanese industry will decline just as its textile industry is currently doing and this will give U.S. producers an opportunity to recover. This latter competitive evolution is extremely unlikely, however. Although it is true that the growth in crude steel production in Japan is levelling off, this does not spell the phasing out of major Japanese steel companies. Rather, it argues that they will shift their resources more and more into the specialty and high quality steels. They will diversify into other metals, plastics, and prefabricated construction as is already apparent from their recent actions and announced moves. In addition, they will increasingly move crude metal production offshore, in response not only to their own economics but also to pressures from their resource locations such as Australia and the Philippines. Hence more Japanese pig iron production will be at the mine head. The major steel companies will also continue to step up their exports of plant and equipment to the LDCs. All in all, these companies will move with the product cycle evolution of their industry and will benefit from it. And because the companies are profitable and because the industry has been rationalized, they have the resources and capability to carry it out. It is also apparent that the government will encourage and facilitate these developments.

This trend will manifest itself over the next ten to fifteen years and will be somewhat accelerated by continuous appreciation of the yen. But due to the high proportion of imported raw material content in the cost of finished steel, the Japanese can be expected to remain highly competitive even in carbon steel.

Appendix: Three Statistical Tables

Table 8A-1
Japan's Crude Steel Production, 1900-1970

(Year)	(Thousand Metric Tons)
1900	1.1
1905	106.7
1910	251.9
1915	514.3
1920	810.8
1925	1,300.2
1930	2,289.3
1935	4,704.5
1940	5,855.7
1945	1,963.8
1950	4,838.5
1955	9,407.7
1960	22,138.4
1965	41,161.1
1969	82,166.2
1970	93,332.0

Table 8A-2
Profiles of Japan's Major Steel Producers (Data for Year Ended March 31, 1971)

	Nippon Steel	Nippon Kokan	Sumitomo Metal	Kawasaki Steel	Kobe Steel
Corporate sales	$3,602M	1,631	1,281	1,144	1,090
Total assets	4,904	2,331	1,627	1,636	1,394
Profit after tax	72	31	26	39	25
Employees	82,046	42,102	31,525	37,834	32,747
Paid-in capital	637M	212	230	248	212
Profit as % Sales	2.0%	1.9%	2.1%	3.5%	2.3%
Annual growth 5-yr. average)	18.9%	22.0%	21.8%	20.2%	16.0%
Market share	36%	14%	12%	12%	10%

Table 8A-3
Crude Steel Production, 1960-1970 (MM Metric Tons)

	Japan	USA	USSR	W. Germany	UK
1960	22.1	90.1	65.3	34.1	24.7
1965	41.2	119.3	91.0	36.8	27.4
1970	93.3	119.4	116.0	45.0	28.3

Competitive Development of the Japanese Automobile Industry

Thomas M. Hout and William V. Rapp

The rise of the Japanese automobile industry during the 1960s radically changed the nature of world and particularly American auto competition. In ten years, Japan grew from a competitively weak, thoroughly protected sector producing less than 100,000 passenger cars annually to the second largest auto producer in the world. Total vehicle production increased by a factor of ten, passenger car output by 20, and passenger car exports by 100. This sudden burst into international prominence, which coincided with and in part caused the compact car boom in the United States, has redefined the nature of the auto business in terms of both product line and the economics of sourcing.

The auto industry's development is perhaps the classic case in postwar Japan. It has all the ingredients of the Japanese pattern. A rapid and sustained growth in domestic demand preceded its impact on export markets. The industry was identified by the government early in the postwar period as a priority and received protection from foreign competition, both imports and investment. Technology was absorbed by purely domestic producers from abroad to assist the development. The government sought to rationalize the producers' structure of the industry to ensure its international competitiveness, and while it largely failed among the major assemblers, the economic impact of consolidation programs on auto parts was critical. Finally, when the industry was strong and export penetration became painful in the United States, the government directed its favors away from the industry. This paper describes the historical development and competitive economics of this performance.

Industry Evolution

Prewar Origins of the Industry

Like the steel industry, the origins of the domestic automobile industry lie in the government's response to the requirements for Japanese military strength and economic autonomy during the first four decades of the century. The major issues of the development period—the threatening presence of foreign capital, the competitive viability of domestic firms, the problem of foreign exchange, and the necessity of military vehicles—required close interaction of government and producing firms. The government's role in the industry's history is a critical one.

Despite assembly of automobiles in Japan as early as 1902 and subsidized production of military trucks during the first world war, passenger car production was negligible into the early 1920s. Ironically, a natural disaster gave the first impetus to the auto business. Tokyo's great earthquake of September 1923 crippled the city's railway and tramcar system. In the absence of domestic substitutes, one thousand buses were shipped from Ford in the United States. Japan's total automotive production in 1923 is estimated at less than 200 units.

Within two years, both Ford and General Motors established wholly-owned onshore assembly operations. Japan Ford Corporation as formed in Yokohama in late 1924, and Japan General Motors, headquartered in Osaka, followed in 1925. By 1929 the two companies combined produced nearly 30,000 automobiles. Parts and subassemblies were imported from the United States for domestic assembly. Each organized a finance company and introduced in Japan installment purchasing. Within five years of their coming, Ford and General Motors controlled 85 percent of the Japanese market with onshore production.

Until the 1930s, neither the government nor the zaibatsu groups showed serious interest in an auto industry. Auto production was regarded as speculative and lower in priority than steel, coal, and other heavy industry. Only small firms were attracted into the business and were inferior in scale, capital, and technology to the resident operations of GM and Ford. Domestic annual production never reached 500 units before 1930.

The 1930s brought a change of attitude on the part of government. Military ambitions in Asia necessitated support of truck producers, of course, but more long-term economic considerations dictated a national automobile development policy. It was apparent that onshore foreign capital, if permitted unlimited production levels, would continue to dominate the domestic market and hence preclude the development of Japanese producers. The domestic manufacturer faced an uncompetitive scale of operation, an inadequate assembly technology, an absence of onshore parts supply, and an inability to finance automobile purchasers at competitive terms. The high failure rate of small domestic producers and the continued unwillingness of the zaibatsu to compete, even at later invitation of the government, convinced planners that protection from foreign capital was the prerequisite of a domestic industry.

The fundamental conclusion was never later seriously questioned in Japanese government or industry. While there was postwar debate within government over the necessity of a domestic automobile industry, the first requirement of any development—protection from foreign capital—was uniformly confirmed. Similarly, the dialogue of 1969-70 within the Japanese economic policy community over capital liberalization of the industry was a debate over the domestic producers' stage of completed development, not a requestioning of the necessity of protection for development.

Another stimulus to the government's reconsideration of autos was the foreign exchange problem. The international monetary crises and trade dislocations of the late 1920s and early 1930s dramatized Japan's precarious import position. Lack of a domestic automobile industry meant importing either finished vehicles or parts for assembly by onshore foreign capital. Both require foreign exchange.

The problem was not merely one of foreign exchange shortage, however, but more importantly, the cyclicality which import dependence forced on the Japanese economy. Japan has a high dependence on imported basic material. Until the past few years the country experienced a chronic deficit on current account in her balance of international payments. Throughout Japan's industrial history, this circumstance has meant a built-in macroeconomic instability: as income cyclically rose and combined basic material and manufactured imports rose in proportion, the resulting foreign exchange deficit required a deflationary countercyclical monetary policy. Japan's modern economic history fully documents this pattern.

The implication for domestic industrial policy was that import-substitute manufacturing industries had to be developed. A domestic automobile assembly and parts industry substantially reduces the net imports per automobile. This reduction is compounded by the secondary effects of domestic auto production on the steel, machinery, and tire industries. These implications were not lost on Japan's economic strategists, particularly as military production requirements rose.

The impact of the new government position on domestic automobile production was felt in the middle and late 1930s. It was felt most keenly by Ford and General Motors. In 1936 the government enacted the Automobile Manufacturing Enterprise Law, which literally and comprehensively aimed at closing down foreign producers onshore. The law's restrictions on foreign producers were severe. Annual production ceilings were imposed. Tariff rates on imported parts were raised. In 1937 a provisional law eliminated the import of strategic commodities. Japan Ford and Japan General Motors were soon closed down.

Japan's currently dominant producers, Toyota and Nissan, began producing during the prewar period. Neither was established at government initiative. Nissan was organized in 1933 under the name of Jidosha Seiyo Company and was an auto producer from the start. Toyota began producing automobiles in the middle 1930s as a diversification venture of Toyota, a leading manufacturer of textile weaving looms. By 1937 the two companies along with Isuzu dominated automotive production with an 80 percent combined market share. Production was nearly all trucks throughout the war, and over half the truck output was for the military. Passenger car output did not reach 2,000 units until 1938. In fact, despite the tremendous passenger car growth of the 1960s, annual car production did not surpass combined truck and bus output until 1969.

The years from the war's end to 1958 form the critical period. During this decade, the government and auto producers first resolved whether the industry should be developed at all. They then determined the competitive environment and technological direction of its development. The achievements of this period are indeed substantial. Japanese manufacturers, largely destroyed during the war, were producing 7,500 military trucks annually at war's end. Passenger car production levels and technology were negligible. By 1958 Japan was producing one-third of a million vehicles and was designing and building her own passenger cars.

The Postwar Policy Question

The immediate postwar condition of the auto industry was understandably weak and confused. The occupation established production limits on vehicles, rationed those available, and controlled prices. Looking ahead to normal economic conditions, the newly emerged Ministry of International Trade and Industry (MITI) recommended redevelopment of the industry, emphasizing passenger cars, using foreign technology, and government financial assistance. There was opposition to this within the government, however. The Bank of Japan, representing the nation's financial priorities, argued that the scarcity of capital and massive reconstruction task required that Japan specialize her industry mix and import automobiles in the short run at least. Inviting wholly-owned foreign capital facilities into Japan was not an alternative.

The opposition of the Bank of Japan to auto development should not be construed as a complete denial of access to the banking system by domestic manufacturers. During the 1949-50 deflation, the bank rescued Japan's largest automobile producer from impending bankruptcy as it did other large Japanese enterprises. In 1949 Toyota was near collapse from uncollected debts and unsold inventory. Toyota and its commercial bankers met with Bank of Japan officials to consider strategies for financial survival. The Bank of Japan responded by approving large credit extensions from Toyota's major commercial banks, Mitsui and Tokai. Financial crisis was thus averted. There was during that period and remains today an important distinction between the government's fundamental commitment to ensure the continuity of major Japanese corporations and the government's deliberate policy of selecting specific economic sectors for rapid growth development.

In 1951 the policy debate was resolved in favor of developing domestic passenger car production. The scarcity of automobiles in Japan during the period and the expectation of continuing foreign exchange constraints strengthened the argument for a domestic industry. MITI pointed out that the amount of foreign exchange drain from imported passenger cars over a short number of years could itself finance domestic production and marketing facilities and hence provide self-sufficiency. The matter was finally settled by the Korean War since the automotive needs of the United Nations forces created a timely opportunity for Japanese producers.

A real development impetus emerged in the 1950s. Military exports and a small but rapidly growing domestic auto market provided the demand base. Production and price controls were removed. The financial stability of the manufacturers improved. In 1951 Prince entered as the fourth domestic manufacturer. Perhaps most critically, MITI in 1957 announced policies which consolidated a comprehensive and imposing structure of protection measures.

Protection from auto imports was accomplished in three ways: quota, tariff, and commodity tax structures. Foreign exchange quotas for automotive imports had been in effect since the war's end to conserve foreign exchange. From the early 1950s, however, quotas were employed chiefly to protect domestic passenger car manufacturers. Japan's tariff rate structure was both absolutely high and relatively geared toward domestic producer interests. Trucks and large cars, where Japanese producers were either fully competitive or not competing at all, had lower rates than small passenger cars where domestic interest lay. The commodity tax structure was again discriminatory against big (in effect, foreign) cars in an attempt to shift demand toward domestic models. All of these protection measures have since been partially or wholly eliminated. Quotas were removed in 1965. Tariff and commodity tax relief came later.

Entry of existing truck producers into passenger car manufacture was heavy during the early 1950s and was made possible through license of foreign technology. Four domestic firms negotiated agreements, mostly with European automakers. Only one, Nissan, had previously made cars. MITI selectively approved these applications to assemble knock-down imported components. Financially precarious firms were discouraged from competing. The role of foreign technology in the industry's development should not be overestimated, however. Toyota and Prince have used domestic know-how exclusively. The four licensees—Nissan, Hino, Mitsubishi, and Isuzu—rapidly improved their own. Assembly of European knock-down cars was not long a factor. The Isuzu-Rootes agreement was the longest, running through 1964, but it produced less than $1 million in royalties over twelve years. By 1958 nearly every passenger car assembled in Japan was designed and manufactured domestically. This technical progress was facilitated by the stable number of producers—Toyota, Prince, Nissan, Isuzu, Hino, and Mitsubishi.

The implications of this autonomy were important for Japan. Decreasing its dependence on knock-down auto parts reduced the foreign exchange drain and the susceptibility to economic cycles through trade imbalance. Domestic production of auto parts advanced the development of the steel, machinery, and rubber industries. During the 1960s, they, along with autos, experienced unparalleled growth and achieved comparable international competitiveness. Design autonomy opened up the opportunity for automobile export in the next decade. During that time Japan's export of necessity shifted from high-labor, low-technology goods toward low-labor, high-technology products. Finally, autonomy vindicated MITI's protection policy and established a significant strategy precedent.

In evaluating MITI's role through the late 1950s, one must say that its contributions were essential. The ministry identified automobiles as an industry critical to Japan's economic future. It defended the industry's position against the opposing strategy of the Bank of Japan. Its elaborate policy of protection was, of course, basic to the industry's development. Also necessary and highly effective was the ministry's admission of unassembled foreign cars in order to build domestic technology.

MITI, however, did not dominate the producers nor monopolize the initiative for development. Its financial assistance to producers, though highly useful, was not critical. MITI played little or no role in the investment policies or technological development activities of the producers. As the decade closed, MITI's role among auto producers waned. By 1958 the highly protected industry was profitably producing one-third of a million vehicles, including 50,000 passenger cars, and was reaching design autonomy.

The government's role was primarily in getting the industry started and in nurturing its development. The industry's competitive development, and the technological and economic success of particular firms, depended on their individual efforts and strategic acumen alone. This is important to recognize since these underlying success factors continued through the 1960s. They are likely to continue into the future despite capital and import liberalization, the emergence of other national priorities, and substantially reduced government support and influence.

The Takeoff of the 1960s

The 1960s decade was one of staggering production growth for the industry during which Japanese automakers rose from a fledgling group producing less than 100,000 passenger cars annually to the second largest auto producer in the world. Total vehicle output increased by a multiple of 10, passenger car output by 20 and passenger car exports by 100 over the ten years. The Japanese emerged from technological inferiority to Western producers to designing their own exemplary assembly plants and competitive automobiles. They now potentially threaten U.S. dominance in world auto production.

The notable competitive developments of the decade were early rapid expansion in the number of producers and subsequent fragmentation of market share, a continuing but largely unsuccessful effort by MITI to consolidate the industry into a small number of large producers, and the emergence of Nissan—and particularly Toyota—as world automaking powers.

From the introduction of foreign technology in 1952 until 1960, the number of conventional passenger car manufacturers had remained stable. By the end of 1962, three more firms—Mitsubishi, Fuji, and Toyo Kogyo—had entered. Four producers newly entered the truck business. While this was a natural outcome of the explosive growth which saw annual car output triple between 1959 and 1961, the impact on Toyota and Nissan market shares was abrupt. Their combined market share dropped from roughly 75 percent to less than 50 percent in less than two years.

Fragmentation of the industry began to concern MITI at this time. The ministry not only wanted to avoid in the short run the problem of small-scale inefficient producers—characteristic of many Japanese industries during this period—but also wanted to preserve a concentration of production which later would make Japanese autos internationally competitive. Liberalization of auto imports and eventually of foreign capital investment was inevitable. Japanese autos in the early 1960s were not yet competitive in quality and price.

The long-run export opportunity was also at stake. Japan was already exporting 50,000 vehicles in 1961, including over 11,500 passenger cars. MITI apparently appreciated the export barriers presented by the chronic nonstandardization of parts (which was already a serious problem among subcontractors in the 1950s), the fragmentation of capital-intensive production among several manufacturers, and the inability of small producers to undertake marketing risks abroad. Resisting imports was also important for developing the export opportunity. Japanese producers had to preempt all domestic market growth in order to gain sufficient production scale and experience to compete in American, and hopefully European, markets.

Consequently, Japan's opportunity to develop an internationally competitive auto business was time-limited. During the industry's takeoff stage, any combination of slow domestic growth or excessive production fragmentation or premature import liberalization could delay and hence prevent Japan's reaching competitive parity before Japan's market was opened.

By the middle 1960s, MITI's concern with structure was acute. The ministry's attempts, both in the form of proposed legislation and administrative guidance, to group the smaller producers into coordinated groups failed. The ministry's efforts were opposed both by significant political elements in Japan and by most of the industry. Consolidation of the auto industry was a major priority of the ministry during this period, but only partial success was achieved. Prince, Hino, and Daihatsu were absorbed into Nissan and Toyota. Three important producers—Isuzu, Mitsubishi, and Toyo Kogyo—remained independent and became MITI's Achilles heel in the foreign capital issue of 1969-70.

It is important to note that financial necessity rather than administrative guidance was the essential stimulant to the affiliations which did occur after 1965—Prince into Nissan and Hino and Daihatsu with Toyota. Total vehicle production rose from 1965 to 1969 at an annual compound growth rate of 26 percent. Production of passenger cars rose at over 30 percent. The total financial and production capacity commitments necessary to merely maintain auto market share were doubling every three years. The recession of 1965, on the other hand, had severely interrupted the cash flow of auto producers. Hence, the industry experienced a period of rapidly escalating capital requirements immediately following a year of severe operating cash-flow strain. The large, dominant firms with superior earnings performance and greater access to the banks increased their market shares during the period. Secondary producers found it difficult to finance comparable growth.

This inability to finance market growth and the failure of the industry to consolidate domestically accelerated the introduction of foreign capital into the industry. Toyo Kogyo, Isuzu, and Mitsubishi's auto division sought affiliation with foreign capital to gain financial as well as marketing, technical, and product strength. In effect, MITI's failure to consolidate the industry had the result not of exposing Japan's secondary producers to the competition of the Big Three, but of forcing them to align with the foreign producers in the Japanese market.

Yet the absence of United States auto producers in postwar Japan until recently still stands out. The lack of technology agreements is understandable. Japan was reluctant to produce under license oversized cars of U.S. dimensions. The Big Three were unwilling to trade technology for anything less than equity. It is curious, however, that U.S. producers did not negotiate an equity position of some form in Japan before 1971, despite foreign investment barriers. It is not only alleged but probable that during the 1950s at least one U.S. producer was informally invited to joint venture with domestic capital in auto production. Japanese producers were weak technologically and competitively. Annual car production in 1955 was a mere 20,000 units. It is reasonable to believe that the Japanese government might have permitted, even welcomed, selected U.S. capital participation under clearly defined constraints regarding share of equity, earnings repatriation, and management prerogative. The basis of Japanese objection to foreign capital is not that it is foreign, but that it is uncontrollable.

The Comparative Economics of U.S.
and Japanese Auto Competition

This section presents a brief comparative U.S.-Japan auto industry analysis which seeks to relate the long-term competitive position of each using a straightforward but instructive analytical tool called the experience curve. The competitive development of two industries is complex, and no single approach fully explains their comparative patterns. The domestic competitive environment and the product mix of each is different. However, remarkable insight into their relative price and cost positions through time can be gained by observing two variables simultaneously. A long-run relationship has been observed in the automobile and other industries in Japan and the United States between real (constant dollar) price per unit and the total accumulated production experience in the product to that point. The experience curve displays this empirical relationship. Real price declines by a characteristic percentage each time accumulated production experience doubles. The double logarithmic paper displays this relationship as a straight line. All real prices are in 1958 dollars or yen.

The implication of this analysis is that the emergence of Japanese auto producers, particularly Toyota and Nissan, as a prominent, if not dominant, factor into international auto competition was not sudden or unpredictable but is rather the outcome of an observable set of circumstances including national development priority, severe domestic competition, and explosive domestic growth. The experience curve displays this development well.

The United States began passenger car production at the turn of the century. Annual production was only about 4,000 vehicles in 1900. Initial costs were high—around $6,000 in 1958 prices. Production and accumulated experience grew quickly, with some drop in prices between 1900 and 1904. The real industry shakeout, however, did not begin until 1908. After that time, there was a fairly uniform decline in real (and current) prices until 1930, reflecting the market dominance of Ford and the Model T. Accumulated experience doubled about every two years until 1916. Between 1916 and 1929, doubling occurred within three, four, and five-year periods successively. Figure 9-1 depicts this development.

The Depression and, later, World War II produced a stagnation in production growth in passenger cars. Despite the growth in the 1950s, accumulated volume of automobiles doubled only twice between 1929 and 1960. More notable than this slowed growth was the leveling of the price decline per unit. Since the war, real average wholesale price per passenger car has remained stable. A number of factors account for it. One is that the American car got bigger and more features were added. The unit of accumulation changed. This is a matter of degree, of course. Autos changed before 1930 when U.S. real prices declined with accumulated volume. Another critical factor was the dominance of General Motors after 1930. After this point, the United States had one clearly dominant and lower cost producer. Comparative financial statements of GM, Ford, and Chrysler bear this out. GM's competitive policies were and remain constrained by U.S. legislation. The U.S. auto business is not fully price competitive, and has not been over the period covered by the horizontal real price line. This leveling of the real price decline parallels a deterioration in the relative competitive position of the United States in world auto market share.

Japanese passenger car production, as already noted, was not significant until the middle 1950s. As late as 1952, only 16,000 passenger cars had been produced. Average current wholesale price for a standard 1000 cc car at that time was about $2900 as compared with $1500 at the time for a U.S. car.

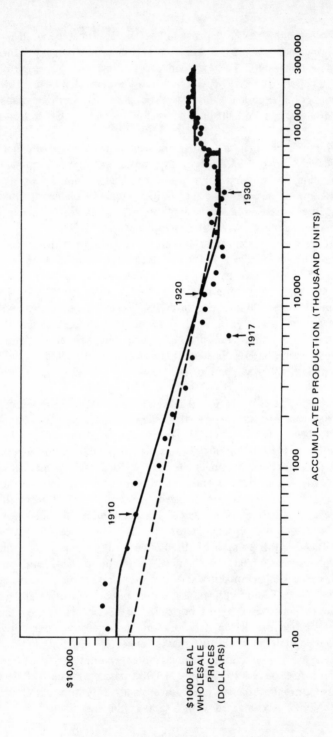

Figure 9-1. U.S. Passenger Car Production Price-Experience Effect: 1900-69.

Subsequently, the Japanese competitive position improved dramatically as real prices proceeded down an experience curve. Real prices declined 12 percent per doubling of accumulated volume—a rate very similar to the United States (Figure 9-1) up until 1930—after the middle 1950s. Japanese real prices before that time actually rose. Passenger car production was small scale and static in technology and design. Prices began to fall when unit costs began to fall. The implicit economics of an experience curve—cost reduction through economies of scale, better organization of production and marketing process, replacement of relatively expensive factors of production, labor, and staff learning—begin to take effect as growth materializes, competitive markets develop, and management begins to relate cost control with competitive position. The Japanese price per unit has continued to decline at this characteristic rate through 1970 despite changes in the product mix and extraordinarily rapid increases in the price of labor. Figure 9-2 is the aggregate (all model) Japanese auto experience curve. Figure 9-3 compares U.S. and Japanese actual (current $) and real (constant $) prices through time.

The combination of maintaining a consistent rate of price decline through accumulated experience and rapid growth in annual production caused Japanese prices to decline very rapidly through time and relative to U.S. prices. Despite a higher rate of inflation in Japan than in the United States (Table 9-1) from the mid-1950s to the mid-1960s, the Japanese were able to lower average current dollar wholesale prices to roughly $1,250 by 1970 from $2,000 in 1958. United States current prices increased over the period.

When industry price data are broken out according to engine size, the downward price patterns are similar or even more pronounced. Figure 9-4 shows the real wholesale price of individual models dropping sharply over time in correspondence with a rapid accumulation of production experience. The 1001-1500 cc engine size is the most popular size car; a large majority of production is in this range. Table 9-2 further points out that the initial cost point for each new model was lower in real and current terms than for the previous model, a smaller and less expensive car.

The competitive interaction between the U.S. and Japanese auto industries parallels their respective price-experience developments. In 1952 current wholesale prices were widely different ($2,900 for a Japanese 1001 cc car versus $1,500 for the average U.S. car), and there was little or no export from Japan. By 1958-60, however, the gap had closed to roughly $1,900 for the average U.S. car and $2,100 for Japanese 1001-1500 cc cars. Nissan was then exporting some 11,000 vehicles (mostly light four-wheel trucks) and Toyota 5,500 vehicles. Still, 86 percent of Nissan's and 84 percent of Toyota's exports were going to less developed countries, mostly in Southeast Asia and Latin America (Table 9-3).

In 1961 current wholesale prices for the two countries were comparable ($1,750 for Japan and $1,850 for the U.S.) although the American cars were of better quality and greater size.[a] By 1964 Japanese current wholesale prices were

---

[a]All Japanese figures in paragraph refer to standard 1001-1500 cc models although as already noted price trends were similar for all car sizes.

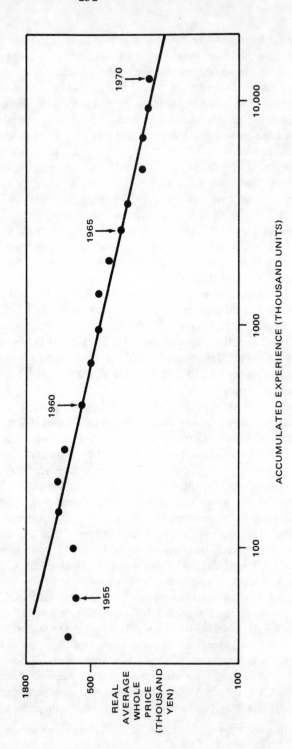

Figure 9-2. Japanese Passenger Car Production Price vs. Accumulated Production Experience: 1954-70 (Constant 1958 Yen). Source: MITI, *Machinery Statistic Yearbook.*

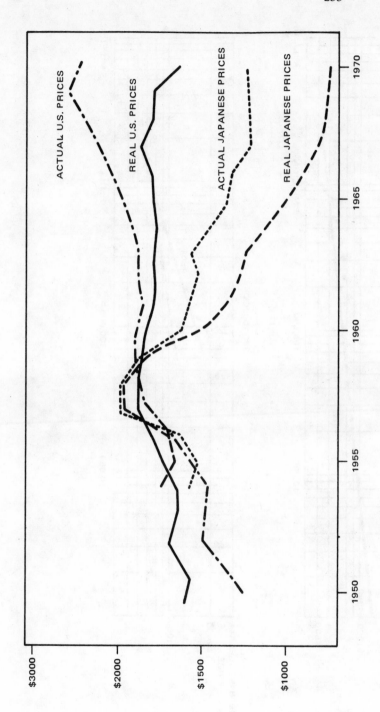

Figure 9-3. Average Wholesale Prices of Automobiles against Time: 1950-70. Source: MITI, *Machinery Statistic Yearbook*. U.S. Census Bureau, *Annual Survey of Manufacturers.*

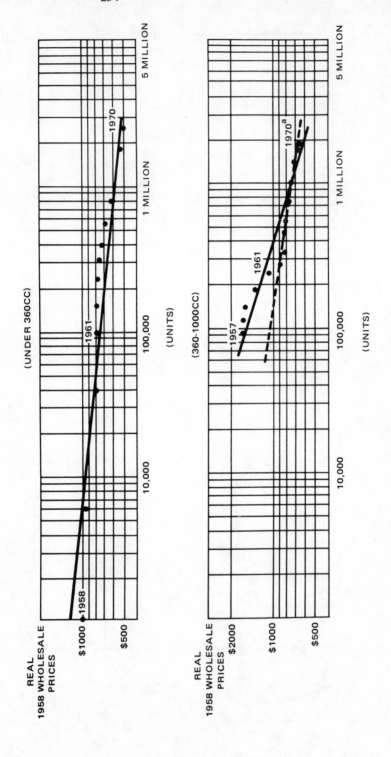

235

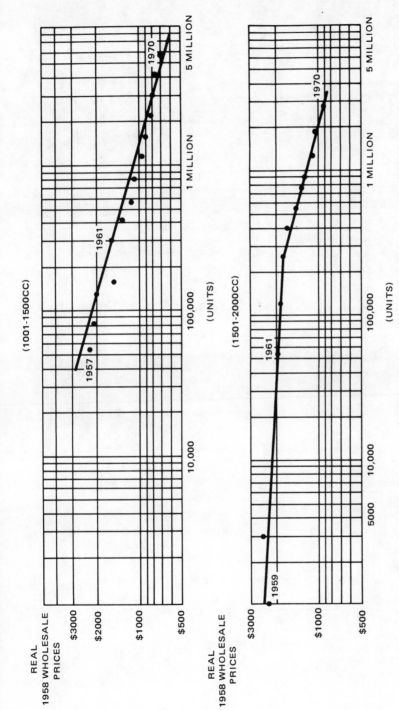

Figure 9-4. Real Prices vs. Accumulated Volume of Production by Model: 1957-70 (under 360 cc)
[a]Rapid reductions in costs and prices may have forced prices down in the late 1950s. The dotted line may reflect more accurately later price movements.

Table 9-1

Competitive Comparison of the Automobile Industry, 1954-1970

	U.S.		Japan	
	1954-70	1965-70	1954-70	1965-70
Annual production growth	1.0%	−7.5%	40.2%	35.4%
Annual experience accumulation rate	4.3	3.9	43.3	37.0
Annual decline in constant dollars or yen (88% experience curve)	−.8	−.7	−7.9	−6.8
Inflation rate	2.6	4.1	4.0	4.6
Annual change in cost in current dollars and yen	1.8	3.4	−3.9	−2.2
Competitor's cost advantage[a]			5.7	5.6

[a]Exchange rate fixed at 360 = $1.00

Source: Calculated from historical data available from MITI and U.S. Census Bureau.

Table 9-2

Average Japanese Initial Factory Prices by Model and for Selected Years: 1957-70[a] (in Dollars)

	1957	1959	1965	1970
Under 360 cc				
Avg. real price	867	939	708	508
Actual price	878	964	972	875
360-1000 cc				
Avg. real price	1,575	1,506	800	628
Actual price	1,597	1,547	1,100	1,078
1001-1500 cc				
Avg. real price	2,250	2,094	956	703
Actual price	2,281	2,150	1,313	1,210
1501-2000 cc				
Avg. real price	–	2,291	1,428	925
Actual price	–	2,353	1,961	1,592
2001 and over				
Avg. real price	–	–	2,300	1,044
Actual price	–	–	3,160	1,797

Note: Exchange Rate 360 = $1.00

Real Prices in 1958 prices

[a]Price not available by model except for standard 1001 cc car before 1957.

Source: MITI, *Machinery Yearbook*.

Table 9-3
Country Direction of Japanese Automobile Exports: 1957-70

	1957	1960	1963	1966	1969	1970
Exports (units)	410	7,013	38,040	153,090	560,431	725,586
Share to less developed countries	93.0%	79.3%	67.8%	36.0%	28.3%	22.7%
Share to advanced countries	7.0%	20.7%	32.2%	64.0%	71.7%	77.3%

Compound Growth in Exports 1957-70: 78.0%
Source: Ministry of Finance, *Export Statistics*.

well below U.S. prices ($1,400 versus $1,900). Most of Japan's exports were still to less developed countries (91 percent for Toyota and 85 percent for Nissan); Toyota and Nissan exported to the United States only 2,000 and 10,000 cars respectively in that year. By 1970 the price gap was substantial ($1,210 for Japan versus $2,215 for the United States), and Japanese exports to the United States had become significant. In that year Toyota sold 196,350 units and Nissan 155,000 units in the U.S. out of total exports of 389 and 325 thousand respectively.

Following the usual pattern, exports first to LDCs and then to the U.S. market, provided the demand stimulus required to accelerate lower costs for the Japanese industry. As can be seen in Table 9-4, passenger car exports grew from 11.6 percent of production in 1964 to 22.8 percent in 1969. Exports to the United States now and in recent years represent the largest portion of this growth. In fact, by 1970 approximately 50 percent (by value) of Japanese passenger car exports were to the United States ($456 million). Toyota and Nissan wisely did not dilute their Japanese experience base by building manufacturing plants in the U.S. Instead they put their efforts into developing large car carriers which reduced transportation costs to a fraction of previous levels. They thereby improved export effectiveness and added to growth in experience and export volume. The net result has been a significant and continued loss in world market share by U.S. producers (Table 9-5).

Table 9-4
Japanese Passenger Car Exports: 1964-70

	1964	1965	1966	1967	1968	1969	1970
Passenger car exports (thousand units)	67	101	153	223	406	560	726
Percentage of total production	11.6	14.5	17.4	16.2	19.8	21.5	22.8
Exports to U.S. market as a percentage of total exports	15.3	26.2	33.0	29.7	41.9	46.9	44.6

Source: Ministry of Finance, *Export Statistics*; and MITI.

Table 9-5
Changes in World Market Share: 1953-70

	1953	1969	1970
World production (thousand units)	8,130	23,124	22,747
U.S. share	75.2%	36.2%	28.8%
Japanese share	0.1%	11.5%	14.0%

Source: *Automobile Facts and Figures*

The Future of Japan's Auto Industry

The future of the Japanese auto producers is difficult to contemplate because, to a greater degree than other major industries, there exists a strong possibility of a fundamental discontinuity between its short and long-run futures. A number of potentially unstable factors—auto technology, Japan's desired mix of industries, and access to export markets—face the industry, and each is so critical and so unresolved that it is very difficult to address the long-run nature of the business.

In the short run, the forces which underlay the dramatic rise of the 1960s will continue to play themselves out. Although domestic demand has leveled off, access to export markets is still sufficient to ensure faster growth than American and European competitors. At the same time, auto technology through 1975 is fundamentally determined. Consequently, Japanese producers will at least maintain competitive position with extensions of current product line, moderate further revaluation notwithstanding. The present number of producers of passenger cars—11—will be reduced as the export emphasis and high cost of emissions reduction narrows the opportunities for marginal producers to survive. This consolidation has been underway since 1965 although its progress has been slow. Finally, some specialization of product mix should occur as General Motors, Chrysler, and eventually Ford source product from their new affiliates in Japan. Nissan and Toyota will strengthen their dominant position in the conventional size segment.

The long-run future, on the other hand, shows the auto industry facing questions as fundamental as that of survival. It is not inconceivable that future national economic policy might call for a gradual phaseout of the auto industry as it is known today in Japan. While this would be heretical and improbable in the U.S., there might be a strong case for it in Japan. The auto sector accounts for only six percent of GNP in Japan (and is now falling steadily) compared with nine percent in the U.S. More importantly, the Japanese commitment to well-managed and well-compensated phaseout is demonstrated today in the textile industry which exceeds the auto industry in both employment and political constituency. In 1972 the Japanese government will spend more on textile dislocation and renovation assistance than the industry will export to the United States.

In addition to having the capacity to execute orderly withdrawal, Japan also has some incentive. The urban density and proximity of major cities to each other are well suited to public, continuous forms of transportation. Existing auto propulsion systems require petroleum fuels, where a reduction is highly desirable in view of Japan's severe environmental problem and her dependence on the politically unstable and potentially confiscatory Middle East. The leading producers—Toyota and Nissan—are strong companies with large cash flows which could be diverted to new major businesses much like the Toyota auto division was started in the 1930s from the earnings of the Toyoda textile loom business. The rate of change over the last fifteen years in both the volume and quality of Japanese industrial output has been staggering, and Japanese policy-makers have made it clear that resource allocation priorities will continue to change.

A great deal may depend on the development of the electric car, one of MITI's currently two largest national research programs. An economical electric car (or suitable alternative) would make a stronger case for reinvestment in the auto business. Socially it is more tolerable than conventional engines. Its probable export life would be longer than that of existing automobiles, which in the coming years may very well face a complex array of nontariff barriers in the developed world. Significant propulsion innovations, then, would prolong the auto industry's prosperity. Regardless of technology, however, the industry will continue to decline relatively in the Japanese economy.

10 Policy Recommendations

The Businessmen's Advisory Committee
Common U.S.-Japan Interests and Aims

The United States and Japan, as top-ranking world-trading economies, share certain clear common interests, both in better management of their bilateral economic relations and in strengthening the multilateral economic structure in which they are both participants and competitors.

1. The interests of both countries will be served by collaboration in achieving, during the 1970s, a nearer balance in their bilateral trade and payments,[a] and by doing so at an expanding (rather than contracting) volume of mutual trade and capital flows.
2. This common objective can realistically be achieved only within the framework of similarly expanding world trade, under increasingly freer and fairer trading conditions, which allow bilateral imbalances to be offset by an approximate multilateral balance in each country's trade and payments.
3. Both the United States and Japan share an urgent common cause, therefore, in further reciprocal worldwide reductions in tariff and non-tariff barriers to trade; in the elimination of discriminatory barriers to agricultural and manufactured exports of the United States, Japan and third countries; in discouraging regional-bloc practices, including preferential tariff groupings which tend to inhibit the free and fair international flow of merchandise trade; and in strengthening multilateral institutions for monetary and trade cooperation.
4. The mutual interests of both countries will also be served by collaboration in reconstructing the international monetary system to provide expanding world liquidity, freer flow of capital investment and returns on investment, and—with the purpose of avoiding future chronic surplus/deficit crises in international payments—greater flexibility in continuing and reasonably automatic and multilaterally applicable currency adjustments

---

[a]Mr. Halaby felt that the effort to achieve a balance in the bilateral trade between Japan and the United States was a matter of some urgency and that the present imbalance could not be dealt with in a leisurely fashion over a period of time such as "the 1970s." The majority of the CEPS economists, on the other hand, felt that trade imbalances should be approached from a multilateral point of view and dealt with by international arrangements which would permit more flexibility in the adjustment of exchange rates, when necessary.

241

which will reflect the actual competitive performance, in world markets, of the major trading economies.

Japan

Having recently achieved an explosive expansion of exports, a very large and continuing trade surplus, and an accumulation of foreign reserves sufficient to disturb world economic equilibrium, Japan now has the obligation to take decisive measures designed to restore a more tolerable balance in its international trade and payments. It has already achieved approximate parity with the United States and the EEC in the extent of its import liberalization.[b] It should also undertake the following initiatives:

1. Japan's unusually powerful surplus position and potential justify the prompt and substantial reduction of its residual tariff and quota barriers to imports, the mitigation of "administrative guidance" to domestic purchasers to the extent that this practice continues to discriminate against imports, and the final dismantling of all remaining export incentives.
2. Japanese government and business initiatives to promote imports, including imaginative programs to inform and assist U.S. exporters in penetrating the Japanese market, are laudable and should be expanded. These efforts also merit positive response from U.S. business and industry.
3. Since Japan as a mature creditor nation is now in a position to divert a growing proportion of its national resources from production for export to production and services for improving the quality of Japanese domestic life, recent government commitments to such a policy should be promptly implemented.
4. Since both the economic and political impacts of Japan's recent export successes have been concentrated in particular markets—especially the United States and Southeast Asia—and in a relatively small number of export-oriented industries, Japan's own long-term interests will be served by greater diversification of its trade, both geographically and in product lines. Achieving this objective presumes, inter alia, improved receptivity to Japanese exports in other major markets, especially Western Europe and perhaps the Soviet Union and People's Republic of China.
5. Japan will also benefit, and possibly avert further imposed or negotiated restrictions on its exports, if it exercises economic statesmanship by avoiding sudden and excessive exploitation of politically sensitive and import-vulnerable foreign product markets. Unilateral restraint in this area is preferable to quotas of any kind, or to foreign retaliation.[c]

[b]This statement assumes a treatment of Japan's voluntary export restrictions as import quotas on the part of the United States.

[c]Mr. McGhee believes that such restraints would be less onerous if they were multilateralized. He feels that the whole problem of "orderly marketing" should be approached on the basis of international multilateral agreements.

6. The large and growing volume of Japan's foreign reserves creates the imperative for substantially increasing the level of official foreign aid, the provision of considerably softer or more generous terms in foreign development-assistance lending and trade-credit arrangements with developing countries, early retirement of accumulated external debt, and significantly higher levels of foreign direct investment—in the United States and elsewhere—including expanded investment in resource development related to Japan's fast-growing requirements for imported fuel and industrial raw materials.

7. In recognition of its strong competitive position, and in order to match the parity in capital liberalization it has already achieved in import liberalization, Japan should accelerate the decontrol of both inward and outward direct foreign investment.[d]

The United States

The seriously deteriorated U.S. foreign trade and payments position is disruptive internationally as well as domestically. The United States also faces certain disciplines and responsibilities which are essential to the restoration of a manageable U.S. balance of international payments.[e] In light of current U.S. national priorities and international commitments, an equilibrium in foreign payments requires a return to surplus in U.S. foreign trade.

1. Highest priority must therefore be given to a restoration of U.S. trade competitiveness, both in world markets and in competition with world exports in the U.S. domestic market. The disciplines required include effective reduction of domestic price inflation, increased levels of investment in R & D and plant modernization, substantial increases in rates of productivity gain (and related reductions in unit labor costs) in export-oriented and import-impacted manufacturing, and more aggressive and effective U.S. export marketing.

2. In the interests of export expansion, competitive (or potentially competitive) U.S. manufacturers should vigorously explore the opportunities available in the increasingly affluent Japanese consumer market and, where equipped to do so, should take advantage of marketing assistance now

[d]Mr. McGhee believes that joint enterprises between United States and Japanese companies would be particularly desirable in the extractive mineral industry along the lines of the recent Mobil-Japanese joint concession in the Luristan province of western Iran. Such joint enterprises would not only help meet Japanese raw material needs but would also enlist the cooperation of American capital in the process.

[e]Mr. MacGregor feels that explicit attention should be called to the part that continuing large federal deficits have played in: (1) promoting inflation, (2) rendering American products less competitive in world markets, and (3) producing disequilibrium and disruptive destabilizing effects on the whole world currency system, making it difficult to maintain currency relationships.

being offered by Japanese government agencies and private organizations, including trading companies. United States exports (to Japan and elsewhere) should be viewed, not as fall-out benefits of surplus domestic production, but rather in terms of a specialized and increasingly competitive world business in which greatly improved U.S. performance is essential to our domestic as well as our international economic interests.

3. Appropriate U.S. industries should also take greater advantage of permissible devices such as joint-exporting ventures, and serious study should be given to changes in U.S. law which would permit the establishment of U.S. trading companies in the Japanese pattern, and other novel mechanisms for the efficient expansion of U.S. exports to the world as well as to Japan.

4. Recent Japanese offers to establish joint-venture trading companies with U.S. partners, to expedite bilateral trade expansion as well as U.S. world-export expansion, should receive careful attention.

5. While acknowledging the substantial contributions of U.S. multinational corporations to U.S. economic strength in foreign markets, to U.S. international payments on current account, and to domestic employment, it may be that the trade-offs affecting the national interest, including the need for export expansion, now call for a reexamination in certain U.S. industries of the alternatives of expanded investment in offshore manufacturing versus expanded domestic investment in export-oriented production.[f]

6. In the interests of import competition, U.S. industry should realistically examine both causes and available competitive remedies (pricing, design, performance, consumer taste, etc.) in those product areas where import penetration of the domestic market has been substantial. In those cases where the competitive advantage (e.g., low wages in a labor-intensive, low-skill, low-technology industry) is heavily in favor of the foreign producer, the United States must resist the temptation to protect the inefficient or obsolescent domestic industry, at the expense of the U.S. consumer and domestic price stability. Where the U.S. producer has the capacity to meet the competition fairly, it is in the national (as well as industry) interest that he attempt to do so.

7. Implicit in the U.S. commitment to fair as well as free trade is the principle that antidumping regulations and countervailing duties should never be invoked as trade barriers, but only when there is clearly demonstrated injury through unfair trade practices.

---

[f]Mr. Freeman and Mr. MacGregor do not feel that such a reexamination is required. They believe that it has been demonstrated that the activities of multinational corporations not only result in export expansion but do not in any way impair domestic employment. It is their view that the investment decisions of the multinational corporations safeguard market positions and that invariably this has protected a great deal of export production which would otherwise have been lost.

Conclusion

Finally, these several recommendations raise cautions and observations which should be made explicit.

1. Although a number of short-term adjustments need to be made in the currently highly distorted U.S.-Japan economic relationship, no short-term remedies should be invoked, on either side or through bilateral arrangements, which may prejudice the longer-term interests of both countries. Over the longer period, the common interest of the wider world-trading community is to achieve a relative balance in multilateral trade and payments, in which no country is in major deficit.
2. Similarly, it is imperative that negotiations affecting structural changes in the trade and monetary systems proceed on multilateral levels, as a precaution against the emergence of blocs and other distortions in what is essentially a unitary and organic international economy.
3. In transition toward our common goals, it is likely that both countries (and others as well) may experience domestic economic and social adjustment problems, requiring public adjustment assistance in the reallocation of both human and capital resources. It is clear that some of these adjustments cannot realistically be made over any short term. Nonetheless, the costs of domestic adjustment are properly domestic costs, and should not be levied directly on foreign trading partners or indirectly on domestic consumers, in the form of protected inefficiency and inflation. In accepting these adjustment costs, each country speeds the qualitative upgrading of its own economy, including the raising of labor skills and incomes, and improved international competitiveness.

Businessmen's Advisory Committee of the Japan Society

The Honorable Henry H. Fowler—Chairman
Partner
Goldman, Sachs & Co.

Mr. Tristan E. Beplat
Senior Vice President
Manufacturers Hanover Trust Company

The Honorable Orville L. Freeman
President
Business International

Mr. Najeeb E. Halaby
International Consultant

246

Mr. James A. Linen
Chairman of the Executive Committee
Time Incorporated

Mr. Ian MacGregor
Chairman of the Board
American Metal Climax, Inc.

The Honorable George Crews McGhee
Chairman
Business Council for International Understanding (BCIU)

The Honorable Robert D. Murphy
Honorary Chairman of the Board
Corning Glass International

Isaac Shapiro, Esq.
Partner
Milbank, Tweed, Hadley & McCloy

Mr. James M. Voss
Chairman of the Board
Caltex Petroleum Corporation

11 Summary and Conclusions

Jerome B. Cohen

We have posed a number of difficult questions. How did Japan achieve its astonishing growth rate over the past two decades? Can it sustain this rate over the decade ahead? What provided the cutting edge for Japan's international competitiveness? Is this competitive capacity likely to diminish or increase? In what ways did and does American economic, industrial, and trade policy differ from the Japanese? What was the impact of the differences? Why did the United States trade and payments situation deteriorate over the past half decade? Why did Japanese trade and payments improve so significantly over the same period? Was there any causal interrelationship between the divergent trends? Is the Japanese trade and payments surplus position likely to persist over the coming decade, and if so what will be its international impact? What is the Japanese trade and payments situation likely to be by 1980? What measures have the Japanese adopted to meet present and prospective imbalances? What policy steps can be taken—by Japan?—by the United States? Should efforts to achieve solutions be unilateral, bilateral, or multilateral? What are the prospects for accommodation?

These are some of the basic and fundamental questions which the economists of the Committee on Economic Policy Studies (CEPS) attempted to answer. While divergent views emerged at times—and such divergences were encouraged and debated—on most of the important economic issues a consensus emerged. This the following pages attempt to portray.

Economic Growth

Two decades ago Japan's gross national product was one-twenty-sixth that of the United States; ten years ago it was one-twelfth; at present it is about one-fifth. According to a recent study made by the Japan Economic Research Center (JERC),[a] projecting both the Japanese economy and the world economy to 1980, the total output of the economy is expected to be in the vicinity of one trillion U.S. dollars, or about one-half that of the United States in 1980. The per

[a]"Social and External Factors Influencing Japanese Foreign Policies during the 1970s: The External Economic Context," by Saburo Okita, Lake Yamanaka, Yamanishi, Japan, March 1972.

247

capita gross national product, the study estimates, is likely to reach U.S. $8,000, about equal to that projected for the United States for that year.

In the past twenty years, the annual growth rate of the Japanese gross national product has, in real terms, increased as follows:

1951-55	8.6 percent
1955-60	9.1 percent
1960-65	9.7 percent
1965-70	13.1 percent

Looking ahead, the Japan Economic Research Center Study declares: "Japan's economic growth in the 1970's may decelerate somewhat compared to the 1960's. However, there are still many factors which are likely to support rates of growth comparatively higher than those of other industrialized countries. Japan's most probable average rate of gross national product growth in real terms during the 1970's is still likely to be around 9 percent."

It seems somewhat unlikely, to a majority of the CEPS economists too, that Japan can continue to sustain in the 1970s the very high economic growth rates attained in the 1950s and 1960s. As we have seen, a confluence of exceptional and unusual circumstances aided the Japanese entrepreneurial drive for economic expansion during this period. The economic advance proceeded from a very low base of postwar reconstruction, unleashing a tremendous burst of productive energy and ingenuity. To close the technological gap which had developed, Japan imported, absorbed and even improved upon a vast store of foreign technology.

National priorities were set for a high rate of economic growth. The banking system was encouraged to finance a heavy business capital investment. Over the 1950-70 period the rate of fixed capital formation in Japan was 30 percent of the gross national product as compared to 24 percent for West Germany, 19 percent for France, and 17 percent for the United States. This high rate of capital investment was supported by a very high rate of personal savings. For Japan in the 1960s personal savings were 20 percent of disposable income as against 12 percent in West Germany and 7 percent in the United States. Taxation was moderate, absorbing 19 percent of Japan's gross national product, compared to 27 percent in the United States and 35 percent in the United Kingdom. Defense expenditures amounted to less than 1 percent of the GNP.

A favorable government maintained a policy of maximizing the rate of growth of aggregate output. It encouraged private capital formation. It maintained a balanced budget in most years and steadily lowered taxes. It favored the high technology, high growth industries. It did this in a variety of ways, some direct and obvious, others subtle and not easily discernible—by controlling foreign exchange allocations, by guiding the inflow of technology, by directing the flow of bank credit, by preferential credit rationing, by protection against foreign imports, by tax exemptions, by extraordinary depreciation allowances, by permitting and even encouraging mergers and consolidations, by aiding the reemergence of the huge international trading companies, and by indefinable "administrative guidance." This is not to suggest any sinister "Japan, Inc." organizational structure. Rather it was a purposeful business-government cooperative effort toward an accepted national goal—rapid economic expansion.

Labor, too, was cooperative. Strikes were relatively few and generally not of long duration. There was a vast transference of manpower (and womanpower) from agriculture to industry, from rural to urban areas. The share of agricultural employment in the labor force fell from 40 percent in 1955 to 15 percent in 1971. Enterprise unionism, the lifetime attachment to a given company, and the wage system based on seniority all contributed to the enhancement of output. Productivity first outstripped and then kept pace with wages. Over two decades workers' *real* income rose steadily.

The external environment was favorable. For a quarter of a century total world trade expanded significantly and relative monetary stability prevailed under Bretton Woods-IMF arrangements. The yen, initially overvalued in relation to the dollar, soon became undervalued as the keen cutting edge of Japanese competitiveness sliced open foreign markets, particularly in the United States and in South and Southeast Asia. Initially U.S. aid, then U.S. military procurement, first for the Korean conflict and then for the Viet Nam War, provided a fillip for Japanese industrial production. Not only did the United States open its own vast market relatively freely to Japanese goods but it also sponsored Japan's reentry into the world trading community. Soon Japan became a member of GATT, the OECD, the IMF, the World Bank, the United Nations, DAC, Ecafe, the Group of Ten, the Asian Development Bank—and a variety of other international institutions, facilitating Japan's emergence as a world economic power. So long as world trade expanded significantly there was little pain caused by Japan's absolute and even relative growth.

A variety of considerations suggest that the rate of growth may be somewhat reduced, say from the 10 to 12 percent level to a 7 to 9 percent range over the 1970s. Some of the factors which aided past growth may not be as readily available. For example, Japan's absorption of foreign technology which permitted rapid productivity improvements is slowing down as Japan has reached technical parity with other advanced industrial nations. The subsequent rate of technological advance, as a result, may not be as rapid as in the past. With labor supply less plentiful and the appearance of cost-push inflation, as well as a desire for shorter hours and longer vacations, labor costs per unit of capital may increase. Japan is on the threshhold of becoming a mass consumption society and the public may demand more and be less willing to sacrifice.

Clearly a new factor which will affect growth in the 1970s is the increasing pressure for amelioration of the adverse environmental consequences of rapid and sustained economic growth. The demand for the alleviation of congestion, overcrowding, and pollution will require more emphasis on social overhead capital and government investment to finance an improvement in the quality of life. More adequate housing, better roads, decentralization to relieve the urban crush, the demand for clean air and clear water, will require Japanese attention and resources in the 1970s and 1980s. A greater availability of resources for the enlargement of social consumption and a higher ratio of public investment seems inevitable. A growth rate which slows for such reasons will be welcomed by the Japanese. This prognostication is not pessimistic at all, since it seems likely that Japan's rate of growth will still be high compared to other advanced countries.

That Japanese energy and resources are, over the near future, likely to be devoted increasingly to improving environmental conditions, seems more probable as a result of the publication of Prime Minister Kakuei Tanaka's book entitled *A Proposal for Remodeling the Japanese Archipelago.* [b] In it he expresses the view that the Japanese people are no longer interested merely in continued industrialization and exporting but want to clean up their air, congestion, and water and to make their land a better place to enjoy life.

Mr. Tanaka favors moving people and industries and everything that supports them away from the urban concentrations of Tokyo, Yokohama, Nagoya, Osaka and Kobe along the Pacific coast. He suggests relocating them along the Sea of Japan in the west, to Japan's less developed island of Shikoku, to the northern reaches of the main island of Honshu and even to the far north of Hokkaido. Within the existing cities he proposes to replace vast sections of cramped one and two-story houses and shops with complexes of high-rise apartments and office buildings with green areas and malls between them.

He proposes that new cities of 250,000 people be built, each having its own industrial, residential, and service areas. Farming, the book indicates, will be changed by having the average farm (now very small) double in size but with a reduction of the labor force on the farms by about two-thirds by increased productivity. Air, rail, and road transport are to be improved, increasing mobility and communications, thereby cutting the cost of moving goods and stabilizing the soaring price of land. Pollution will be strictly controlled by adopting the principle that the polluter is to pay the costs of cleaning up his mess.

He envisages a five-day week, with younger people living primarily in high-rise apartments, moving to houses in exurbia later in life. If his program requires deficit financing this does not seem to worry Mr. Tanaka. It would be more shameful, he contends, to leave a polluted, unlivable Japan to future generations than to leave them with debts. Continued economic growth, he holds, is necessary for the economic and financial success of his plan. He envisages that Japan's economy will more than treble by 1985 to a $1 trillion gross national product. Economic growth should not be subordinated to welfare but coordinated with it, he argues.

[b]See *Nippon Retto Kaizo Ron*, as reported in the New York Times of August 23, 1972 and the *Japan Times Weekly* of September 23, 1972.

If we put together our sweat and power, [he writes,] as well as the wisdom and technology that enabled us to construct the Japan of today from the debris of fire in World War II, I do not think it impossible to have a new era of 'human restoration' in which society, man, sun and green will take the initiative away from big cities and industries.

When more than 100 million competent, bright, and diligent Japanese, [he adds] put all of their strength together to solve inflation, pollution, overpopulation (in cities), underpopulation (in rural areas), stagnant agriculture, and the generation gap, common to developed countries, while avoiding militarism, the people of the world will find Japan in the van of civilization.

Whether the Tanaka plan, by shifting capital investment from business investment to the public and social sector investment, will maintain, increase, or decrease Japan's growth rate over the next decade, remains, of course, to be seen.

Yet another constraint on prospective Japanese growth arises from world trade considerations. Externally, resistance may continue to grow to Japanese export expansion. World capacity to absorb Japanese exports and provide needed imports may become a problem. As Professor Rosovky notes in Chapter 1: "A Japanese economy growing at 6.5 percent per year presents considerable problems for the world, and possible international repercussions must be considered in any estimate of the future. Japan's sustained rapid growth will almost certainly continue to be led by manufacturing. As a result the growth of exports will have to be large and above the growth of world trade. Whether or not the rest of the world can or desires to swallow the flood of Japanese manufactures has to be a matter of grave concern."

On the import side, Japan faces equally serious international constraints. Professor Rosovsky declares: "It is true that Japan is anxious to exchange her excellent manufactures for the raw materials of less developed countries, and that her large purchases are beneficial to many nations. But few countries see their future as raw material exporters, and Japan's enormous needs now—and more enormous needs in the future—create economic and political apprehensions in diverse parts of the globe. Japan has to face the very real possibility that the world may be unwilling to supply, under any reasonable conditions, the raw materials necessary to sustain for twenty-five years a growth rate of 6.5 percent. A growth rate of 10 percent, as at present, is almost surely out of the question with this constraint."

Japanese Competitiveness

Japan will be able to maintain a 10 percent annual growth rate throughout the 1970s, Drs. Abegglen and Rapp maintain, because the Japanese understand the competitive process better than the United States. This manifests itself in Japan's increased competitiveness in world markets, particularly in manufactured goods. In Southeast Asia, Japan has become the dominant supplier of manufactured goods. In the American market itself, Japanese imports have penetrated a wide range of industries from steel, textiles, and automobiles to toys, rubber footwear, and consumer electronics.

In the world market, Japan's export growth rate over the past decade has been two and a half times that of the United States (17.2 percent versus 7.7 percent). The United States has been steadily losing world export market shares and in recent years U.S. export growth, especially in manufactures, has been below world averages. Along with these world market developments, Japan has increased her share of total United States imports from 7.8 percent in 1960 to 14.7 percent in 1970.

The traditional explanation of Japan's ability to compete so effectively in world markets has focused on Japan's lower wage rates, special export incentives together with controls on imports, administrative guidance, and even on "dumping" practices. To the extent that this may have been partially the case at one time, it is no longer the fact and the real explanation for the effectiveness of Japanese competition must be sought elsewhere.

Drs. Abegglen and Rapp explain Japan's superior competitive power in terms of a variety of factors, stressing the cost, price, volume relationship. For Japanese industry total cost per unit in constant yen declines by a characteristic amount (usually 20 to 30 percent) each time accumulated productive experience (total amount ever produced) doubles. The faster a company or an industry grows, using new machinery and equipment and the most modern technology, the more rapidly are its unit costs reduced. The implication of the cost-experience effect for Japanese competition is that growth directly determines the Japanese firm's ability to accumulate experience and to lower costs. Thus market share, particularly combined domestic and world market share, becomes a primary objective, even at the expense of short-term profitability. To obtain larger market share to reduce unit costs, there is an added incentive to reduce price. The reduced price obtains a larger market share. This lowers unit costs which in turn permits lower selling prices.

The way in which Japanese industry finances, in contrast to U.S. industry, for example, accelerates the growth process. Most Japanese companies have a much higher debt level than comparable U.S. companies. This means a higher level of fixed costs, a higher breakeven point and therefore an inducement to operate at full capacity and to reduce prices, if necessary, to accomplish this, as long as the product is sold at prices above variable costs. Since the breakeven point is high and cannot be significantly reduced in the short run, management is constantly pressed to lower prices as necessary to ensure full operations as long as these prices do not drop below variable costs. In the United States, this price point is reached much sooner than in Japan, since a substantially larger share of United States company costs are variable and can be reduced.

Taken together with Japanese financial practices, this "full-capacity policy" means that Japanese firms can price lower while maintaining required levels of return and a high growth rate, and has a powerful incentive to price lower to maintain full capacity.

Product and industry life cycles are a logical and recognized economic phenomenon, with new industries beginning in the most advanced countries, then being diffused abroad to other advanced countries, and in due course, over the longer run to the less developed countries. This process is well known. Take the cotton textile industry. First, European dominance gave way to U.S. competition and this, in turn, was faced with Japanese competition. Later competition from Hong Kong, Korea, and Taiwan invaded foreign markets, and more recently China, India, and Pakistan have developed cotton textile industries. Imports of textile goods from other Asian countries into Japan increased from $5.8 million in 1965 to $130 million in 1970. Raw silk was an important export item for many decades for Japan, but a few years ago Japan became a net importer.

In each country one finds a constantly changing spectrum of industries in various stages of development—initial entry, early development, rapid growth, export, maturity, import, decline. Because this is an ongoing process, it is illogical to expect a particular country to dominate production in a given manufactured product forever. Comparative advantage implies changes. That the Japanese may understand this, or be willing to recognize it, more than the United States, is indicated by their willingness to phase out and rationalize declining industries, such as cotton textiles or sewing machines, in favor of newer high-growth industries. It is these high-growth industries, such as computers, for example, that the Japanese have protected and favored. Japan has consciously pursued a policy of shifting its economic and industrial emphasis from low-growth, less sophisticated products toward high growth, more complex products—a rational policy that has contributed to Japan's competitive efficiency. In contrast, United States policy has been to protect slow-growth, or declining industries, leaving high growth industries to shift for themselves. This may have been self-defeating in terms of resource allocation, economic growth, and meeting Japanese competition.

The cutting edge of Japanese competitiveness in international markets is the giant trading company and it epitomizes the drive for volume rather than profit. Of the 6,000 or so trading companies there are 6 major ones with offices all over the world. Last year the "Big Six" brought in about 40 percent of Japan's imports and were responsible for approximately 50 percent of Japan's exports. They are multifaceted, multipurpose international companies, not only dealing in commodity imports needed by other Japanese manufacturers, and handling exports of manufactured goods for diverse and numerous Japanese manufacturers, but also handling shipping, financing, and insurance arrangements, channeling foreign investments by Japan in resource developments in overseas areas, arranging investment, merger, and acquisition deals between Japanese and foreign firms, and most recently offering to help United States companies market their products in Japan. They are at once private commercial attaches, importers, exporters, shippers, expediters, salesmen, investment and venture capital experts, raw material developers, etc. They are immensely flexible and adaptable as the eyes and ears for Japanese industry. Perhaps more than any other single factor they are responsible for the global reach of Japanese business. The United States has no comparable instrument.

Trade and Payments—Achievements and Prospects

Japan's emergence as one of the world's leading economic powers was not only based upon the very rapid rate of the growth of domestic output but was also accompanied by a massive penetration of world markets and the achievement of both trade and payments surpluses so large as to threaten to disturb international economic and financial equilibrium.

Not only did Japan's foreign trade grow at a faster rate than her gross national product, but also at a rate in excess of the growth of world trade as a whole. At the same time U.S. total trade expanded at a rate slightly below that of total world trade. As Professor Hunsberger has noted, the average annual rate of growth for the two decades, 1951-71, for total Japanese trade was 12.9 percent compared to total world trade growth over the same period at an average annual rate of 6.9 percent. Total United States trade grew at a 6.1 percent average annual rate.

Furthermore, Japanese exports, over the two decades, grew at a more rapid rate (14.7 percent) than did Japanese imports (11.4 percent). And this was particularly true for the American market, which absorbed Japanese exports at about twice the rate it provided Japanese imports. United States imports from Japan rose at an average annual rate (1951-71) of 18.5 percent while U.S. exports grew at a rate of 9.5 percent. The culmination of this trend came in 1971 when the United States experienced its first overall trade deficit of the twentieth century, and its trade deficit with Japan of $3.2 billion was in excess of its overall trade deficit of some $2.8 billion. In 1971 Japan's overall trade surplus reached a $7.9 billion level on a multilateral basis, and its foreign-exchange reserves rose from $4 billion at the end of 1970 to some $16 billion by the end of 1971.

Members of the Committee on Economic Policy Studies are in general agreement that stresses and policy conflicts in United States-Japan economic relations are deep-seated and likely to continue throughout the 1970s and could indeed worsen in the immediate future. For example, over the first seven months of 1972, Japan's trade surplus exceeded $4.7 billion, and many experts felt that, barring major policy changes, Japan's trade and current account surpluses would exceed $8 billion and $5.5 billion, respectively, in its fiscal year—April 1, 1972 to March 31, 1973. The U.S. trade deficit with Japan was projected at about $3.8 billion for calendar 1972, larger than for 1971, and it was at this point that President Nixon and Prime Minister Tanaka agreed in Hawaii in August 1972 that Japan would absorb an extra billion dollars of U.S. exports in order to reduce the prospective U.S. bilateral trade deficit with Japan.[c] This agreement, however, may be regarded as a short-term, stop-gap measure since Mr. Tanaka did not commit Japan to any significant long-term changes in export or import policy.

Whether this bilateral trade gap was due to the ingenuity of Japanese businessmen, or to trade barriers of various types, or to the ineffectiveness of U.S. export performance, the bilateral stresses, in fact, may be treated as indicators of Japan's wider and longer-range problem of becoming assimilated into the world trading community. The recent "explosive expansion" of Japanese exports have created multilateral as well as bilateral frictions and have been so large as to call for new policies and programs, some of which have already been adopted and others of which appear to be in the making.

During the 1950s and part of the 1960s Japan was subject to a balance-of-

---

[c]The three relevant paragraphs of the Nixon-Tanaka Communique issued at Honolulu on September 1, 1972 were as follows. (For the Trade Announcement issued at the time, see Appendix A.):

[5]

The Prime Minister and the President exchanged views in a broad perspective on issues related to economic, trade and financial matters. The Prime Minister and the President emphasized the great importance of economic relations between Japan and the United States. Both leaders expressed their conviction that their talks would contribute to closer cooperation between the two countries in dealing with economic issues of a bilateral and global nature.

[6]

The Prime Minister and the President shared the view that fundamental reform of the international monetary system is essential. They committed their Governments to work rapidly to achieve such reform. In trade, they reaffirmed the February, 1972 commitments of both countries to initiate and actively support multilateral trade negotiations covering both industry and agriculture in 1973. In this connection they noted the need in the forthcoming trade negotiations to lay the basis for further trade expansion through reduction of tariff and non-tariff barriers as well as formulation of a multilateral non-discriminatory safeguard mechanism.

[7]

The Prime Minister and the President agreed that both countries would endeavor to move toward a better equilibrium in their balance of payments and trade positions. In this regard, the President explained the measures undertaken by the United States to improve its trade and payments position and stated that the Government of the United States was urging U.S. firms to expand the volume of exports through increased productivity and improved market research, particularly to Japan. The Prime Minister indicated that the Government of Japan would also try to promote imports from the United States and that it was the intention of the Government of Japan to reduce the imbalance to a more manageable size within a reasonable period of time. The Prime Minister and the President agreed that it would be most valuable to hold future meetings at a high level to review evolving economic relationships, and that they intend to hold a meeting of the joint United States-Japan Committee on Trade and Economic Affairs as early in 1973 as feasible.

payments constraint. As Dr. Kuwayama has indicated, each time the Japanese economy began expanding rapidly, imports rose sharply and export goods were drawn into the home market. Since foreign exchange reserves were never large, compared with Japan's annual imports, the drain could not be allowed to continue. Japan's foreign exchange reserves were, during this period, subject to severe fluctuations which at times brought them down to less than the value of three months imports. When the domestic boom brought the balance of payments into deficit temporarily and drew down reserves, Japanese monetary authorities moved to check the domestic boom. Money and credit were restricted, interest rates rose, imports were reduced and export efforts by Japanese firms intensified, thus bringing the payments balance back into surplus. This chain of economic events occurred in 1953, 1957, 1961, and 1964-65.

During the last half of the 1960s and continuing to the present, however, a fundamental change occurred in the Japanese balance of payments. The occasional troublesome periodic deficit turned to a chronic and ever-increasing surplus. This change has freed Japan from an external constraint which dominated postwar economic policy for a long period: the need to insure that the increased import requirements attendant upon economic expansion did not outrun export earnings. From 1968 on Japan's balance of payments on current account was in growing surplus, reaching a striking $5.9 billion in 1971. If Dr. Kuwayama's projections are reasonably correct, it will be in surplus for all of the 1970s, even increasing in current dollars in the late 1970s. By 1980, she estimates that Japan's trade surplus will reach $9.1 billion and the balance-of-payments current account surplus $7.3 billion. Thus the 1970s would appear to present for Japan and for the countries dealing with her new dilemmas and problems.

Thus far the main thrust of Japan's expanding trade and payments situation has been felt by East and Southeast Asia and by the United States. Western Europe appears to have parried Japanese market penetration to a degree. Japan's trade relations with Communist countries have been relatively minimal, but under the new Tanaka initiatives this may change, particularly with respect to China.

Japan has become the dominant economic force in East and Southeast Asia, in trade, in foreign investment, and in economic aid. Paradoxically, the area is becoming more dependent on Japan, while at the same time Japan is becoming relatively less dependent on the region. As indicated in Professor Okita's study, cited earlier, in 1960 one-third of Japan's exports went to non-communist Asia from South Korea to Burma. By 1970, in relative terms, the figure was down to one-fourth and by 1980 it is expected to be about one-fifth of much larger total Japanese exports. Yet because of Japan's explosive export expansion, the market share of Japanese products has risen from 14 percent in 1960, to 26 percent in 1970 and is expected to reach 40 percent in 1980.

Japan's imports from the region are growing in absolute amounts but decreasing in proportion to her total needs. The region's share of Japan's imports dropped from 20 percent in 1960 to 15 percent in 1970 and is expected to be about 13.5 percent in 1980. Yet to individual countries of the area, Japan's economic power is most important. For example, as Professor Sato's paper indicates, in 1971 Japan supplied 69 percent of Burma's imports, 61 percent of Taiwan's, 43 percent of Indonesia's, 40 percent of Korea's, 39 percent of the Philippines' and 39 percent of Thailand's. In the same year, Japan took 55 percent of Indonesia's exports, 35 percent of the Philippines', 27 percent of Australia's, 21 percent of Thailand's, and 19 percent of Korea's. With a trade imbalance in Japan's favor of $2.2 billion in 1971, the Japanese provided aid amounting to $1.1 billion, most of which was tied to purchases in Japan.

One popular account of the widespread Japanese presence in Southeast Asia reads:

Today Japan does more business, gives more aid, sends more tourists and even plays more golf in the region than any other country. Her steel builds virtually all the buildings, her cars and motorcycles dominate the roads, her ships fill the ports, her radios bring the news, and her advertising keeps both the region's press afloat and its cities lit up at night. It is almost impossible in Hong Kong and Singapore to look out a window without seeing a great neon plug for Sanyo, Seiko, National, Sony, Teijin, Datsun or Mitsubishi.

In Bangkok, a Thai businessman wakes up by a Japanese alarm clock, looks out a window made of Japanese glass, puts on trousers made of fibers supplied by Japan, puts on a Japanese watch, drives to work in a Japanese car, and watches on a Japanese television set a Japanese melodrama dubbed in Thai. Using designers from Tokyo, Japanese companies in Bangkok are building two golf courses of their own. The Japanese tend to move in bunches, frequenting Japanese bars, restaurants, night clubs, and hotels. Because of this, Japanese restaurants find it profitable to fly in raw fish from Tokyo once a week via—naturally—Japan Air Lines. Entire blocks of Bangkok that formerly housed Americans now house Japanese.[d]

The Japanese face a dilemma in their prospective dealings with other Asians over the next decade. On the one hand there will be the incentive for Japan to invest further in raw material development, oil, copper, timber, etc. in the Asian arc of nations, as well as to build branch plants of less sophisticated industries, using the cheaper labor of Asian neighbors but providing Japanese capital. To pay for the greater volume of imports, more exports from Japan may be expected. But this revives memories of the pre-World War II discredited Greater East Asia Co-prosperity Sphere, and the Japanese presence is already so extensive that any extension of it may produce the adverse reaction and possible expropriation that Americans have long endured in dealings with Latin America. Pursuit of economic logic may lead to undesirable political consequences.

[d] James P. Sterba, "Japan Tightens Her Economic Grip on Nations of East and South Asia," *New York Times*, August 28, 1972.

Nor is further penetration of the American market to any significant degree a likely possibility for Japan, unless the Japanese are prepared to absorb a much greater volume of American goods than presently seems probable. As Professor Hunsberger's chapter indicates, trade between the two countries has expanded rapidly over the past decade, and while the share of the United States in total Japanese world trade has been more or less stable, accounting for about 30 percent of both Japanese exports and Japanese imports, the share of Japan in total United States trade has increased rapidly. In 1960 Japan provided about 7 percent of United States imports, but by 1971 this had increased to almost 16 percent. These trends have been attributed to a variety of factors, to the difference in the growth rates of the two economies, to the undervaluation of the yen, to the greater openness over most of the decade of the United States market to Japanese goods than of the Japanese market to American goods, to the greater and more intensive concentration of the Japanese on exports, in contrast to an allegedly less intensive interest by major United States industries in sales abroad.

According to the Japan Economic Research Center projections, the Japanese share of United States imports is likely to increase to about 23 percent in 1980, while the United States share of Japanese trade is likely to decline slightly. Since this projection is based on past trends and would mean an even larger bilateral U.S. trade deficit with Japan in 1980 than at present, it does not seem probable or possible.

Assuming an 8 percent annual growth rate of Japanese gross national product over the 1970s, Professor Sato's chapter provides some striking conclusions for Japanese total trade in 1980. On the import side Japan will in 1980 require over one-quarter (26.8 percent) of the world's output of crude materials, as compared to 15 percent in 1970 and 8.7 percent in 1960. Additionally, it will require one-fifth of the world's petroleum output (19.8 percent), as against 10.6 percent in 1970 and 4.2 percent in 1960. He foresees a serious problem for Japan to attain so substantial a share of world raw material and petroleum resources. Even with massive foreign investment by Japan to obtain an uninterrupted supply of needed resources at stable prices will be a difficult task.

On the export side, he demonstrates that while 74 percent of Japan's required 1980 exports can be sold without altering its present marginal market shares, the remaining 26 percent must be absorbed by expanding its market shares. Where to sell this additional 26 percent of 1980 exports? He assumes that, as we have indicated earlier, additional marginal shares cannot be obtained in either Southeast Asia or in the United States and suggests that Japan will have to diversify further its export markets and mount trade drives to obtain greater market shares in Western and Eastern Europe, in the USSR, in Latin America, in Africa, in Oceania, and in China.

The Outlook

Whether the Japanese economy grows at a 6.5 ± 1 percent annual rate (Prof. Rosovsky), or at an 8 percent rate (Drs. Kuwayama and Sato), or at a 9 percent rate (Dr. Okita), or at a 10 percent rate (Drs. Abegglen and Rapp), Japan's role in the world economy is bound to increase significantly in the course of this decade. Japan's share of total world gross national product may rise from 6 percent in 1970 to perhaps 12 percent in 1980. If so, this will mean a doubling of Japan's share of the world economy by 1980. Thus Japan's economic policies will have a more substantial impact as the 1970s unfold.

If Dr. Kuwayama's and Dr. Sato's projections on trade and payments are reasonably correct, and assuming continuously expanding world trade over the decade, the magnitude of Japan's projected payments surplus, the need for expanded and more diversified export markets, and the large increase in import requirements—especially in raw materials and petroleum—are likely to pose major problems over the decade. In a fully open multilateral international economy it might not matter that Japan's manufactures are exported principally to the industrialized countries, while its raw material imports come primarily from the developing countries. Or if its incremental raw material imports could be developed from sources which would accept Japanese manufactures in return, there might be less strain and tension. But Japanese and world trade and payments are not so neatly nor conveniently ordered.

Neither Southeast Asia nor the United States can be expected to absorb annual trade deficits running into the billions. Perhaps with more extensive economic aid and increased foreign investment by Japan in the area, the situation in Southeast Asia can be carried a while longer. But it has become clear that the United States can no longer convert other countries' trade surpluses into gold it no longer has; that the enlarged European Community will not much longer finance U.S. payments deficits by absorbing an avalanche of dollars; and thus that the United States cannot finance Japan's surplus by passing it on through its own deficit. With $60 billion dollars of U.S. external short-term liabilities overhanging world financial markets, even the newly established Smithsonian exchange parities, have already come under continuing pressure, and it would be optimistic to expect them to be maintained.

Clearly, as the previous chapter suggests, a new and evolving order of world trade and payments must emerge during this decade, in which greater equilibrium in trade balances, possibly via greater flexibility in exchange rate adjustments from time to time, must be sought. While solutions are to emerge from the newly formed Group of Twenty, there is much that Japan and the United States can do in the interim to facilitate the move to more rational international trade and payments arrangements.

Japan has clearly moved to lower its trade barriers and to open its domestic market more widely to imported goods. It has acted to utilize its recently acquired large foreign exchange reserves to increase foreign investment, to extend more foreign aid, and to pay off external debts. It has revalued the yen and may have to do so again if trade and payments surpluses continue at present levels. It has moved to diversify its exports and expand its import sources and to temper its export drive by turning attention and resources to environmental improvement and to the betterment of its living standards. It is turning more to its own research and development efforts and to a lessened dependence upon the United States. As Drs. Abegglen and Rapp observe: "The further prediction may be offered that through the decade Japan will seek steadily to effect a disengagement from its very deep commitment to the United States and search actively for viable alternatives to the United States in both the economic and security areas." The perceptiveness of this forecast became apparent early in the Tanaka regime.

In the last analysis, however, there is a limit to what Japan can do on its own in the international economic sphere. It cannot either by unilateral or bilateral action reorder the world's monetary or trade arrangements. It cannot affect inflationary conditions in other countries, or fiscal disarray which leads to balance-of-payments difficulties. It cannot, by itself, contain the landslide of dollars which threatens to engulf the world's leading reserve currency. It cannot mandate the end of international conflicts or the maintenance of armaments so extensive as to burden the international economic order. It cannot reorder world priorities to promote economic improvement in the developing countries. It is contained by the international environment and such initiatives as it undertakes must of necessity have limited scope. Only by multilateral and multinational agreements and arrangements can the world economy continue to expand and to prosper. This is as true for the United States as it is for Japan, except that greater scope for world initiatives still rests with the United States—at least in the 1970s. Beyond that who would be bold enough to venture?

Appendix to Chapter 11

The Nixon-Tanaka Trade Announcement issued at Honolulu on September 1, 1972 was as follows:

The Trade Announcement

[1]

On the occasion of their meeting in Hakone the United States and Japan exchanged views on their respective balance-of-payments objectives. In this context both Governments discussed various measures, both short-term and long-term, that could assist the improvement of their mutual trade imbalance.

[2]

Since their meeting in Hakone, the two Governments have closely cooperated and worked together in an attempt to quantify some of the specific short-term measures that have been discussed at the time of Hakone. President Nixon,taking the opportunity of his meeting with Prime Minister Tanaka, welcomed the following results thus worked out in a series of meetings between Deputy Vice Minister Tsurumi and Ambassador Ingersoll, including purchase of U.S. goods and services of over $1-billion:

A. The estimated increase in Japan's purchases of agricultural, forestry and fishery products from the United States during Japanese Fiscal Year 1972, ending March 31, 1973, is expected to be about $390-million. In addition, it is expected that there will be about $50-million in special grains purchases on the basis of reasonable prices. These purchases total $440-million more than the purchases in the previous year. These would bring total Japanese purchases of agricultural, forestry, and fishery products from the U.S. to $2,218,000,000 in J.F.Y. 1972, the highest such export by the U.S. to any country.

B. Japanese commercial airlines are planning to purchase civil aircraft, including wide-bodied aircraft, valued at approximately $320-million from the United States. Such orders would be placed in J.F.Y. 1972 and J.F.Y. 1973. The Government of Japan will facilitate the purchase of these aircraft upon finalization of purchase contracts. The Government of Japan also intends to purchase, subject to budgetary appropriation, helicopters and aviation-related facilities amounting to $20-million from the U.S.

C. The Japanese power companies will purchase $320-million in uranium-enrichment services from the United States with payment to be facilitated by the Government of Japan.

D. Finally, it was also agreed by both the U.S. and Japanese Governments that they would use their best efforts to facilitate the establishment at an early date of a joint Japan-U.S. working group to begin study of the feasibility of a joint venture for construction in the United States of a gaseous-diffusion enrichment facility for peaceful uses, which would involve a total investment of approximately $1-billion.

261

[3]

The President also noted with appreciation the recent decisions by the Government of Japan to liberalize access to the distribution system by allowing improved investment opportunities in retailing, processing and packaging as well as the decision to allow greater sales of American computer products in Japan.

Index

263

About the Authors

Dr. James C. Abegglen, Vice-President of The Boston Consulting Group, is also President of The Boston Consulting Group K.K. and Director of The Boston Consulting Group Ltd.

Dr. Abegglen has worked intensively as management consultant on international management problems in Western Europe, Africa and Australia, as well as in East Asia, which has remained the focus of his interest. Prior to joining The Boston Consulting Group, he was with McKinsey & Co., Inc. in New York, and before that with Arthur D. Little, Inc.

Dr. Abegglen was a Ford Foundation Fellow (1955-1956) working in Japan. This led to the publication of his well-known study of Japanese management methods, *The Japanese Factory*. He was also with The Center for International Studies at MIT, where he directed research into Mexico's economic development. He is author of *Warudo Bijinesu no Keiei Senryaku, Big Business Leaders in America, Occupational Mobility in American Business and Industry*, and numerous monographs in addition to *The Japanese Factory*. He edited *Business Strategies for Japan*, published by Sophia University, Tokyo, 1970.

Dr. Abegglen received the Ph.D. from the University of Chicago, with postdoctoral study at Harvard. He has been a member of the faculties of the University of Chicago and the Massachusetts Institute of Technology. He is presently a Director of The Japan Society and a member of The Council on Foreign Relations. He now resides in Japan.

Dr. Jerome B. Cohen, who served as Chairman of the Committee on Economic Policy Studies, was a Japanese Language Officer in U.S. Naval Intelligence in World War II. He has his M.A. and Ph.D. in Economics and Finance from Columbia University. His previous publications on Japan include: *Japan's Economy in War & Reconstruction*, University of Minnesota Press, 1949; *Economic Problems of Free Japan*, Center of International Studies, Princeton University, 1952; "International Aspects of Japan's Economic Situation," in *Japan Between East and West*, edited by Hugh Borton, published for the Council on Foreign Relations by Harper, 1957; *Japan's Postwar Economy*, Indiana University Press, 1958. He has served in Japan with the United States Strategic Bombing Survey, with the Shoup Tax Mission, as a consultant to American Airlines, etc. He was Dean of The School of Business, Dean of Graduate Studies, and Acting President of Baruch College of The City University of New York until his recent retirement. He is a member of Phi Beta Kappa, Beta Gamma Sigma, the Council on Foreign Relations, the Asia Society, the Japan Society, the American Economic Association, etc.

267

James van B. Dresser, Jr. is Managing Director, The Boston Consulting Group Ltd. He received the B.A. with honors and distinction in government from Wesleyan University; the M.A. in international relations from the Fletcher School of Law and Diplomacy; and the M.B.A. with high distinction from the Harvard Business School, where he was a Baker Scholar and was awarded the Loeb Rhoades Fellowship Prize for excellence in finance.

Mr. Dresser has worked on several major assignments in Japan on behalf of U.S. clients. Before joining The Boston Consulting Group, Mr. Dresser served in Japan for several years as an intelligence officer in the U.S. Air Force.

Thomas M. Hout is presently in Japan with The Boston Consulting Group K.K. He received the M.B.A. from Stanford University. His B.A. in economics is from Yale University. Mr. Hout has also done graduate study in mathematics and economics at the University of Manchester under a Rotary Foundation Fellowship. Before that, he served as an officer in the U.S. Navy.

Warren S. Hunsberger is Professor of Economics and Director of the Center for Asian Studies at American University in Washington, D.C. He holds the Ph.D. in economics from Yale University. He is the author of *Japan and the United States in World Trade*, published for the Council on Foreign Relations. He has had extensive administrative and research experience in various Asian countries, including Japan.

He has been Professor of International Economics at the University of Rochester; Professor of Economic Programming for the School of Advanced International Studies, The Johns Hopkins University; Research Fellow at the Council on Foreign Relations; Chief of the Division of Research for Far East, United States Department of State; Far East Regional Economist for the United States International Cooperation Administration; Economist for the Board of Economic Warfare; and Advisor to the Economic Planning Unit, Prime Minister's Department, Kuala Lumpur, Malaysia for the Ford Foundation.

Lawrence B. Krause is a Senior Research Fellow at The Brookings Institution, Washington, D.C. He holds the B.A. and M.A. degrees from the University of Michigan and the Ph.D. in economics from Harvard. He has served as a staff member of the Cowles Foundation for Research in Economics at Yale University and at the Growth Center at Yale. He was on the Senior Staff of the Council of Economic Advisors and is a Lecturer at the School for Advanced International Studies at Johns Hopkins University. He is the author of numerous books and articles on international economic and international monetary problems, the most recent of which is *Sequel to Bretton Woods: A Proposal to Reform the World Monetary System*, The Brookings Institution, 1971.

Patricia Hagan Kuwayama has her A.B. degree from Radcliffe College, 1962 and her Ph.D. in economics from the City University of New York, 1970. She is currently economist in the Foreign Research Division of the Federal Reserve Bank of New York, specializing in analysis of the Japanese economy.

William V. Rapp received the M.A. and Ph.D. in economics from Yale University as a National Science Foundation Fellow. His dissertation dealt with the relationships between Japanese industrial development and changes in Japanese trade patterns. Dr. Rapp spent two years with the Agency for International Development in Korea and Vietnam as an economist. After leaving AID, he received the M.A. in Far Eastern Studies from Stanford University as a Ford Foundation Foreign Area Fellow.

Dr. Rapp graduated from Amherst College, where he received the B.A. in economics *magna cum laude* and was elected to Phi Beta Kappa. He has taught economics at Yale and has worked for Philips Gloeilampen in the Netherlands and Toyo Menka Kaisha Ltd. in Japan. His publications include *A Theory of Changing Trade Patterns Under Economics Growth: Tested for Japan; Effective and Protective Rates for Korean Industries; Japanese Managerial Behavior and Excessive Competition*, and "Implications of Japanese Competition for U.S. Business."

He is currently living in Japan, associated with The Boston Consulting Group, K.K.

Henry Rosovsky is Professor of Economics at Harvard University and Chairman of its Economics Department. From 1967 to 1969 he served as Associate Director of Harvard's East Asian Research Center. He received the A.B. degree in 1949 from the College of William and Mary. He holds the A.M. (1953) and the Ph.D. (1959) degrees from Harvard.

Before coming to Harvard in 1965 he was Assistant, Associate, and Professor of Economics and History, and Chairman of the Center for Japanese and Korean Studies at the University of California, Berkeley (1958-65). He has also served as Visiting Professor at Stanford University, Hitotsubashi University, Tokyo University, and the Hebrew University of Jerusalem.

Professor Rosovsky is the author of *Capital Formation in Japan* (1961) and editor of *Industrialization in Two Systems* (1966). He has also contributed articles to the *American Economic Review*, the *Journal of Economic History, Explorations in Entrepreneurial History, Economic Development and Cultural Change, The American Scholar*, the *Business History Review*, and others, including many Japanese journals.

He is a member of the American Economic Association, the Economic History Association, the Association of Asian Studies (Board of Directors, 1963-66), Chairman of the Council on Research in Economic History, and Chairman of the Policy and Advisory Board of the Economics Institute.

Kazuo Sato is currently professor of economics at the State University of New York at Buffalo. He received the B.A. (1953) from Hokkaido University, Japan, and the Ph.D. (1960) from Yale University. He was on the faculty of the Institute of Social and Economic Research, Osaka University (1959-62), an economist with the Centre for Development Planning, Projections, and Policies of the United Nations (1962-70), and a visiting professor at the Massachusetts Institute of Technology (1969-70). He has written a number of articles on economic theory and on the Japanese economy. He is the editor of *Japanese Economic Studies.*

Gary Saxonhouse received the A.B., M.A., and Ph.D. in economics from Yale University. He is currently Assistant Professor of Economics at the University of Michigan. He is the author of a number of papers and articles on Japanese economic problems and is currently engaged (with Professor Hugh Patrick) in a study of Japanese-American economic relations under a grant from The Twentieth Century Fund. He served as a member of the American Delegation to the Third Japanese-American Assembly in Shimoda, Japan in June 1972.

234567890